TEAC[I1028729]

THIRD YEAR LATIN

CHARLES JENNEY, JR.

ROGERS V. SCUDDER

DAVID D. COFFIN

PRENTICE HALL

Needham,
Massachusetts

Englewood Cliffs,
New Jersey

ISBN: 0-13-918822-3

2 3 4 5 6 7 8 9 97 96 95 94 93 92 91 90 89

Prentice-Hall of Australia, Pty, Ltd., Sydney
Prentice-Hall Canada Inc., Toronto
Prentice-Hall Hispanoamericana, S.A., Mexico
Prentice-Hall of India Private Ltd., New Delhi
Prentice-Hall International (UK) Limited, London
Prentice-Hall of Japan, Inc., Tokyo
Prentice-Hall of Southeast Asia Pte. Ltd., Singapore
Editora Prentice-Hall Do Brasil Ltda., Rio de Janeiro

A Simon & Schuster Company

CONTENTS

Introduction

The purpose of this Teacher's Guide is to assist teachers of *Third Year Latin* to plan the year's work, to develop day-by-day procedures to accomplish their objectives, to make the most of every student's capability for acquiring a mastery of Latin, and to promote a lively interest in the classics. In addition to suggestions for planning the year's work, this guide also contains a suggested Third-Year Word List, a classified bibliography of resource materials, and translations of all the Latin selections in the text. It is true of course that there are many possible variations from the translations given here. While the translations attempt to combine the literal rendering with a smooth translation of Latin into English, the emphasis is on trying to help the teacher who wants help, rather than on providing the best literary English.

TEACHING FEATURES
IN THIRD YEAR LATIN

Valuable teaching aids have been included in the make-up of Jenney's *Third Year Latin*. Each feature will be particularly helpful in the degree that it is consciously utilized by the teacher.

Organization. *Third Year Latin* is made up of five sections of Latin reading—Cicero, Sallust, Pliny, Ovid, and Later Latin—plus an Introduction which gives a concise survey of the political and social constitution of the Roman Republic in the first century B.C. The appendix includes a complete review of Latin inflectional forms and of grammar constructions, with particular attention to those usages especially characteristic of Cicero's language. The grammar review is followed by a two-page résumé of rhetorical terms used in the footnotes. This list is, in turn, followed by the Latin-English vocabulary and by the index and list of illustrations.

To facilitate reading of Latin selections, especially in the Cicero section,

1

pages of Latin text are not broken up with art work. Footnotes, with whatever help the authors out of their experience as teachers considered useful, appear on the same page as the Latin.

Illustrations. *Third Year Latin* has been enriched with an unusual collection of illustrations derived largely from ancient sources: arches, funeral monuments, bas reliefs, wall paintings, mosaics, coins, artifacts, and portrait sculpture. These illustrations of ancient life as represented by the ancients themselves are invaluable sources of information in helping students to a vivid conception of the Romans of long ago who created Latin literature. Students may be surprised to discover how familiar they would find many features of ancient Rome and its government and civilization. An example of this is the modern look of the apartment block in Ostia. Most words used in picture captions are from the vocabulary used in selections; in the few cases in which the caption word is not in the text vocabulary, the students' curiosity should be aroused to send them to their Latin dictionary (any students going on to third-year Latin should be encouraged to acquire a dictionary of their own). A description of all illustrations is given in the list of illustrations, following the index in the text.

Helpful Books. A short list of books, selected from the bibliography in this manual, precedes the grammar review in the text. Students' attention should be called to this booklist early in the year, perhaps in connection with assigning topics for investigation and class reports.

Outlines and Charts. Three outlines and charts have been provided to help students get a clear idea and firm grasp of background information necessary for placing in perspective the various Latin selections they will be reading. The first of these is "Political and Religious Structure of the Roman State in the Late Republic," pages 2 and 3 of the text. The information summarized on these two pages is well worth the student's memorizing; it will be invaluable help in understanding references and allusions in his Latin reading throughout the coming year and in future Latin courses as well.

The next chart is "Outline of Roman History 107-43 B.C.," pages 20 and 21 of the text, covering the main events of the years spanning Cicero's lifetime, arranged especially to point up contemporaneous events of a given year in Cicero's life.

The third chart is "Writers in the Classical Period of Roman Literature," pages 58 and 59 of the text, arranged to help students see at a glance writers in chronological order and to relate each writer to other writers living at the same time, as well as to place each one in his respective background of the Republic or the Empire.

Maps. The series of maps in *Third Year Latin* has been carefully prepared for the purpose of enabling students to locate any city, town,

2

or geographical feature mentioned in the Latin selections or their accompanying notes. By regularly expecting students to be able to locate an item in the day's lesson on the map in their text or a classroom map, teachers can train students to an awareness of geographical orientation that will enrich their learning in many fields.

Speech Outlines. Each of Cicero's orations is introduced with an outline of the speech, matching the main headings from the typical speech outline (page 52 of text) with the corresponding part of the specific speech. Students should be asked to copy the outline in their notebooks, substituting for the chapter and line references a brief résumé in English (or possibly in Latin) of each part of the oration. This activity, more than any other type of review, will help students to see the oration as a literary whole and to remember its essential content.

PLANNING AHEAD

It is rather unlikely that any class will cover all the Latin selections included in *Third Year Latin*. The purpose of the authors has been to include enough reading so that a teacher may choose among the selections according to his preferences and the special interests of the class. Some classes will read the First Oration and the Third Oration Against Catiline; others, the First and the Fourth; still others, all four speeches, with emphasis on rapid reading. Most teachers will want to read the speech for the Manilian law, surely a classic. Some will want to spend time on the letters of Cicero and of Pliny, which give firsthand pictures respectively of Roman life and history in the last decades of the Republic and in the last part of the first century of the Empire. Most teachers will want to read some of the Ovid stories, especially if the class has not yet read anything but Latin prose, in order to introduce their students to Latin poetry.

Special attention is called to the new section of Latin written during the centuries that followed the classical period of Cicero and Augustus. The renewed interest in Latin has included interest in later Latin literature, for Latin continued to be the universal language of the literate almost to our own times and indeed continues to this day as the official language of one great section of Christendom. The selections in the Later Latin section are actually easier reading than Cicero, with ample notes to clear up quickly the few spelling differences and meanings of new words or, in a few instances, new meanings of familiar words. One interesting way to use the material from the section is as a change from the more imposing prose of Cicero.

But whatever the readings to be covered, the teacher should so far

3

as possible lay out a plan for the whole year. Suppose there are 36 weeks, divided into four terms of nine weeks each, or three of twelve weeks each, or possibly two of eighteen weeks each: decide what is to be covered each term and each week of the term.

THE FIRST WEEK

The first week is, of course, extremely important, both to give students a clear idea of what is expected of them, and also to show them how they can profit from, and enjoy, the course.

The First Day. It is to be hoped that members of the class will have in their hands their texts as they begin the year. Examine the books together. Notice the organization: a general Introduction which describes the political and constitutional structure of the Roman Republic, followed by sections of Latin reading from Cicero, Sallust, Pliny, Ovid, and Later Latin. Each section of reading begins with background material in English, with many instructive illustrations of Roman life from ancient sources. As is consistent with the standard curriculum for third-year Latin, the bulk of the book is devoted to Cicero. The Cicero section includes all four Catilinarian orations in full, the speeches for the Manilian law and for Archias in full, plus a more extensive selection from the Fourth Verrine Book than is usually found in a high school text, and twenty-two letters that provide a fascinating, first-person account of Cicero's mature years. In addition, there is ample reading from Sallust, Pliny, Ovid, and Later Latin to provide considerable variety in the course.

Call attention to the particular sections of the text which will be covered during the coming year; then turn to the first item, in most cases the First Oration Against Catiline. Go over the helps provided — the discussion of the background of the speech, footnotes, and the vocabulary at the end of the book — so that students know where to find study aids. Explain the general procedures that you will be following in the course and in day-to-day class sessions.

TRANSLATION. Will you make use of written or of oral translation of reading assigned as homework? Probably some of both. Written translations make it easier, in some ways, to check which students have done the most, and the best, work; written work, if handed in, need not always be graded before it is returned. Another way to use written work is to ask a student to read his translation all the way through, then another, and another, and after this to let the class compare differences and decide why one translation is preferable to another.

4

Another day the teacher may collect the papers, read one or two sentences from a number of papers, then discuss differences. At least some time during the year should be spent simply on rapid reading, as a means of increasing facility in direct comprehension of Latin.

Some time, too, should be spent on reading Latin aloud; advantage should be taken of opportunities for dramatizing parts of the orations. Reading aloud serves to confirm habits of accurate pronunciation and to establish ability to understand spoken Latin. Practice in reading should emphasize phrasing which shows understandings of the passage and should help students to recognize such rhetorical devices as Cicero's balanced phrases, repetition, invective, irony, antithesis, climax, and rhetorical questions. Students should always supply the complete word or phrase, with the appropriate inflectional ending, when they meet abbreviations of the praenomen, of phrases giving the date, and of numerals. There are some recordings available as a model for reading Latin aloud and for practice in understanding oral Latin (page 21).

HOMEWORK. Some teachers assign a certain number of lines as the work to be prepared outside of class; others prefer to say, "Do as much as you can in 40 or 45 minutes"—or whatever the presumed amount of study time may be. This type of assignment is practical with a class that is cooperative and trustworthy; it gives students a chance to see their own increasing ability to translate, and makes certain that students will not say, "I spent two hours on Latin and didn't have any time left for math."

COMPOSITION. English-to-Latin translation will be a regular part of the course, for there is no better way to reinforce a student's knowledge of forms, constructions, and vocabulary. How much time should be devoted to composition? Some teachers include composition as part of the classwork one day each week, others prefer to wait until the reading of an oration is completed and then to spend a day or two on composition. Sentences and paragraphs assigned for translation into Latin should consistently review basic vocabulary, constructions, and forms. There should also be opportunity for original writing. One device is to let students read a selection silently (narratives lend themselves best to this method), then close their books and write a résumé *in Latin*. When the first composition is assigned, call attention to the summary of forms and grammar in the appendix of the text.

VOCABULARY. How will vocabulary study be handled? The general Latin vocabulary, at the end of the text, has been marked to show words

5

included in first-, second-, and third-year lists, respectively. Some teachers prefer to let the learning of vocabulary come as the natural concomitant of reading Latin selections, with a test at intervals to check on learning. Others will assign a set number of words — perhaps the first 15 or 20 words marked • • • in the vocabulary — for the first Friday, to be followed each week with a group of 15 or 20 additional words.

TESTS. It should be explained to students that tests will feature sight translation passages, and the only way by which they can prepare for tests is to do their own outside assignments, regularly, alone, from day to day. The use of a "trot" or "pony" is self-defeating, for the student fails to develop the ability to do his own translating. In addition, a certain amount of recognition-of-constructions type of question may be expected.

ASSIGNMENT FOR THE SECOND DAY. Students can profitably spend the first two or three days reading the material in the Introduction to the text, which outlines the political constitution of the Late Republic and gives information about voting assemblies and the qualifications and duties belonging to the various offices, and then provides important biographical and critical information on Cicero himself. The text of the orations, for satisfactory understanding, requires students to be aware of this background. Assign some part of the Introduction, perhaps the first 19 pages of the section, to be read for the next class session.

The Second Day. Beginning with the assigned reading, discuss the political organization of the Republic. Have in the classroom such supplementary material as you can provide from your files or from the library, including pertinent picture material. Let students ask such questions as they may have about government and offices, or ask questions yourself if they have none. Call attention to reference books in which the interested student may find out more about matters discussed.

Move on to a discussion of the particular times in which Cicero lived. Let students tell what they have gathered from history courses they may have studied. Study the chart on pages 20 and 21. Emphasize the crisis nature of the decades of Cicero's active public life: the fact that the Republic had by then existed nearly 500 years, the pressing and unsolved problems which had come with the expansion from a city-state to a world empire, the growing importance of single powerful personalities like Sulla, Marius, and Pompey who tended to place themselves outside constitutional procedures, the factors that were undermining genuinely democratic government, and similarities and contrasts to our own political and social problems.

As time permits, start reading together the biography of Cicero.

6

Assign further reading of this biographical material before the next class session.

The Third Day. Continue the discussion, or questions and answers, or reading together of the life of Cicero. Note in particular such important factors in Cicero's career as his unusual position in politics as a "new man," his preparation for his career, his progress through the *cursus honorum*, and the very unsettled nature of his times. Pin down a few key dates, such as 63 B.C

Devote some time to helping students realize the place of oratory in ancient times, the training of the orator, the importance of the study of rhetoric, and the typical outline of a classical oration.

Assign chapter 1 of the First Oration. Do not expect a finished translation. Explain that the prose is very different from Caesar's, with such obvious items as more use of the first and second persons, imperatives, direct address; much longer sentences; word order that is flexible, often with the most emphatic words at the beginning and the end of sentences; and deliberate use of rhetorical devices and of emotional language.

The Fourth Day. Review the special background of the First Oration. Turn to the speech itself. One can lead into the translation by sketching the immediate situation — the assembling of the senate under crisis conditions and Catiline's possibly unexpected appearance — and then delivering from memory the first few phrases of the oration, accompanied by dramatic hand-pointing toward a student on the right.

Take the translation sentence by sentence. Do each one two or three times, trying out suggestions to see which one best suits the Latin and the setting. Continue to dramatize the directness of the speech with appropriate gestures. When problems arise, refer to the notes — they are there to be used.

Questions on syntax help students to review what they have learned about the structure of Latin and also point up differences between Cicero's and Caesar's styles.

The following questions might be asked on chapter 1 of the First Oration:

1. What is the case of **audacia** in l. 3? (Nom., the subject of **iactabit**: note the emphatic position at the end of the sentence, a typical Ciceronian device.)

2. What is the case of **te** in l. 4? (Acc., obj. of **moverunt**, the last word in the sentence.)

3. What is the case of **ora** in l. 6? (Nom., one of the series of subjects of **moverunt**.)

7

4. What is the case of **vultus** in l. 6? (Also nom.; together with **ora** it is an example of hendiadys and should be translated "expressions on the faces.")

5. What is the form of **sentis** in l. 7? (Second person sing., pres. tense of **sentio.**)

6. What does **proxima** in l. 9 agree with? (**Nocte** understood, an abl. of time when.)

7. What is the mood of **egeris** in l. 9? Why? (Subjunctive in an indirect question after **ignorare:** note the sequence.)

8. What is the case of **consili** in l. 10? (Gen. of the whole with **quid** — see § 56 in the appendix of the text.)

9. What is the case of **tempora** and **mores** in l. 11? (Acc. of exclamation.)

10. What is the case of **particeps** in l. 13? (Predicate nom. after **fit.**)

11. What is the form of **duci** in l. 16? (Pres. pass. infinitive of **duco,** after **oportebat.**)

12. What does **privatus** in l. 19 modify? (**Scipio:** translate "as a private citizen.")

13. What is the case of **nos consules** in l. 21? (Nom., subject of **perferemus.**)

The following words from chapter 1 should be learned: **abutere, patientia, furor, iactabit, concursus, ora, vultus, patere, scientia, ignorare, mores, vivit, notat, vitamus, iam pridem, pestem, orbem terrae, caede, incendiis, praetereo, studentem, occidit, quondam, suppliciis, acerbissimum, senatus consultum, aperte, desumus.** These are in addition to the common words of first- and second-year lists, which perhaps should be reviewed. There are many English derivatives from these words; derivatives should always be noted by students, or by the teacher if students cannot think of any.

These questions might be asked in chapter 2 of the First Oration:

1. What kind of clause is **ne . . . caperet,** ll. 1 and 2? (Negative purpose clause.)

2. What is the case and the use of **detrimenti** in l. 2? (Gen. of the whole; note the use of **quid** for **aliquid.**)

3. What is the case and the use of **patre** in l. 4? (Abl. of description.)

4. What is the case and the use of **consulibus** in l. 6? (Dat. of indirect object.)

5. The particle **num,** l. 7, expects what answer? ("No." The clause is a fine example of the rhetorical question.)

6. What is the case and the use of **diem** in l. 7? (Acc., duration of time.)

8

7. Is **deponendam** in l. 14 a gerund or a gerundive? (Gerundive, agreeing with **audaciam**.)

    8. What is the case of **patres conscripti** in l. 15? (Vocative.)

    9. Who is meant by the term **ducem hostium** in ll. 19 and 20? (Catiline.)

    10. What is the case and use of **mihi** in l. 23? (Dat. of agent with the passive periphrastic **erit verendum**.)

    11. What is the mood and the reason for the mood of **dicat** in l. 24? (Subjunctive [pres. tense] in a clause of fearing.)

    12. What is the form of **interficiere** in l. 27? (Second person sing., fut. pass.)

    13. Why is **fateatur** subjunctive, l. 29? (Verb in a result clause.)

    14. Why is **possis**, l. 31, subjunctive? (Verb in a purpose clause.)

The following words from chapter 2 should be learned: **decrevit, quondam, detrimenti, clarissimo, maioribus, consularis, convenit, vivis, deponendam, clementem, inertiae, condemno, crescit, moenia, perniciem, molientem, verendum, potius, crudelius, nondum, improbus, perditus, fateatur, quam diu, audeat, aures, sentientem, custodient.** Words which appear on first- and second-year lists should also be reviewed, and various derivatives noted.

With the completion of chapters 1 and 2 students have covered Cicero's introduction to his speech. Draw attention to the outline on page 70 and direct students to copy the outline headings in notebook and to summarize Cicero's *exordium* and *narratio*. It may be advisable to do this in class this time, to show students what is expected as they fill in outlines of speeches studied.

These questions might be asked on chapter 3 of the First Oration:

    1. Why is **exspectes** subjunctive, l. 1? (Verb in clause of characteristic.)

    2. What is the form of **muta** in l. 4? (Imperative.)

    3. What is the case and the use of **mihi** in l 4? (Dat. after **crede**.)

    4. What is the form of **obliviscere** in ll. 4 and 5? (Imperative sing. of a deponent.)

    5. What is the case and the use of **caedis** in l. 5? (Gen. after a verb of forgetting.)

    6. What is the form of **teneris** in l. 5? (Pres. indicative, second sing., pass.)

    7. What is the case and the use of **luce** in l. 5? (Abl. of comparison, following **clariora**.)

    8. How do you find the day of the month by our reckoning? (Count

backwards from the Calends — the first day of November — and remember to count the Calends as the first day in the twelve.)

9. What answer does the particle **num,** l. 11, expect? ("No.")
10. What is the form of **est admirandum** called, ll. 12 and 13? (Pass. periphrastic.) How is it translated? ("Ought to be admired.")
11. What is the case and the use of **Roma** in l. 15? (Abl. of place from which. Remember that there is no preposition with names of towns, cities, small islands, **domus,** and **rus.**)
12. Why is **remansissemus** in l. 19 subjunctive? (Verb in subordinate clause in indirect discourse.)
13. Locate Praeneste. (It is about 20 miles east of Rome, modern Palestrina.)
14. What is the mood and the use of **audiam** in l. 24? (Subjunctive, the verb in a clause of characteristic.)

The following words in chapter 3 should be reviewed, or learned if they are new, and English derivatives and related Latin words noted: **tenebris, nefarios, parietibus, coniurationis, erumpunt, muta, crede, obliviscere, recognoscas, meministi, satellitem, fefellit, atrox, incredibilis, admirandum, infitiari, circumclusum, sensisti, coloniam, vigiliis, moliris, cogitas.**

Third-Year Word List

The following list of words, in addition to those listed in *Second Year Latin* and to the words in lesson vocabularies of *First Year Latin*, is suggested for mastery by students who have taken Latin for three years.

abhorreō	adipīscor	aequitās
accūsō	adiungō	aerārium
acerbus	admoneō	aerārius
adaequō	adulēscēns	aeternus
adeō, *adverb*	adulēscentia	afferō
adhūc	adversārius	afficiō
adimō	aedēs	agrestis

āiō	clēmēns	custōdia
aliquandō	clēmentia	custōdiō
alō	cōgitō	
āmēns	cognōmen	damnō
āmentia	colō	dēbilitō
an	colōnus	dēcēdō
appetō	comes	dēcernō
aptus	comitātus, *noun*	decet
āra	comitia	dēclārō
ārdeō	Comitium	dēdecus
argentum	complector	dēficiō
argūmentum	comprobō	dēlectō
ars	conciliō	dēleō
ascrībō	concitō	dēlictum
assequor	concordia	dēlūbrum
assiduus	concurrō	dēmēns
atrōx	condō	dēnique
attendō	cōnfiteor	dēnūntiō
auris	coniūnx	dēpellō
aurum	coniūrātiō	dēposcō
auspicium	coniūrātus	dēprecor
avāritia	coniūrō	dēprehendō
avidus	cōnscientia	dēscrībō
avus	cōnsīderō	dēserō
	cōnstantia	dēsīderō
beātus	cōnsulāris	dēsignō
bellō	cōnsulātus	dēsinō
benevolentia	cōnsultum	dictitō
bīnī	contemnō	dignus
	contentus	dīlēctus
carcer	contingō	dīligō
careō	cōntiō	dīripiō
cārus	convīvium	discō
caveō	corrumpō	discrīmen
celeber	crēdibilis	dissentiō
celebrō	crēscō	dissimulō
cēnseō	cruciātus	dīvīnus
cēnsor	crūdēlis	dīvitiae
cernō	culpa	doctrīna
certō, *verb*	cūnctus	domesticus
circā	cupiditās	dubius
cīvīlis	cūria	dulcis

11

ecquis	foedus	incrēdibilis
efferō	formīdō	index
egeō	fors (forte)	indicium
ēgregius	fortasse	indicō, –āre
emō	frequēns	indīcō, –ere
ergā	frētus	indignus
ērudiō	frīgus	industria
etenim	frūctus	inertia
ēvertō	fruor	īnferus
exanimō	furō	īnfestus
exaudiō	furor	ingenium
excellō	fūrtum	ingēns
excelsus		ingredior
excitō	gradus	innocēns
exemplum	gravitās	innocentia
exigō	grex	īnsidior
eximius		īnsigne
exitium	hesternus	īnsignis
expetō	hinc	interdum
exsilium	hodiernus	interitus
exsistō	honestās	intersum
exstinguō	honestus	intrōdūcō
exsultō	hospes	intueor
externus	hūmānus	invideō
	humus	invidia
facilitās		īrāscor
facinus	iaceō	iste
fallō	iactō	iterum
fānum	idcircō	iūcundus
fateor	Īdūs	iūstitia
fātum	igitur	iuvenis
faucēs	ignōminia	
faveō	ignōscō	Kalendae
fax	illūstris	
fēlīcitās	imāgō	lacessō
ferrum	immineō	laetitia
fingō	immō	laetor
flāgitium	impendeō	largior
flāgitō	imperītus	latrō
flagrō	improbus	latrōcinium
flamma	incendium	lēnis
flōreō	inclūdō	levō

12

libenter	nōminō	penitus
līberālis	Nōnae	percipiō
libīdō	nōscō	perdō
locuplēs	notō	perīculōsus
longinquus	nūper	perniciēs
lūdō	nūtus	perniciōsus
lūmen		pertimēscō
lūxuria	obeō	pestis
	oblīvīscor	plācō
macula	obscūrus	plēnus
maeror	obsecrō	pontifex
manifestus	occultō	posteritās
mānsuētūdō	ōdī	prae
mātūrus	odium	praecipuus
mediocris	ōmen	praeclārus
meminī	ōminor	praedicō, -āre
mereō	omittō	praeditus
metuō	onus	praedō
mīlitia	opīnor	praeferō
misceō	ops	praesēns
misericordia	optimās	praetereō
mītis	optō	praetermittō
moenia	ōra	praetūra
molestus	ōrnāmentum	prīvō
mōlior	ōrnō	prōdō
monumentum	ōs, ōris	profectō
morbus	ōtium	proinde
mortālis		proprius
mōtus	pactum	prōsum
mūnicipium	paenitet	prūdentia
mūtō	palam	pudet
	parēns	pudor
nāvālis	pariēs	pūniō
necessitūdō	pariō	
necō	parricīda	quaestiō
nefārius	partim	quaestus
neglegō	patefaciō	quālis
negō	patientia	quamquam
nēquitia	patrēs cōnscrīptī	quamvīs
nervus	patrius	quandō
nex	peccō	quārē
nimius	pendeō	quasi

querēla	scriptor	tēctum
quia	sēcernō	temeritās
quiēscō	secūris	temperantia
quīn	sēdēs	tenebrae
Quirītēs	sēmen	tenuis
quisnam	senectūs	terminus
quisquis	senex	testāmentum
quīvis	sēnsus	testimōnium
quoad	sententia	testis
quondam	sepeliō	togātus
quoniam	sermō	tolerō
quotiēns	serviō	totiēns
	sevēritās	tractō
recitō	sevērus	trānsmittō
recordor	sīca	trīstis
rēctē	simulācrum	triumphō
redimō	simulō	triumphus
rēgius	sinō	tumultus
rēgnō	societās	turpitūdō
religiō	soleō	
repetō	sors	ulcīscor
reprehendō	spīritus	ūtilitās
reprimō	splendor	utinam
repudiō	spoliō	utrum
requīrō	stabilis	
resistō	stimulus	valeō
restō	strepitus	varietās
retardō	stultus	varius
reus	stuprum	vectīgal
revocō	suādeō	vēndō
rīdeō	subiciō	venēnum
rōbur	suffrāgium	veneror
rūs	sūmptus	venia
	superbus	verber
sācrificium	supplex	vēritās
sānctus	supplicātiō	versor
sānē		versus
sānō	tabella	vertō
sapiēns	tabula	vērus
scelerātus	taceō	vestīgium
scelus	tametsī	vexō
scīlicet	tamquam	vidēlicet

14

vindicō	virgō	voluptās
vīnum	vīsō	vultus
violō	vitium	

Bibliography

ARCHAEOLOGY, BIOGRAPHY, HISTORY, ROMAN LIFE

Abbott, Frank F., *The Common People of Ancient Rome*. Biblo & Tannen, Cheshire, CT
———— *Roman Politcal Institutions*. Biblo & Tannen, Cheshire, CT
———— *Society and Politics in Ancient Rome*. Biblo & Tannen, Cheshire, CT
Barrow, Reginald H., *The Romans*. Penguin Books, 1949
Boak, Arthur E. R., *A History of Rome to 565* A.D. Macmillan, 1955
Breasted, James H., *Ancient Times: A History of the Early World*, 2nd ed. rev. Ginn, 1944
Buchan, John, *Augustus*. Greenwood Press, Westport, CT, 1975
———— *Julius Caesar*. Appleton, 1932
Cambridge Ancient History. Cambridge University Press, 1939–1950
Carcopino, Jérome, *Daily Life in Ancient Rome*. Yale University Press, 1940
Cary, Max, *History of Rome Down to the Reign of Constantine*. Macmillan, 1935
Casson, Lionel, *The Ancient Mariners* (ships, to the Byzantine era). Macmillan, 1959
Church, Alfred J., *Roman Life in the Days of Cicero*. Biblo & Tannen, Cheshire, CT, 1959
Davis, William S., *A Day in Old Rome*. Biblo & Tannen, Cheshire CT
DeBurgh, William G., *The Legacy of the Ancient World*. Macmillan, 1924. Reprint, Barnes and Noble
Dudley, Donald R., *The Civilization of Rome*. Mentor Books, 1960
Duff, John W., *A Literary History of Rome*. Barnes & Noble, 1954
———— *A Literary History of Rome in the Silver Age*. Greenwood Press, Westport, CT

Everyday Life in Ancient Times (full-color art recreations of ancient civilizations). The National Geographic Society, 1951, 1953

Ferrero, Guglielmo, *Life of Caesar,* tr. by A. E. Zimmern. Greenwood Press, Westport, CT, 1977

_____ *Women of the Caesars.* Norwood Editions, Norwood, PA

Foster, Genevieve S., *Augustus Caesar's World.* Scribner, 1947

Fowler, William Warde, *The City-State of the Greeks and Romans.* Macmillan, 1895. Reprint, St. Martin's Press

_____ *Rome.* Oxford University Press, New York, 1967

_____ *Social Life at Rome in the Age of Cicero.* Richard West, Philadelphia

Frank, Tenney, *Aspects of Social Behavior in Ancient Rome.* Cooper Square, New York, 1969

_____ *A History of Rome.* Holt, Rinehart, & Winston, 1923

_____ *Life and Literature in the Roman Republic.* University of California Press, 1930

Friedlaender, Ludwig, *Roman Life and Manners under the Early Empire.* Arno Press, New York, 1980

Glover, Terrot Reaveley, *The Ancient World.* Greenwood Press, Westport, CT, 1980

Grant, Michael, *Roman History from Coins* (excellent). Cambridge University Press, 1968

_____ *Roman Imperial Money.* Cambridge University Press, 1954

_____ *Roman Literature.* Cambridge University Press, 1954

_____ *The World of Rome (133 B.C.–A.D. 217).* Mentor Books, 1960

Gwynn, Aubrey O., *Roman Education from Cicero to Quintilian.* The Clarendon Press, Oxford, 1926

Hadas, Moses, *Ancilla to Classical Reading.* Columbia University Press, 1954

_____ *History of Latin Literature.* Columbia University Press, 1952

Hamilton, Edith, *The Roman Way.* Norton, 1932 (also in paperback, Avon, New York, 1973)

Highet, Gilbert, *The Classical Tradition—Greek and Roman Influence on Western Literature.* The Clarendon Press, Oxford, 1951

_____ *Poets in a Landscape.* Alfred A. Knopf, 1957

Hutchinson, Lester, *The Conspiracy of Catiline.* Barnes & Noble, New York, 1967

Johnston, Mary, *Roman Life* (successor to *The Private Life of the Romans).* Scott, Foresman, 1957

Labande, Yvonne and Emond-René, *Rome,* tr. and adapted by George Millard. The Clarendon Press, Oxford, 1961

Lofstedt, Einar, *Roman Literary Portraits,* tr. by P. M. Fraser. Greenwood, Press, Westport, CT 1978

McCartney, Eugene S., *Warfare by Land and Sea.* Cooper Square, New York

McKendrick, Paul, *The Mute Stones Speak* (excellent, well illustrated). W. W. Norton, New York, 1976

Mainzer, Ferdinand, *Caesar's Mantle: The End of the Roman Republic.* Viking Press, 1936

Marek, Kurt W. (pseud. C. W. Ceram), *Gods, Graves, and Scholars.* Alfred A Knopf, 1951

_____ *The March of Archaeology.* Alfred A. Knopf, 1958

Moore, Frank G., *The Roman's World.* Biblo & Tanner, Cheshire, CT

Odahl, Charles M., *The Catilinarian Conspiracy.* College & University Press, New Haven, 1971

Plutarch, *The Lives of Noble Grecians and Romans* (many editions available)

Robathan, Dorothy M., *Monuments of Ancient Rome.* Bretschneider, 1950

Showerman, Grant, *Eternal Rome.* Yale University Press, 1925

_____ *Monuments and Men of Ancient Rome.* Appleton-Century, 1935

_____ *Rome and the Romans.* Macmillan, 1931

Starr, Chester G., *The Roman Imperial Navy, 31 B.C.–A.D. 324.* Greenwood Press, Westport, CT 1975

Taylor, Lily R., *Party Politics in the Age of Caesar.* University of California Press, 1949

Treble, Henry A., and K. M. King, *Everyday Life in Rome in the Time of Caesar and Cicero.* The Clarendon Press, Oxford, 1930

Woolley, Charles L., *Digging Up the Past.* Greenwood Press, Westport, CT 1977

17

LIFE OF CICERO

Bailey, D. R. Shackleton, *Cicero*. Scribner's, New York, 1971

Boissier, Gaston, *Cicero and His Friends,* tr. by Jones. Cooper Square, New York, 1970

Cowell, Frank R., *Cicero and the Roman Republic*. Penguin Books, 1956

Forsyth, William, *Life of Marcus Tullius Cicero*. Richard West, Philadelphia

Frank, Tenney, *Cicero*. Humphrey Milford, 1932

Haskell, Henry J., *This Was Cicero: Modern Politics in a Roman Toga* (written by a Washington, D.C., political reporter). Alfred A. Knopf, 1942

Hunt, Harold A. K., *The Humanism of Cicero,* Melbourne University Press, 1954

Jeans, George E., *The Life and Letters of Marcus Tullius Cicero*. Macmillan, 1925

Petersson, Torsten, *Cicero, A Biography*. University of California Press, 1920

Richards, George C., *Cicero, A Study*. Greenwood Press, Westport, CT

Rolfe, John C., *Cicero and His Influence*. Cooper Square, New York

Sihler, Ernest G., *Cicero of Arpinum*. Cooper Square, New York, 1969

Smith, R. E. *Cicero the Statesman*. Cambridge University Press, 1966

Stockton, David, *Cicero: A Political Biography*. Oxford University Press, 1971

Strachan-Davidson, James L., *Cicero and the Fall of the Roman Republic*. Arno Press, New York, 1972

Taylor, Hannis, *Cicero: A Sketch of His Life and Works*. Dynamic Learning Corp., 1978

Wilkin, Robert N., *Eternal Lawyer*. Macmillan, 1947

MYTHOLOGY

Bulfinch, Thomas, *Bulfinch's Mythology* (many editions available)

Coolidge, Olivia, *Greek Myths*. Houghton Mifflin, 1949

———— *Roman People*. Houghton Mifflin, 1959

Gayley, Charles M., *The Classic Myths in English Literature and in Art*. John Wiley & Sons, New York

Hamilton, Edith, *Mythology*. Little, Brown, 1942. Mentor Books, 1953 edition, p. 390

Herzberg, Max J., *Myths and Their Meaning*. Allyn and Bacon, 1984
Norton, Daniel S., and Peters Rushton, *Classical Myths in English Literature*. Greenwood Press, Westport, CT
Sabin, Frances E., *Classical Myths That Live Today*. Silver, Burdett, 1958

DICTIONARIES AND ATLASES

Greene, Amsel, *Word Clues* (derivatives). Harper & Row, New York, 1962
Harper's Dictionary of Classical Literature and Antiquities. Cooper Square, New York
Heyden, A. A. M., and H. H. Scullard, eds., *Atlas of the Classical World*. Nelson, 1959
Historical Atlas, C. S. Hammond, 1954
Historical Atlas of the World, Rand, McNally, 1961
Kidd, D. A., *Collins Latin Gem Dictionary* (very good pocket-size Latin-English, English-Latin dictionary). Collins, 1957
Oxford Classical Dictionary. The Clarendon Press, Oxford, 1949 (2nd edition, 1970)
Oxford Companion to Classical Literature. The Clarendon Press, Oxford, 1937
Simpson, D. P., *Cassell's Latin Dictionary*. Macmillan, New York, 1977
Smith, W., *Smaller Classical Dictionary*. E. P. Dutton (Everyman Series), 1958

HISTORICAL FICTION

Anderson, Paul L., *Pugnax the Gladiator*. Biblo & Tannen, Cheshire, CT
———— *Slave of Catline*. Appleton-Century, 1930
Bulwer-Lytton, Sir Edward, *The Last Days of Pompeii* (many editions available)
Crozier, William P., *Fates Are Laughing*. Harcourt, 1949 Story of the beginnings of the Empire
Doyle, A. Conan, *The Last Galley*. Doubleday, 1911

Duggan, Alfred, *He Died Old*. Peter Davies, London, 1975 Story of Mithridates the Great, 120–64 B.C.

_____ *Three's Company*. Peter Davies, London,, Story of the Second Triumvirate

Fast, Howard, *Spartacus*. Dell, New York, 1980

Gray, Charles E., *Murder Defies Roman Emperor*. Humphries, 1958 Mystery, set in the time of Hadrian

Green, Peter, *Sword of Pleasure*. John Murray, London, 1959 A psychological study of Sulla the dictator

Kellner, Esther, *The Bride of Pilate*. Appleton-Century-Crofts, 1959 Story about Augustus's granddaughter

Lindsay, Jack, *Rome for Sale*. Harper, 1934 Story of Catiline

Mason, Alfred E. W., *The Three Gentlemen*. Doubleday, 1932

Sienkiewicz, Henryk K., *Quo Vadis*. Airmont Publishers, New York, 1968

Wagner, John and Esther, *The Gift of Rome*. Little, Brown, 1961 Story based on Cicero's *Pro Cluentio*

Warner, Rex, *The Young Caesar*. Little, Brown, 1958

_____ *The Imperial Caesar*. Little, Brown, 1960

Wilder, Thornton, *The Ides of March*. Avon Books, New York, 1975 Caesar's story told through a series of imaginary letters, reports, and documents: well liked by students

_____Audio-Visual Materials

A very useful source of visual aids is your local museum of fine arts. Most institutions of this kind are able to supply a school with exhibits at little or no cost except transportation of the items loaned, and sometimes it is even possible to book a lecturer from the museum. In the New England area this service is available from the Museum of Fine Arts, Boston, Massachusetts; in the East, from the Metropolitan Museum of Art, New York; in the Midwest, from the Art Institute, Ryerson Library, and the Natural History Museum, Chicago, Illinois. *Be sure to investigate the resources of nearby museums.*

American Classical League Service Bureau, Miami University, Oxford, Ohio, 45056
The Service Bureau is a very useful source of helpful materials for classical teachers. There are dozens of inexpensive mimeograph sheets on every possible aspect of teaching of the classics, sets of pictures, plays, projects, games, posters, and books. Send for free folder of offerings.

American Library Colorslide Co., PO Box 5810 Grand Central Station, New York, 10017 Large selection of 2″ × 2″ and 3″ × 4″ slides.

Coronet, The Multimedia Company, 65 East South Water St., Chicago, IL 60601

EMC Recordings Corporation, 180 East 6th St., St. Paul, Minnesota Tapes presenting dramatized 15-minute programs in which Roman characters speak in Latin.

Encyclopedia Britannica Educational Corp., 425 N. Michigan Ave., Chicago, IL 60611

Folkways Records and Service Corp., 43 W. 61st St., New York, 10023 Readings from Cicero by Moses Hadas.

McGraw-Hill Films, 110 15th St., Del Mar, CA 92014

Society for Visual Education, Inc., Singer Education Division, 1345 Diversey Pkwy., Chicago IL 60614

Techniques for Teaching Reading

The literary selections in THIRD YEAR LATIN are designed for intensive reading. However, there are many different ways to teach reading extensively and some of these should be used at various intervals to add variety and interest to the classroom. Some suggestions follow:

(a) The teacher translates various phrases or sentences in the selection and asks students to find the corresponding Latin.

(b) The teacher selects various sections in Latin (a paragraph or two) and asks students to provide an English summary.

(c) The teacher teaches for comprehension by asking questions on the reading and having students answer in English.

(d) The teacher uses the reading to reinforce grammatical concepts by asking questions such as "Why is **telō** in line 3 translated as *with a spear?*"

(e) Reading selections can be used to make the "Latin-English Connection" by choosing isolated sections and providing English derivatives of specific Latin words to ascertain meaning. This technique, added to the basic content of the selection, enables students to guess intelligently at unfamiliar vocabulary and thus to read with more ease.

First Oration Against Catiline

1. How long, pray, will you abuse our patience, Catiline? how long will that madness of yours make sport of us? to what end will your unbridled audacity (go in) vaunt(ing) itself?

Have not the nightly garrison of the Palatine, nor the watches of the city, nor the fear of the people, nor the gathering of all good (*worthy*) citizens, nor this very well fortified place for convening the senate, nor the expressions on the faces of all these (senators) moved you at all? Do you not realize that your plans are made public (*laid open*), do you not see that your conspiracy is held and bound fast (*completely in check*) by the knowledge of all these (people around you)? — who of us do you think is ignorant of what you did last night, and the night before, where you were, whom you called together, and what plan you adopted?

Oh, the times! Oh, the morals (*customs*)! — the senate understands these things, the consul sees them; yet this man lives. Lives? he even comes into the senate, he is made a sharer in the public debate, while he notes and marks out with his eyes each one of us for murder. We brave men, however, think that we are doing enough for the state if we (personally) avoid the madness and weapons of that man.

You ought to have been led to death long ago, Catiline, by order of the consul; that destruction which you have been planning for all of us for a long time should have been visited upon you. In truth, that very distinguished man, Publius Scipio, as pontifex maximus and (merely) a private citizen, killed Tiberius Gracchus when he was only moderately weakening the condition of the republic: shall we consuls put up with Catiline who is desiring to lay waste the whole world with murder and fires? For I pass over those other (incidents) as too ancient, (for example) that Gaius Servilius Ahala killed with his own hand Spurius Maelius, who was desiring a revolution.

There was, once there was, in this state such courage that brave men punished a dangerous citizen with more severe penalties than a very bitter enemy. We have a decree of the senate against you, Catiline, vehement and stern; the planning and support of this body is not lacking; we, I admit openly, we consuls are remiss (*found lacking*).

2. The senate formerly decreed that Lucius Opimius, the consul, should see to it that "the state should not suffer any harm." Not a night passed; Gaius Gracchus, with the most distinguished father, grandfather, and ancestors, was killed on account of certain suspicions of treason, and Marcus Fulvius, of consular rank, (also) was cut down along with his children.

By a similar decree, the (safety of the) state was entrusted to the consuls Gaius Marius and Lucius Valerius: and death and the vengeance of the state did not have to wait for a single day, did it, for the punishment of Lucius Saturninus, a tribune of the people, and Gaius Servilius, a praetor?

But we now for the twentieth day allow the edge of our authority to grow dull. For we have a decree of the senate of the same kind, put away indeed in the archives, like a sword in its sheath, a decree of the senate according to which, Catiline, you ought to have been killed at once. But you still live, and you live not to put aside, but to strengthen, your boldness.

I desire, senators, to be merciful; I desire in such great perils of the state not to seem remiss, but I now blame myself for inaction and criminal carelessness. There is a camp situated in the mountain passes of Etruria, hostile to the Roman people, (and) the number of the enemy is increasing from day to day; you see, however, the general of that camp and the leader of the enemy inside the walls and even here in the senate, threatening every day some internal danger to the state.

If now I order you to be arrested or killed, Catiline, I suppose that I shall have to fear, not that all good men may say that I have done this too late, but that anyone will say that I have done it too cruelly. But I am not yet convinced, for a certain reason, that I should do that which should have been done long ago.

You will finally be killed (only) then when at last no one can be found so wicked, so abandoned, so like yourself that he will not admit that it was done justly. As long as there is (*will be*) anyone who dares (*will dare*) to defend you, you will live, and you will live, just as you are now living, surrounded by my many strong guards, so that you will not be able to make any move against the state. The eyes and ears of many people will watch and guard you, though you do not realize it, just as they have done up to this time.

3. For what is there, Catiline, which you expect further, if night with its darkness cannot shut in your wicked meetings, nor a private house with its walls can contain the voices of the conspiracy, if all things are brought to light, if everything has burst forth?

Do you remember my saying on October 21, in the senate, that Gaius Manlius, a follower and tool of your boldness, would be in arms on a certain day, which day would be October 27? I was not mistaken, was I, not only about such an important, atrocious, and incredible a matter, but even — what is much more to be wondered at — the very day itself? I also said in the senate that you had set October 28 as the day for the slaughter of the leading citizens, a time (*then*) when many of the leaders of the state fled from Rome, not so much for the sake of saving themselves as for checking (*foiling*) your plans.

You cannot deny, can you, that surrounded by my guards and watchfulness you were not able to make any move against the state, when at the departure of the others you said that you were satisfied with the slaughter of those of us who remained? What of this? — when you were confident that you would seize Praeneste on the first day of November in a night attack, did you realize that that town had been fortified by my guards and watchmen and troops? You do nothing, you plan nothing, you think of nothing which I not only hear about but see and clearly understand.

4. Recall with me, then, that night before last; (and) at last you will understand that I am watching even more keenly for the safety, than you are for the destruction, of the state. I say that you came on that night before last — I will not speak darkly (*obscurely*) — into the street of the scythe makers, to the house of Marcus Laeca; and that there came together to the same place many of your companions of the same madness and crime. You do not dare to deny it, do you? why are you silent? I will convince you if you do deny it. For I see here in the senate certain people who were with you.

Oh, ye immortal gods! Where in the world are we? what sort of a state do we have? in what kind of a city are we living? Here, here in our own number, senators, in this most dignified and sacred council of the whole world, are (men) who are planning for the ruin of this city and even of the whole world. I the consul see them and inquire about their feelings about the state, and (yet) I do not, as yet, injure with my

25

voice those who ought to be killed with swords!

You were, then, at Laeca's house that night, Catiline, you apportioned parts of Italy, you decided where you wanted each man to go, you chose those whom you would leave at Rome and those whom you would take with you, you assigned parts of the city to be burned, you stated that you yourself would be going soon, but you said that there was for you a matter of a slight delay, because I was still living. Two Roman knights were found who were to free you from this anxiety, and they promised that they would kill me in my bed a little before dawn.

I discovered all of this almost before your meeting had been dismissed; I strengthened and fortified my house with stronger guards, and I kept out those whom you had sent to greet me in the morning when they came, the very men whom I had predicted to many eminent gentlemen would come at (just) that time.

5. Since these things are so, Catiline, continue where you have begun: now finally get out of the city; the gates are open, depart. That Manlian camp of yours has been longing for you, its commander, for too long a time. Lead out with you all of your men; if not all, as many as possible; cleanse the city. You will free me of a great fear, provided there is a wall between you and me. You cannot stay with us any longer; I will not tolerate (bear) it, I will not allow it, I will not permit it. Great thanks are owed to the immortal gods, and especially to this Jupiter Stator (himself), the most ancient guardian of this city, because we have escaped so often this plague of the state so foul, so horrible, so deadly.

The safety of the state ought not to be endangered too often for the sake of one man. As long as you plotted against me when I was consul-elect, Catiline, I protected myself by my own caution, not by a public bodyguard. When at the last consular elections you wanted to kill me the consul and your competitors, in the Campus Martius, I checked your wicked attempts with a garrison of friends and my own forces, without publicly stirring up any tumult; finally, as often as you aimed at me, I withstood you through my own efforts, although I saw that harm to me personally was bound up with great calamity to the state. Now you are openly attacking the whole state, you are calling down to ruin and devastation the temples of the immortal gods, the buildings of the city, the lives of all the citizens, and all of Italy.

Therefore, since I do not yet dare to do that which is of first importance, and which is appropriate to this nation's sovereignty and to traditions of our ancestors, I shall do that which is more lenient in the point of severity and more useful for the common safety. For if I order you to be killed, there will remain in the state the rest of the band of conspirators; but if you go out, as I have long been urging you to do, the abundant and pestilent bilge water of the state — (that is,) your accomplices — will be drained off from the city.

What is there, Catiline? — you do not hesitate, do you, to do at my order what you were already doing of your own accord? The consul orders an enemy to go out of the city. You ask me whether (this means to go) into exile. I do not order it, but if you ask my advice, I advise it.

6. What is there, Catiline, which can delight you any longer in this city? — (a city) in which there is no one except for your fellow conspirators, ruined men, who does not fear you, no one who does not hate you?

What mark of personal disgrace has not been branded upon your life? what outrage in your personal affairs does not cling to your ill fame? what lust has ever been absent from your eyes, what crime from your hands, what outrage from your whole body? to what young man whom you have ensnared by the allurements of your corrupt practices have you not offered a weapon for his crimes or a torch for his lust? What then? — when recently, by the killing of your former wife, you made a place for a new marriage, did you not add to this crime another unbelievable crime? — I pass over these events, and easily allow them to be kept still, lest it appear in this state the hugeness of such a great crime (was suffered) either to have existed or not to have been punished.

I pass over the ruins of your private fortunes, which you will feel threatening you at the Ides of the next month: I come to those things which concern not the private disgrace of your own affairs, not your domestic difficulty and baseness, but rather (concern) the welfare of the state and the life and safety of all of us. Can this light or the breath of this air be pleasing to you, Catiline, when you know that there is no one of all these men here who does not know that you, on the day before the Calends of January, in the consulship of Lepidus and Tullus, stood armed in the assembly, and that you had prepared a gang for the sake of killing the consuls and the leading men of the state; and that it was not any change of mind or fear on your part which put a stop to this crime and madness, but rather the good fortune of the Roman people?

And now I pass over those crimes — for they are not unknown and many have been committed since that time — how many times you attempted to kill me when I was consul-elect, and how many times when I was consul! how many of your thrusts, so aimed that they seemed unavoidable, did I escape by a slight twist of the body (*a bit of "fancy footwork"*), as they say! You do nothing, you accomplish nothing, and still you do not stop trying and hoping. How often has that dagger been snatched from your hands; how often has it fallen by an accident and slipped (out of your hand)! I do not know by what sacred rites this dagger has been consecrated by you that you think it necessary to plunge it into the body of a consul!

7. Now, in truth, what is that life of yours? For I shall speak with you now, not to appear moved by hatred as I ought, but by pity, which is not anything owed you at all.

You came a little while ago into the senate: who among all your friends and associates greeted you? If this has happened to no one before within the memory of man, do you await the insult of vocal utterance when you have already been crushed by this gravest judgment of silence? What of the fact that at your arrival all the seats near you were left empty, that all men of consular rank, who have very often been marked out for murder by you, as soon as you sat down, left that (entire) section of seats bare and unoccupied, how do you think that you ought to feel about this?

By Hercules, if my servants feared me as all the citizens fear you, I would think that I ought to leave my house; don't you think that you ought to leave the city? and if I saw that I was so grievously suspected, even unjustly, and that I was so offensive to my fellow citizens, I would prefer not to be seen by my fellow citizens (rather) than to be gazed at with the hostile eyes of all: now you, since you know by the conscious-ness of your crimes that the hatred of all is just and long owed you, do you hesitate to avoid the sight and presence of those whose mind and sensibilities you wound?

If your parents feared and hated you and you could not win them over by any appeal, you would, I believe, take yourself from their sight. Now (our) country, which is the common parent of all of us, hates and fears you, and judges that you now for a long time have been planning nothing except its destruction: will you not revere her authority, nor obey her judgments, nor fear her power?

This country now pleads with you and, though silent, speaks in a certain way: "Now for some years no crime has come into existence except through you, no outrage without you; the murder of many citizens, the plundering and harassing of our allies has been for you alone free and unpunished; you have been able not only to neglect lawsuits and trials, but even to thwart and destroy them. I bore those former acts of yours as well as I was able, although they ought not to have been endured; but now, the fact that I am wholly in a state of fear on account of you alone, that at the slightest sound Catiline is feared, that it seems no plan can be undertaken against me which is not related to your crime, (all this) is not to be endured (further). Therefore, depart and free me from this fear; if it is a well-grounded fear, so that

28

I will not be overcome; but if it is groundless, so that I can at least cease to fear."

8. If the country should speak with you in this way, as I have said, should it not gain its request, even if it is unable to use force? What of the fact that you gave yourself into voluntary custody, that for the sake of avoiding suspicion you said that you wanted to live at the house of Manius Lepidus? When you were not received by him, you dared to come to me and asked me to keep you at my house. When you had received this answer from me that I could not possibly be safe with you inside the same house walls, when I was in great danger because we were held in the same city walls, you came to the praetor Quintus Metellus.

Having been rejected by him, you moved on to that fraternity friend of yours, Marcus Metellus, a fine (!) man, whom you apparently thought would be most diligent in guarding you, most sagacious in suspecting, and most courageous in punishing! But how far away from prison and chains do you think a man should be who already judges himself worthy of custody?

Since these things are so, Catiline, if you are not able to die with a calm mind, do you hesitate to go off to some other lands and devote that life of yours, rescued from many just and long-deserved punishments, to flight and solitude?

You say, "Refer it to the senate"; for you demand this and say that if it is pleasing to this order (*the senate*) that you go into exile, you will comply. I will not refer it to the senate, for it is not in accord with my practice, and yet I will let you know what these men think about you. Get out of the city, Catiline, free the state of fear; set out for exile, if this is the word you are waiting for.

What is it? what are you waiting for? don't you notice the silence of these men? They allow me to say this to you, and they are silent. Why do you await the authority of these men speaking, when you can see their wishes silently expressed? If I had said this same thing to that most excellent young man, Publius Sestius, or to this very brave man, Marcus Marcellus, the senate would have laid violent hands upon me, the consul, and rightly so, here in this very temple.

But about you, Catiline, when they are quiet they are showing their approval, when they allow me to say this they are voting, when they keep still they are shouting against you, not only these men whose authority is apparently so dear to you (though their) lives are quite worthless (to you); but also these most honorable and noble Roman knights, and all the rest of the very brave citizens who are standing about the senate (meeting place), you were able to see the crowd of

29

them, to perceive their zeal, and hear their voices a little while ago. For a long time now I have scarcely kept their hands and weapons away from you, and I shall easily persuade them to escort you, leaving behind these things which you have long been anxious to destroy, right to the gates (of the city).

9. And yet, why do I speak? — that anything will change you, that you will ever reform, that you will meditate any flight, that you will plan exile? Would that the immortal gods would give you that intention! — and yet I see that if terrified by my voice you make up your mind to go into exile, what a great storm of ill feeling will await me, if not at the present time because of the fresh memory of your crimes, certainly in later times. But that is worth while, provided only that is a personal calamity and is separated from any danger to the state. But it is not to be expected that you will be dissuaded from your own vices, or that you will fear the penalty of laws, or that you will yield to the needs of the state. For you are not the kind of man, Catiline, that shame has ever called away from disgrace, or fear from danger, or reason from madness.

Wherefore, as I have often said, set out and if you wish to stir up ill will against me, your personal enemy as you say, go straight into exile; I shall scarcely bear the talk of men, if you do this; I shall scarcely sustain (*bear up under*) the load of that hatred if you go into exile at the order of the consul. But if you prefer to minister to my praise and glory, get out (along) with that wretched band of criminals, betake yourself to Manlius, stir up reprobate citizens, separate yourself from good citizens, make war on your country, exult in your impious brigandage, so that you will seem to have gone not (as though) expelled by me (to join) aliens, but rather invited to join your friends.

Though why do I urge you, by whom I know men have been sent ahead already to await you in arms at Forum Aurelium; when I know that a day has been set and fixed with Manlius, and when I know that that silver eagle which I trust will always be deadly and fatal to you and all your men, for which you set up a shrine in your own house, that this too has been sent ahead? Can you be without this any longer, which you were accustomed to worship when setting out for a murder, and the altar from which you often transferred that impious right hand of yours to the slaughter of citizens?

10. You will go, then, at last, where that unbridled and mad desire of yours has long been hurrying you; and still this fact does not bring sorrow to you, but a certain incredible pleasure. For nature bore you for this madness, your own wish has trained you, and your luck has preserved you. You have never desired, not merely peace, but not even

30

a war unless wicked. You have gathered together a band of wicked men, who have given up all hope not only of any further fortunes, but even of hope itself. Now with what happiness will you rejoice, with what joys will you exult, in how much pleasure will you revel, when you neither hear nor see a single good man in all of your company of associates!

For those toils of yours which are commonly bragged about have trained you for a life of this sort, namely, to lie on the ground, not only to lay siege to the object of your lust, but also to undertake (any) shameful affair, to stay awake (at night) not only to plot against the sleep of husbands, but also the worldly goods of (all) peaceful citizens. You have a chance of showing that extraordinary endurance of hunger, cold, and a lack of all things, by which you will realize in a short time that you have been finished. I accomplished so (*this*) much, when I beat you out of the consulship, that you as an exile would be able to attack the state rather than as consul to shake it, and that that which was undertaken and criminally conceived by you would be called brigandage (*outlawry*) rather than (civil) war.

11. And now, so that I may defend myself and protest against a certain just complaint of (our) country, senators, listen carefully, I ask you, to what I have to say and store these things deep in your hearts and minds. For if my country, which is much dearer to me than life itself, if all of Italy, if the whole republic should say:

"Marcus Tullius, what are you doing? Will you allow to go out a man whom you know to be an enemy, whom you see is the leader of the future war, whom you know is awaited as the commander in the camp of the enemy, the author of this crime, the chief of the conspiracy, the recruiter of slaves and reprobate citizens, (in such a way) that he seems, not cast out of the city by you, but let loose against the city? Will you not rather (*Aren't you going, instead, to*) order him cast into chains, to be seized for death, to be punished with the supreme penalty? What, pray, is preventing you? the customs of your ancestors? But very often even private men in this state have punished dangerous citizens with death. Or is it the laws which have been enacted regarding the punishment of Roman citizens? But never in this city have those who have revolted against the state enjoyed the rights of citizens.

"Or do you fear unpopularity in the future? But you would be repaying fine gratitude to the Roman people, who have raised you, a man known only by your own achievements, with no recommendation from your ancestors, at so early an (*the earliest legal*) age to the highest office through all of the steps of office, if you neglect the safety of the citizens on account of any fear of ill will or danger. But even if there is any fear

31

of (adverse) criticism, that of (*coming from*) sternness and severity is no more greatly to be feared than that which comes from inertia and laxness. Or, when all of Italy shall be ravaged by war, when the cities be plundered, and the houses be burned, do you not think that you will then be scorched by a fire of unpopularity?"

12. I will answer a few words to these most sacred utterances of the state and to the minds of those people who feel the same way. If, senators, I judged that the best thing to do was to have Catiline punished by death, I would not give to that scoundrel the enjoyment of one hour for living. For if the most noble men and illustrious citizens have not only not stained their names by the killing of Saturninus and the Gracchi and Flaccus and several others, but have even gained honor from it, certainly I shall not have to fear that any unpopularity would attach itself to me by the killing of this murderer of citizens. But even if that did seriously threaten me, I have always been of the opinion that unpopularity gained by uprightness is really glory, not unpopularity.

And yet there are some in this body who either do not see the things which are threatening, or they hide what they do see; these men have nourished the hopes of Catiline by their faint measures, and they have strengthened the growing conspiracy by disbelieving it; with the backing of these (men) many others, not only the wicked, but also the ignorant, if I had punished this man, would now be saying that I had acted cruelly and in the manner of a tyrant.

(But) now I realize, that if he reaches that Manlian camp as he intends, no one will be so stupid as not to see that a conspiracy has been formed, no one so wicked as not to admit it. Moreover, I realize that if this one man is killed, the danger to the state can be checked for a little while, but (by this means) it cannot be checked forever. But if he thrusts himself out and leads out with him his (friends) and all the other shipwrecked men collected from all sides, then there will be destroyed and wiped out not only this plague to the state, (now) so full grown, but the root and seed of all evil.

13. For a long time now, senators, we have been living in the midst of the dangers and plots of a conspiracy, but somehow or other the fruition of all these crimes and old madness has broken out in the time of my consulship. If this one man is taken away from such a big crowd of robbers, we shall perhaps seem relieved of our care and fear for some short time, but the danger will remain. and it will be deeply inclosed in the veins and vitals of the state. Just as often men who are sick with a serious disease, when they are tossing around with the heat of fever, if they drink cold water, they seem at first to be relieved, but then they are afflicted much more seriously and violently, so this disease which is

32

in the state, if relieved at first by the punishment of that man yonder, would grow much worse since the rest are living.

Wherefore, let the wicked depart, let them separate themselves from decent men, let them finally be separated from us by a wall, as I have often said; let them stop plotting against the consul in his own house, standing around the tribunal of the city praetor, besieging the senate house with swords, and preparing torches and firebrands for the burning of the city; let there finally be written on the forehead of each one what he thinks about the republic. I promise you this, senators, that there will be so much diligence in us consuls, so much authority in you, so much fortitude in Roman knights, and so much agreement in all good men, that at the departure of Catiline you will see everything made clear, brought to light, suppressed, and punished.

With these prophetic words, Catiline, set out to that nefarious and impious war, with (*in the interests of*) the highest welfare of the state and the plague and destruction of yourself and the finish of those who have joined themselves to you in every crime and murder.

You, Jupiter, who was established by Romulus under the same auspices by which the city was established, whom we call Protector of the city and the national sovereignty (*empire*), you will repel him and his associates from your temples and the other temples, from the buildings of the city and its walls, from the lives and fortunes of all the citizens, and you will punish with eternal punishments these men, living or dead, who are enemies of the upright, foes of their native land, plunderers of Italy joined by a compact of crime and abominable association.

Second Oration Against Catiline

1. Now at last, fellow citizens, we have thrown out of the city, or sent out, or followed with words as he was going, Lucius Catiline, blazing with audacity, breathing out wickedness, shamefully planning the destruction of the state, and threatening you and the city with fire and sword. He has gone, he has departed, he has escaped, he has burst out.

No longer will any deadly destruction be prepared by that monster and criminal inside the walls against these walls. And we have, in fact, defeated this one leader of this domestic war without a controversy. No longer will that dagger dwell within our sides, we shall no longer be afraid in the Campus Martius, nor in the Forum, nor in the senate house, nor finally within our house walls. He was forced from his vantage point when he was driven out of the city. Now we shall wage a just war openly with a public enemy, with no one hindering us. Without doubt we destroyed the man and gloriously defeated him, when we drove him from hidden ambush into open outlawry.

With what great grief do you think that he has been struck down and afflicted, because he did not take out a blood-stained dagger, as he wanted to, or because he left with us alive, or because we have wrenched his weapon from his hands, or because he left behind the citizens unharmed and the city standing? He now lies prostrate, citizens, and he realizes that he has been driven forth and cast out, and he certainly often turns his eyes back to this city which he mourns has been snatched from his jaws; but it (*on the other hand the city*) now seems to me to rejoice because it has ejected and thrown out that pestilence.

2. And if there is anyone such as all ought to be, who in this very matter in which my speech exults and boasts, violently accuses me because I have not arrested such a deadly enemy, but rather sent him out, this is not my fault, fellow citizens, but rather the fault of the times. Lucius Catiline ought to have been killed and to have suffered the most terrible punishment long ago, and the custom of our ancestors and the dignity of this government and the state demanded this of me.

But how many are there, do you suppose, who would not believe what I was reporting, how many who on account of stupidity would not think as I did, how many who would even defend him, how many who on account of wickedness (actually) favored him? And if I judged that all danger was being removed from you by putting him out of the way, I would have removed Catiline long ago, not only at the risk of personal enmity but even of life. But since I saw that not even then had the matter been made clear even to all of you, that if I had punished him by death as he deserved, then I, oppressed by (bitter) criticism, would not be able to prosecute his companions, I brought the matter to the point where you would be able to fight openly when you saw the public enemy clearly.

You may realize, fellow citizens, how greatly I think this enemy is to be feared outside, from this fact that I am greatly vexed that he went out of the city with too small a retinue! Would that he had led out all of his troops! He did take with him, I see, that Tongilius, whom he had begun to love in early boyhood, and Publicius and Minucius, whose debts contracted in eating-houses were not able to bring any disturbance to the state: what men he has left behind, how greatly in debt, how valiant, how noble!

3. And I greatly scorn that army of his, compared with the Gallic legions and that levy of troops which Quintus Metellus has (raised) in the Picenic and Gallic lands, and these troops which are being prepared daily by us: (his army) collected from ruined old men, landholders bankrupt because of their extravagant high living, men who preferred to abandon their bail rather than that army of his; these will collapse if I show them, not the battle line of our army, but merely the edict of the praetor.

I see these men flitting about in the Forum, standing near the senate house and even coming into the senate, men who glisten with unguents, who are refulgent in their purple; I would prefer that he had taken them out with him as soldiers: if they remain here, remember that we must fear not so much that army as those who have deserted that army. And I think they are more to be feared because they realize that I know what they are thinking and they are still unmoved. I see (him) to whom Apulia has been allotted, (him) who has Etruria, (the one) who has the country of the Picenes, (the one) who (has) the country of the Gauls, (the one) who demanded for himself the (maturing of) plots for murder and burning within the city. They know that all of their plans of that former night have been brought to me, for I exposed them in the senate yesterday; Catiline himself was afraid, he fled: but what are these men waiting for? Surely they are very much mistaken if they hope that my earlier leniency will be everlasting.

4. I have now accomplished what I was waiting for, (namely,) that you would all see that a conspiracy has been openly formed against the state; unless perhaps, there is anyone who thinks that men like Catiline (*of Catiline's ilk*) do not agree with Catiline. There is now no place for leniency; the matter itself demands severity. But even now I will make one concession: let them go out, let them set out, let them not allow poor Catiline to waste away from longing for them. I will point out the way: he started by the Aurelian Way; if they wish to hurry, they will overtake him by evening. Oh fortunate republic, if it will throw out this bilge water of the city!

By Hercules, the state already seems to me to be relieved and refreshed with Catiline alone removed. For what evil or crime can be

35

imagined or planned which he did not conceive of? — what poisoner in all of Italy, what gladiator, what robber, what assassin, what parricide, what forger of wills, what cheat, what glutton, what spendthrift, what adulterer, what shameless woman, what corrupter of youth, what profligate, what abandoned character can be found, who will not confess that he has lived on very intimate terms with Catiline? What murder has been committed through recent years without him, what foul debauch without him?

Now in truth, what (so) great enticement of youth was ever so great in any man as in him? — who himself loved others most basely, served the love of others most shamefully, to some promised fulfillment of their lusts, to others the death of their parents, not only by encouraging them but even by helping them. Now again how quickly he has collected a great crowd of abandoned men, not only from the city but also from the fields! No one not only in Rome but even in any corner of Italy has been oppressed by debt whom he did not enroll in his incredible alliance of crime.

5. So that you may perceive his different pursuits in an altogether different sphere, there is no one in the gladiatorial school a little too eager for crime who does not admit that he is intimate with Catiline; no one on the stage more trivial or a little inclined to vice who does not claim that he is almost his boon companion. And this same man, hardened as he is by the training of vices and crimes, by enduring cold, hunger, thirst, and lack of sleep, was heralded by these men as brave, although he was wasting in his lust and wantonness the forces that (ought to) make for industry and assist virtue. If his companions will follow him, if these outrageous bands of desperate men will get out of the city, oh how happy we will be, how fortunate the state, how glorious the praise of my consulship!

For the lusts of these men are not now moderate, their audacity is not human and tolerable: they think of nothing but murder, fire, and pillage. They have squandered their patrimonies, they have mortgaged their properties; ready money began to fail them long ago, recently their credit; however, that same lawlessness which they had in their better days still remains. But if they were only seeking revelry and harlots in their wine and gambling, they should certainly be despaired of, but nevertheless they should be borne: but who can bear this, that cowards should plot against the bravest, that the stupidest should plot against the wisest, the drunk against the sober, and the sleeping against the watchful? — it seems to me that these men, reclining at their banquets, embracing shameless women, stupid from wine, stuffed with food, crowned with wreaths, smeared with ointments, weakened by their vice, belch forth in their conversation the murder of good citizens and the burning of the city.

I am confident that some fate hangs over these men, and the punishment long due them for their wickedness, iniquity, crime, and lust is now either right at hand for them or is certainly approaching. If my consulship, since it is not able to cure them, will remove them, it will add to the life of the state not some brief time, but many ages.

There is, indeed, no nation that we should fear, no king that can make war on the Roman people; all foreign enemies on land and sea have been subdued by the valor of one man: the civil enemy remains, the plotting is now from within, the danger is shut up within, the enemy is within. We must fight with extravagance, with madness, with crime. I offer myself, fellow citizens, as a leader for this war; I take on myself the hatred of the wicked men; I will cure in some way or other what can be cured; but I will not allow to remain as a danger to the state what must be cut off. Therefore, let these men go out or keep quiet; if they remain in the city with the same attitude, let them expect what they deserve.

6. There are some who may say, citizens, that Catiline was thrown out by me; if (only) I could accomplish this by words, I would throw out those who say these things. Apparently (he was) a very timid or modest man (who) was not able to endure the voice of the consul; as soon as he was ordered to go into exile, he obeyed!

But yesterday, when I had almost been killed in my house, I summoned the senate into the temple of Jupiter Stator, and I revealed the whole matter to the senatorial council. When Catiline came there, what senator addressed him, who greeted him, finally who regarded him merely as a vicious man, and not rather as a very dangerous public enemy? Nay, more, the chief men of the (senatorial) order left that part of the seats, to which he had approached, bare and unoccupied.

Then I, that violent consul who thrusts citizens into exile by a mere word, asked Catiline whether he had been at a night meeting at the house of Marcus Laeca, or not. When that very bold man, at first convicted by his conscience, became silent, I revealed the other things: I showed what he had done that night, where he had been, what he had planned for the next night, and how he had arranged the plan for the whole war. When he hesitated (and) was held trapped, I asked him why he hesitated to set out there where he was preparing (to go) for a long time, when I knew that his arms and axes, the fasces, trumpets, military standards, and the silver eagle for which he had made a shrine of crime in his own home, had all been sent ahead.

Did I cast into exile a man whom I saw had already set out for war?

I suppose that centurion Manlius who pitched camp in the district of Faesulae declared war on the Roman people in his own name, and that that camp is not now awaiting Catiline as its leader, and that he, having been thrown out, is taking himself to Marseilles, driven into exile, as they say, and not to that camp!

7. Oh, wretched lot not only of governing but also of saving the republic! If now Lucius Catiline, surrounded and weakened by my plans, labors, and dangers, suddenly becomes afraid and changes his mind, and deserts his friends, and casts aside his plans for making war, and turns his journey away from this course of crime and war to exile, he will be said not to have been deprived of the arms of boldness by me, not to have been stunned and terrified by my watchfulness, not driven from his hope and attempt, but innocent and uncondemned to have been thrust into exile by the consul, by threats of force; and if he does this, there will be those who want him to be considered not wicked but unfortunate, and me to be considered not a very diligent consul, but a very cruel tyrant! But it is worth while for me, citizens, to bear the storm of this false and unjust hatred, provided only the danger of this horrible war and wicked peril is driven away from you.

Let it be said, indeed, that he was thrown out by me, provided he goes into exile. But believe me, he is not intending to go. I shall never hope from the immortal gods, citizens, that for the sake of lessening my unpopularity you will hear that Catiline is leading an army and is flitting around in arms, but you will hear this, however, within three days; I am much more afraid that I may sometime be unpopular because I have sent him out than because I threw him out.

But since there are some who will say that he was thrown out when he went out, what would these same men say if he had been killed? And yet those who keep saying that Catiline is going to Marseilles do not so much complain of this as they dread it. There is no one of them so merciful that he would not prefer that he go to Manlius's camp rather than to Marseilles. But if he, by Hercules, had never before planned what he is now doing, still he would prefer to be killed a bandit rather than to live in exile. But now, since nothing has happened to him other than what he wished and planned, except that he did set out from Rome with me alive, let us hope rather than complain that he may have gone into exile.

8. But why do we speak so long about one enemy, and (moreover) about that enemy who now confesses that he is an enemy, and whom I no longer fear because, as I have always wished, there is a wall between us: shall we say nothing about those who are in hiding, who stay at Rome, and who are still here with us? — them indeed I do not so much

want to punish, if it can be done in any way, as to cure them for themselves, to win them back to the state, and I know how this can be done if they are willing to listen to me. For I shall show you, fellow citizens, from what classes of men those troops are raised; then I shall bring to each of them, if I am able in any way, the healing of my counsel and discourse.

The first class consists of those who, though greatly in debt, have still greater property, to which they are so devoted that they can in no way be separated from it. The appearance of these men is very honest, for they are rich, but their intentions and cause is most shameless. Do you, rich and possessing abundant fields, buildings, silver, slaves, and all things, hesitate to take away from your property to acquire (good) credit? What are you waiting for? — war? What then? — in the devastation of everything do you think that your property will be sacred? — or (perhaps) a cancellation of debts?

Those are mistaken who expect this from Catiline: by my figuring, new (*clean*) accounts will be offered, but they will be those of the auctioneer; for those who have possessions cannot be separated from them in any other way. But if they had been willing to do this earlier, and had not most stupidly tried to pay the interest on their debts from the income of their estates, we should find them now both richer and more useful citizens. But I think that these men are the least to be feared, because either they can be induced to abandon their opinions or, if they remain with them, they seem to me to be more likely to make vows against the state than to bear arms.

9. A second class is (made up) of those who, although they are oppressed by debt, still expect to rule, they wish to get control of affairs, and they think that they are more likely to gain the honors that they despair of when the state is quiet, when the state is in turmoil. It seems to me that these men should be shown this, just the same as all the others, that they should give up hope of attaining that which they are trying to accomplish: first of all, that I am watchful, am present, and am providing for the state; in the second place, there is great courage in decent (*good*) citizens, great harmony, a very great number (of them), and besides (*in addition*), large military forces (*a great crowd of soldiers*); finally, that the immortal gods will bring help to this undefeated people, most illustrious sovereign nation (*empire*), and very beautiful city, against such a great violence of crime, with their immediate presence.

But even if they should gain that which they desire with the greatest madness, they do not hope, do they, that in the ashes of the city and the blood of the citizens, things which they have longed for in their depraved and nefarious minds, (that) they will be the consuls or dictators,

39

or even kings? Do they not see that if they were to gain this which they desire, it would (soon) be necessary to surrender it to some runaway slave or gladiator?

There is a third class, composed of men already affected by old age, but still robust from training; from this class is that Manlius whom Catiline is now going to join. These are men from those colonies which Sulla established; I realize that these colonies in general are composed of very fine (*good*) citizens and very brave men, but still there are some colonists who, in their sudden and unexpected wealth, have made themselves conspicuous by displaying too much extravagance and pride. While they build houses as if they were wealthy, while they delight themselves in their choice estates, large retinues of slaves, (and) well-prepared banquets, they have fallen so greatly into debt that if they wish to be solvent, Sulla himself must be raised from the dead: these (men) also have induced some poor countrymen of little wealth to indulge in the same hope of more of the old confiscations.

I put both of these classes in the category of pirates and robbers, but I give them this warning, let them stop being mad and plotting proscriptions and dictatorships. For so much sorrow of those times has been branded upon the state that it seems to me that not only human beings but even the cattle will not suffer them any more.

10. The fourth class is certainly varied, mixed, and turbulent; they have long been oppressed, and they never emerge, and they stagger under their old debts, partly from sloth, partly from bad managing of their business, partly from extravagance; many of these, worn out by their bail, court judgments, and by the siezure of their property (for debts), are said to be taking themselves from the city and the countryside to that camp. I think that these men are not such fierce soldiers as they are slow defaulters.

Let these men collapse as soon as possible, if they are not able to stand, but in such a way that not only the state, but even their nearest neighbors will not know about it. For I do not know why, if they cannot live honorably, they wish to perish disgracefully, or why they think that they will die with less pain with (*in the company of*) many others than if they should die alone.

The fifth class is composed of parricides, assassins, and all sorts of criminals. I do not call these men away from Catiline; for they cannot be torn from him, and indeed let them perish as outlaws, since there are so many of them that a prison cannot hold them.

The last class is, moreover, last not only in number but also in the type of its life which is Catiline's own type, (levied) from his own chosen kind, (taken) indeed even from his embrace and bosom; you see them

40

with their hair combed, sleek, with either no beards or long beards, with tunics that reach to the ankles and wrists, clad in veils, not togas; all their industry in life and toil of keeping the night watches are spent in all-night banquets. In these gangs are all gamblers, all adulterers, all impure and shameless rascals. These boys, so delicate and soft, have learned not only how to love and be loved, to dance and sing, but also to brandish daggers and to sprinkle poison.

Unless they leave the city, unless they die, even if Catiline dies, be assured that there will be in this state (still) a school of (new) Catilines. But what do these wretches want? — they are not going to take their lady friends with them to camp, are they? How are they going to do without them, especially on these (cold) nights? How will they endure the cold and snows of the Apennines? — unless indeed they think that they will stand the winter more easily, because they have learned to dance with no clothes at their banquets.

11. Oh, war greatly to be feared, since Catiline is going to have as his bodyguard these unmanly men! And now, citizens, draw up (*put on parade*) your own guards and armies against these troops, so illustrious, of Catiline. First put your consuls and your generals against that worn-out and wounded gladiator; then against that banished and weakened band of shipwrecked men, lead out the flower and strength of all Italy. Now, in truth, the cities of the colonies and free towns will answer (*serve to offset*) the wooded heights of Catiline. For I do not have to compare your other resources, equipment, and garrisons with the want and poverty of that bandit.

But if, omitting all other resources with which we are supplied (and) he lacks, the senate, the Roman knights, the city, the treasury, the revenues, all of Italy, all the provinces, and foreign nations, if without mentioning these things we wish to compare the causes which are in opposition to each other, from this we can realize how utterly (helpless) they lie. For on this side modesty is fighting, on that shamelessness; on this honor, on that vice; on this faith, on that fraud; on this righteousness, on that crime; on this constancy, on that madness; on this honesty, on that disgrace; on this self-restraint, on that lust; on this side finally, justice, temperance, fortitude, prudence, and all the virtues contend with injustice, extravagance, cowardice, rashness, and all the vices; lastly, abundance fights with poverty, a sane mind (*sanity*) with madness, and finally good hope with despair in all things.

In a struggle and battle of this kind, even if the efforts of men should fail, would not the immortal gods themselves compel so many and such great vices to be defeated by these most notable virtues?

12. Since these things are so, fellow citizens, defend you your homes with guards and watches, as I have said before; it has been arranged and provided for by me that the city will have sufficient protection without your (suffering) fear, and without any disturbance.

All of the colonies and your municipal free towns, having been informed by me about this night attack of Catiline, will easily defend their cities and territories; the gladiators, a band which he surely thought would be on his side, although they are of better minds than some of the patricians, will still be restrained by my authority. Quintus Metellus, whom foreseeing this I sent ahead into the district of Gaul and Picenum, will either crush the man or will forestall all of his movements and attempts. We shall now refer to the senate, which you see is being summoned, concerning arranging, expediting, and acting on the remaining matters.

Now those men who have stayed in the city and have been left by Catiline in the city (to work) against the safety of the city and all of you, because they were born citizens, although they are (now) enemies, I want warned again and again. If this leniency of mine has up to this time seemed to anyone too remiss, it has been waiting for this, that what was lying hidden would burst forth.

As for the future, I cannot forget that this is my country, that I am the consul of this (assembled company) and that I must either live with them or die for them. There is no guard at the gate, no one is lying in ambush along the way; if any are willing to go, I can arrange it; but whoever busies himself in the city and I detect, I will not say any actual act of his, but even any first move or attempt against the country, he will realize that there are vigilant consuls in this city, that there are outstanding magistrates, a brave senate, and that there are arms (and) a prison which our ancestors wanted to be the avenger of wicked and clearly shown crimes.

13. And all of these things will be so carried out that the greatest of affairs will be settled with the least disturbance, utmost dangers with no tumult, and this most cruel and momentous internal and domestic war within the memory of man (settled) with me, the leader and commander, wearing (only) the garb of a civilian. But I will so arrange matters, fellow citizens, if it can be done in any way, that not even any wicked citizen in this city will pay the penalty of his own crime. But if the violence of his obvious boldness, if the danger threatening the state shall necessarily force me from this leniency of mine, I will certainly bring it about — what seems scarcely to be hoped for in so great and insidious a war — that no upright man shall perish and that you shall all be saved by the punishment of (only) a few.

I promise these things to you, fellow citizens, relying not on my own wisdom nor on human planning, but on not (*by no means*) doubtful portents of the immortal gods, under whose leadership I have entered upon this hope and purpose; these gods, no longer far removed as they were accustomed to be from a far-distant and foreign enemy, but here present with their divine will and aid, are defending their own temples and the buildings of the city. You ought to pray to them, fellow citizens, and beseech them and implore them to defend from an outrageous plot of nefarious traitors this city which they have wished to be the most beautiful, the most flourishing, and the most powerful (in the world), now that all the forces of foreign enemies on land and sea have been defeated.

Third Oration Against Catiline

1. You see, fellow citizens, the state and the lives of all of you, your property, fortunes, your wives and children, and this home of the most glorious government, this most fortunate and beautiful city, snatched from fire and sword and almost from the jaws of fate and saved and restored to you today by the greatest love of the immortal gods for you, and by my labors, planning, and perils.

And (*Indeed*) if the days on which we are saved are no less pleasant and illustrious in our sight than those on which we are born, because the joy of safety is a certain one and the condition of being born is uncertain, and because we are born without feeling, whereas we are saved with (conscious) happiness, certainly (*especially*) since we have raised to the immortal gods with good will and praise that man who founded this city, he who has saved the same city, founded and now enlarged, shall deserve to be (held) in honor among you and your posterity. For we have extinguished the fires which were kindled and almost surrounded the whole city, the temples, shrines, buildings and walls, and we have also struck back swords drawn against the state and knocked aside the sword points from your throats.

Since these events have been brought into the open, exposed, and recounted in the senate, I will now reveal them to you, fellow citizens, so that you, who (are) uninformed and eager for news, may know how great and how manifest are the things that have been investigated, and in what way they have been suppressed. To begin with, when Catiline rushed from the city a few days ago, since he had left at Rome the allies of his crime and the fiercest leaders of this nefarious war, I always (*continually*) watched and made provision, citizens, for ways in which we could be safe in these plots so great and so secret.

2. For at the time when I thrust Catiline from the city — I no longer fear (any bitter) criticism arising from this word since it is (now) more to be feared that he got out alive — but at the time when I wanted him to be banished, I thought that either the rest of that band would go out at the same time or that those who stayed here would be weak and helpless without him.

And also, as I saw that those whom I knew were inflamed with the greatest fury and madness were still with us and had remained at Rome, I spent all my days and nights in this purpose to (*so that I might*) find out and see what they were doing and planning, in order that — since my speech would have less credence in your ears because of the incredible magnitude of the crime — I might get the matter so in my grasp (*get in hand [concrete] evidence*) that you would then at last make provision for your safety with (good) heart (*courage*) when you actually saw the crime itself with your own eyes.

And so when I found out that ambassadors of the Allobroges had been offered bribes by Publius Lentulus to stir up a Transalpine war and a Gallic insurrection, and that these envoys had been sent with letters and orders to Gaul to their own citizens, and on the same journey to Catiline Titus Volturcius had been assigned to them as an escort, and that a letter had been given to him for Catiline, I thought that an opportunity had been presented to me, so that what was most difficult and what I had kept hoping for from the immortal gods, the whole matter would be grasped not only by me but also plainly by the senate and you.

Accordingly, yesterday I called to me the praetors Lucius Flaccus and Gaius Pomptinus, very brave and patriotic men, I explained the situation, and I showed them what I wanted done. They, moreover, as men of pure and noble patriotism, undertook the task with no hesitation nor delay, and when it began to get dark, they came secretly to the Mulvian Bridge, and there they stayed in the nearest houses in two divisions, so that the Tiber and the bridge was between them. These men had brought to the same place, without anyone suspecting it, many brave men, and I had also sent from the prefecture of Reate several picked young men with swords, whose help I continually use in protecting the state. Meanwhile, when the third watch was nearly past (and) when at length the envoys of the Allobroges, and along with them Volturcius, were beginning to go on the Mulvian Bridge with a great retinue, an attack was made on them. Swords were drawn by their men and by ours. The plan was known to the praetors alone, it was not known by the others.

3. Then, at the intervention of Pomptinus and Flaccus, the battle which had been started was settled. Whatever letters there were in that company were handed over to the praetors with the seals unbroken; the arrested men themselves were brought to me when it was beginning to get light. And I called to me at once the most wicked contriver of all these crimes, Gabinius Cimber, who did not yet suspect anything; then Lucius Statilius was likewise summoned, and after him Cethegus; slowest (of all) moreover, came Lentulus, I suppose because he had been up so late the night before working on the letters!

Although it was pleasing to many well-known and high-minded men of this state, who had come to me in large numbers in the morning after hearing about the affair, that the letters should be opened by me before they were given to the senate lest, if nothing was found in them so great a tumult would not seem to be thrown upon the state, I said that I would not take any other course than to refer the whole question of the public crisis (*danger*) to a public council. For, citizens, even if those things which were reported to me were not found, I still thought that in such great dangers to the state I did not have to fear (exercising) too much care. I quickly summoned the senate in large numbers, as you saw. And meanwhile, at the suggestion of the Allobroges, I at once sent that brave man Gaius Sulpicius, the praetor, to bring from the house of Cethegus whatever weapons were there; he brought out from there (*the house*) a very large number of daggers and swords.

4. I introduced (*brought in*) Volturcius without the Gauls; by order of the senate, I gave him a pledge (of immunity) in the name of the state; I urged him to reveal whatever he knew without fear. Then, when he had with difficulty recovered from his great fear, he said that he had instructions and a letter for Catiline to the effect that he use a bodyguard of slaves and approach the city with an army as soon as possible; and moreover, this was to be the plan, that when they had set fire to the city on all sides, as it had been assigned and allotted, and murdered countless numbers of citizens, he would be nearby to take those who were fleeing and (then) to join himself with the leaders in the city. Further, when the Gauls were brought in, then they said that an oath had been given them and also letters from Lentulus, Cethegus, and

45

Statilius addressed to their own tribe and they had been instructed by these men and by Lucius Cassius to send cavalry into Italy as soon as possible, adding that infantry troops would not be lacking for them.

They said, moreover, that they had been given assurance by Lentulus that according to the Sibylline fates and the responses of the soothsayers he was that third Cornelius to whom the rule and power of the city was destined to come: that Cinna and Sulla had been before him. And the same man had said that this year was fated for the destruction of the city and the government, this being the tenth year after the acquittal of the Vestal Virgins, and moreover the twentieth after the burning of the Capitol. They said that Cethegus had had an argument with the others, because it seemed best to Lentulus and the others that the slaughter be carried out and the city burned on the Saturnalia, but that this had seemed to Cethegus too long to wait.

5. To be brief, citizens, I ordered the letters to be brought in which were said to have been given them by each. First I showed (one) to Cethegus; he acknowledged the seal. I cut the thread (and) read it. It was written in his own hand to the senate and people of the Allobroges, saying that he would do what he had assured their envoys he would do; and he begged them to do what their envoys had promised him. Then Cethegus, who a little earlier had made some reply about the swords and daggers which had been seized in his house and had stated that he had always been a fancier of good ironware, overwhelmed by the reading of the letters and stricken by a sense of guilt, suddenly became silent.

Brought in (next), Statilius acknowledged both his seal and his handwriting. His letter was read, with its contents about the same; he confessed.

Then I showed tablets to Lentulus, and asked him whether or not he acknowledged the seal; he nodded (assent). "It is, in truth," I said, "a well-known seal, the image of your grandfather, a most famous man, who loved his country and its citizens with all his heart; this silent image should have called you back from so great a crime." His letter to the same effect, to the senate and people of the Allobroges, was then read.

If he wished to say anything about these matters, I gave him the chance. At first he refused; after a little time, however, when the whole evidence had been produced and laid before us, he stood up and asked the Gauls, and likewise Volturcius, what business he had with them, as a reason why they had come to his house. When these had replied briefly but firmly through whom they had come to him and how often, and they asked him whether or not he had spoken with them about the

46

Sibylline fates, then he, maddened by crime (*suddenly losing grip on himself*), showed how great is the power of conscience.

For when he still might have denied it, suddenly, contrary to the expectation of all, he confessed. Thus not only that ability and practice in speaking, in which he always excelled, but also his boldness and impudence (*brazen demeanor*) in which he surpassed everyone failed him, because of the effect of revealing the crime and its detection. Volturcius indeed suddenly ordered the letter to be brought in and opened, which he said had been given him by Lentulus for Catiline. And then, greatly agitated, Lentulus admitted both his own seal and handwriting.

The letter was without address or signature, but (ran) thus: "You will know who I am from him whom I have sent to you. Take care that you be a man, and consider into what situation you have brought yourself. See what you may need and take care to join to you the auxiliary troops of all classes, even the lowest." Gabinius then was brought in, and although he had at first begun to reply brazenly, at the end he denied none of the things which the Gauls charged him with.

And, citizens, not only do these things seem to me the most certain arguments and proof of their guilt, the letters, the seals, the (individual) handwriting, and finally the confession of each one of them, but much more certain proof (was) their pallor, their eyes, their expressions, and their silence. For they were so stunned, they thus gazed at the ground, sometimes they exchanged glances at each other thus furtively, that they seemed not to be testified against (*indicted*) by others, but to be testifying against (*indicting*) themselves.

6. When the evidence had been set forth and drawn up in final form, citizens, I asked the senate what they wanted done about the highest safety of the state. Very pointed and courageous speeches were uttered by the principal men, and their motions were adopted without any dissenting (voice). And since the decree of the senate has not yet been written out, I will deliver from memory, citizens, (the essentials of) what the senate voted.

First, thanks were given to me in very generous terms, because the state was saved from the greatest of perils by my courage, wisdom, and foresight. Then Lucius Flaccus and Gaius Pomptinus, the praetors, were deservedly and rightly praised because I had used their courageous and useful assistance. And also praise was accorded to my colleague, a brave man, because he had removed from his counsels and those of the state those men who had been participants in this conspiracy.

And so (*Next*) they voted that Lentulus should be handed over to custody, after he had resigned from the praetorship; likewise that

Cethegus, Statilius, and Gabinius, who were all present, should be given into custody; and the same thing was decreed for Lucius Cassius, who had demanded for himself the supervision of the burning of the city; and against Ceparius to whom, it was shown, Apulia had been assigned for stirring up the shepherds; against Publius Furius, who is one of those colonists whom Sulla settled at Faesulae; against Quintus Annius Chilo, who had been along with this Furius in bribing the Allobroges; and against Publius Umbrenus, a freedman, who it was evident had first introduced the Gauls to Gabinius. And so the senate used such leniency, citizens, that out of so great a conspiracy and such a large crowd of domestic enemies, with the republic saved by the punishment of these nine most (*especially*) criminal men, it thought that the (perverse) minds of the rest could be made sane.

And also a thanksgiving was decreed to the immortal gods in my name, for their singular favor, a thing which (thus) happened to me, a civilian official, for the first time since the city was founded, and was decreed in these words: "because I had saved the city from burning, the citizens from murder, and Italy from war." If this thanksgiving should be compared with others, there is this difference, that others have been decreed for skillful ordering of the state (in war), (but) this is the only one decreed for saving the state.

And that which had to be done first was done and finished. For Lentulus, although by the judgment of the senate he had lost not only the rights of his office as praetor but also of a citizen, through the giving of the evidence and his own confession, still he resigned his office so that we might be freed from scruple in punishing Lentulus as (other than) a private citizen, though no such scruple prevented that noblest of men, Marius, from killing Gaius Glaucus, a praetor, (though) no action had been taken against him by name.

7. Now, fellow citizens, since you have the nefarious leaders of this most criminal and dangerous war captured and arrested, you should believe that all of Catiline's troops, all his resources, all of his hopes have (as good as) collapsed, now that these dangers in the city have been driven away.

Indeed, when I drove him from the city, I foresaw this, citizens, that with Catiline removed, I did not have to fear the sleepiness of Lentulus, nor the fat (*obesity*) of Cassius, nor the mad fury of Cethegus. He was the only one of all of these men that had to be feared, but only so long as he was inside the city walls. He knew everything, he had all approaches to everyone; he was able and he dared to summon, tempt, and entice. He had a mind set on crime, and neither his tongue nor his hand failed his purpose. He had certain men picked and assigned to accomplish

48

:ertain tasks. Nor in truth when he had commanded something, did ie think the job was done; there was nothing which he himself did not supervise, inspect, watch, and toil for; he was able to bear cold, :hirst, and hunger.

If I had not driven this man, so bitter, so bold, so ready, so watchful in crime, so energetic in evil enterprise, from domestic plots into the :amp of bandits — I shall say what I think, citizens — I would not easily have removed from your necks this burden of disaster. That one would not have fixed upon the (still faraway) Saturnalia for us, nor would he have announced so far ahead the day of the destruction and fate of the republic, nor would he have allowed his seal, his letters to be seized as obvious proof of crime.

Now, with him away, these things were done in such a way that no theft in a private house has ever been detected so plainly as this conspiracy in the state has been clearly found out and suppressed. But if Catiline had remained in the city till this time, although as long as he was here I met and opposed all of his plans, still, to put the case very mildly, we would have had to fight him to the finish, and we would not ever, while that enemy was inside the city, have freed the state of such great dangers with so much quiet, peace, and silence.

8. And yet, fellow citizens, all of these things have been carried out by me in such a way that they seem to have been managed and provided by the immortal gods. Not only can we assume this by inference, because the direction of such great affairs seems scarcely able to have been managed by human counsel, but the gods in person have brought such help and assistance to us that we are able to see them almost with our very eyes. For, not to mention other things, the torches that were seen in the west at night, the glow in the sky, the hurling of thunderbolts, the earthquakes, and to omit other things which have happened in such great numbers in my consulship that the immortal gods seem to foretell the events which have come to pass, certainly this which I am about to tell of, fellow citizens, must not be omitted or passed over (in silence).

For you surely remember that in the consulship of Cotta and Torquatus many things on the Capitol were struck by lightning, when both the images of the gods were thrown down and the statues of the men of olden times were overturned, and the bronze tablets of the law were melted, and even (the statue of) Romulus, the founder of the city, was struck, a gilded (statue) which you remember had been on the Capitoline, (portraying him) as small and suckling at the udders of the wolf. At this time, when the soothsayers had assembled from all of Etruria, they said that slaughter and burning and the destruction of the laws,

49

and civil and domestic war, and the downfall of the whole city was approaching, unless the immortal gods, appeased in every way possible, could avert by their divinity almost fates themselves (*fate itself*).

Accordingly, because of their predictions games were held at that time for ten days, and nothing was left undone which might placate the will of the gods. These same men ordered that a larger statue of Jupiter should be made and set up in a high place, and turned to the rising sun, a direction opposite to its previous position; and they said that they hoped that if this statue which you see looked on the rising sun and the Forum and the senate house, it would come to pass that those plans which were secretly formed against the safety of this city and the republic would come to light so that they would be seen clearly by the senate and the Roman people. And so those consuls contracted for the erection of that statue; but such was the slowness of the work that it was not set up during any previous consulships nor during ours until today.

9. But who here can be so averse to the truth, so headstrong, so depraved in mind, as to say that all of these things which we see, and especially this city, are not being governed by the will and power of the immortal gods? For when the answer had been given that murder, arson, and the ruin of the state were all being planned, and that by citizens, such things seemed at that time unbelievable because of the magnitude of the crime; but you have realized that these things had not only been plotted by nefarious citizens, but that they had even been undertaken; but is it not such an immediate manifestation that it seems to have been done by the command of the great Jupiter Optimus Maximus, that when this (*today in the*) morning the conspirators and the witnesses (against them) were being led through the Forum into the temple of Concord, at my order, at that very time the statue was being erected?

When this had been erected and faced towards you and the senate, both you and the senate saw that everything which had been plotted against the safety of all was made clear and disclosed. Those men, therefore, are worthy of an even greater hatred and punishment who tried to bring their foul and cursed fires not only to your homes and buildings, but even to the temples and shrines of the immortal gods.

If I should say that I resisted these men, I would be taking too much on myself, and I would be unbearable; he, Jupiter, resisted them; he wanted the Capitol, these temples, the whole city, and all of you, to be safe. Under the guidance of the immortal gods I settled on this purpose and determination and I reached such great decisions.

For never, surely, would that attempt to win over the Allobroges —

and the entrusting by Lentulus and the other domestic enemies of such great and important affairs (would) never have been so rashly committed to such unknown and barbarous men, unless all sanity had been taken from him by the gods themselves. What now? — (the fact) that men of Gaul, a state not thoroughly pacified, the only people which seems able and not unwilling to make war on the Roman people, would disregard the hope of power and such great rewards offered to them voluntarily by men of noble rank, and put your safety ahead of their interests, do you not think that this was done with divine aid, especially when they could win not by fighting but by keeping still?

10. Therefore, citizens, since a thanksgiving has been decreed at all the shrines, you shall celebrate these days with your wives and children. For many honors, just and deserved, have been often held for the immortal gods, but never more deserved. For you have been rescued from the most cruel and wretched destruction, rescued without murder, without bloodshed, without an army, without a struggle; you in civilian clothes have conquered with me, your leader and commander, also in civilian clothes.

Now recall, fellow citizens, all of the civil dissensions, not only those which you have read about, but also the ones that you remember and have seen. Lucius Sulla overcame Publius Sulpicius; and he cast out from the city Gaius Marius, the guardian of the city; many brave men he threw in part out of the state, in part killed. Gnaeus Octavius as consul drove his colleague from the city by force of arms. This whole place was filled with the piles of bodies and the blood of citizens. Afterwards Cinna with Marius prevailed: at this time indeed, with many very notable men of the state killed, the lights of the city were extinguished. Sulla later avenged the cruelty of that victory, it is not necessary for me to say with what great slaughter of citizens and calamity of the state.

Marcus Lepidus quarreled with Quintus Catulus, a very famous and brave man: not so much his death brought sorrow to the state as did the death of the others involved.

And all of these civil dissensions aimed, citizens, aimed not at the destruction of the state, but at a change in the government: they did not want that there be no government, but in that which there was, they wanted to be the leaders; not that the city should be burned, but that they should (be the ones to) flourish in the city. And yet all of these civil wars, none of which sought the ruin of the state, were settled not by peaceful reconciliation but by the bloodshed of citizens.

However, in this one greatest and most cruel war within the memory of man, such a war as no barbarian ever waged with his own tribe, a war in which the rule had been established by Lentulus, Gabinius, Cethegus, Cassius, that all who could be safe in the safe city should be considered in the number of the enemy, I have conducted myself, citizens, in such a way that you all are safe, and when your enemies thought that only those citizens would remain who could survive the infinite slaughter, and only so much of the city as the flames could not destroy, I have kept the city and its citizens safe and unharmed.

11. In return for these great services, citizens, I ask from you no reward of courage, no insignia of honor, no monument of praise, except the eternal memory of this day. I want all my triumphs, decorations of honor, the monuments of glory, and the insignia of praise to be stored away and enshrined in your hearts. Nothing mute can please me, nothing silent, nothing, finally, of such a kind that less worthy men can attain it. Our (*My*) deeds will be cherished in your memories, fellow citizens, they will grow by being talked about, and they will grow older and stronger in the monuments of literature; and I know that the self-same time, which I hope will be eternal, has been prolonged for the safety of the city and the memory of my consulship, and that at one time there have existed two citizens in this state, one of whom was destined to define the borders of your empire, not by earthly boundaries but by limits of the sky, and the other was destined to save the home and seat of the government.

12. But since the fortune and lot of these things which I have done is not the same as those who have carried on foreign wars, because I must live with those whom I have conquered, whereas they leave their enemies either killed or oppressed, it is your duty, citizens, to see to it that, if other men rightly profit by their deeds, my deeds may not at any time injure me. For I have provided that the criminal and nefarious minds of the boldest men may not be able to harm you; now it is your duty to see to it that they not harm me.

And yet, citizens, no harm can be done to me now by these men. For there is in good men great protection, which has been prepared for me forever, (and) there is great majesty in the state, which though silent will always defend me; and great power of conscience, and those who neglect this, when they wish to injure me, will be betraying themselves.

For there is such determination in us (*me*), citizens, that we will not only yield to the boldness of no man, but we will always of our own accord always attack all wicked men. But if the attack of our domestic enemy, having been turned away from you, should turn itself on me alone, you will have to consider, citizens, what you want the lot of those to be who have exposed themselves for your safety to enmity and all hazards: as for me, indeed, what is there which can be added to the enjoyment of life, especially when I see no loftier honor that you have to bestow, nor any greater height to which I can ascend? I will surely accomplish it, citizens, that I as a private citizen will support and dignify the things which I have accomplished in my consulship, so that if any enmity has been gained in my saving the state, it may injure the envious and will increase my fame.

I will, finally, so conduct myself in the state that I will always remember what I have done, and take care that those things are seen to have been by courage, not by chance. You, fellow citizens, since it is now night, after worshiping Jupiter, the guardian of the city and of you, go back to your homes, and although the danger has now been driven away, defend them just the same as the night before, with guards and sentinels. I will take care that you will not have to do this too long (*much longer*), and that you may be able to live in lasting peace.

Fourth Oration Against Catiline

1. I see, senators, the faces and eyes of all of you turned toward me, I see that you are all worried not only about your own danger and that of the state, but if that has been driven away, about my danger. Your anxiety about me is pleasing to me in my bad times and gratifying in my sorrow, but by the immortal gods, put it aside and, forgetful of my safety, think about yourselves and your children. If this consulship has been bestowed upon me on these terms, that I should endure all bitterness, all sorrows and tortures, I will bear them not only bravely but even gladly, provided that by my labors dignity and safety may be gained for you and the Roman people.

For I am that consul, senators, to whom not the Forum, in which all justice is centered; not the Campus Martius, consecrated by consular auspices; not the senate house, the greatest protection of all nations; not the home, the common refuge; nor the couch, a place for rest; nor finally this chair of office, the seat of honor, has ever been free from plots and the danger of death. I have been silent about many things, I have put up with many things, I have made many concessions, and I

53

have remedied many things, with some suffering on my part and fear on yours.

Now, if the immortal gods have wanted this to be the result of my consulship, that I should save you and the Roman people from very wretched slaughter, your wives and children and the Vestal Virgins from the cruelest outrage, the temples and shrines and this most beautiful fatherland of all of us from the most terrible conflagration, and all of Italy from war and devastation, then let me alone endure whatever fortune may have in store for me. For if Lentulus, convinced by the soothsayers, thought that his name would be destined to destroy the state, why should not I rejoice that my consulship has been destined almost by fate to save the Roman people?

2. Therefore, senators, take counsel for yourselves, protect the country, save yourselves, your wives and children, your fortunes, and defend the name and safety of the Roman people; stop sparing me and thinking about me. For first of all, I should hope that all of the gods who preside over this city will repay me gratitude in such measure as I deserve; then, if anything shall happen to me, I will die with a calm and resigned mind. For a base death cannot come to a brave man, nor an early one to a man of consular rank, nor an unhappy one to a philosopher.

Still, I am not so hardhearted as not to be moved by the sorrow of my most fond and loving brother who is here in person, and by the tears of all of these men by whom you see me surrounded. And often my thoughts are called homeward by my terrified wife, and my daughter prostrated with fear, and my small son, whom it seems to me the state is embracing as a hostage of my consulship, nor by my son-in-law, whom I see standing there awaiting the outcome of this day. I am moved by all of these things, but only to the determination that they shall all be safe, along with you, even if any violence overwhelms me, rather than that they and we perish in the destruction of the state.

Wherefore, senators, bend to the oars, for the safety of the state, look around at all of the storms which are threatening unless you make provisions. It is not a case of a Tiberius Gracchus, because he wanted to be a tribune of the people for a second time, or Gaius Gracchus because he tried to stir up the people on farms, nor a Lucius Saturninus because he killed Gaius Memmius being brought to trial and the judgment of your severity: those are being held here now who have stayed in Rome to burn the city, to kill all of you, and to receive Catiline back; we have their letters, seals, and handwriting, and finally the confession of each; the Allobroges are being offered bribes, the slaves invited to enlist, Catiline is summoned back, (and) this is their plan, that when they have killed everyone, no one will be left even to mourn the name of the Roman people and to lament the destruction of so great a government. **3.** The witnesses have disclosed all these facts, the defendants have confessed, you have already by many decisions made judgments, first because you voted thanks to me in most remarkable terms, and you proclaimed that the conspiracy of traitors was exposed by my courage and diligence, then because you forced Publius Lentulus to resign from his praetorship; then because you voted that he and the others about whom you passed judgment should be given into custody, and especially because you decreed a thanksgiving in my name, an honor which no one has ever before received as a civilian; and finally yesterday you gave most ample rewards to the envoys of the Allobroges and to Titus Volturcius. All of these things are of such a kind that they seem to show that those who have been put in custody by name, without any doubt have been condemned by you.

But I have decided to refer the whole matter to you, senators, as if it were still a fresh question, both as to what you may judge about the crime, and then what you may vote about the punishment. I will say only what is befitting a consul to say. I long ago saw that some great madness was in our state, and that new pernicious schemes were brewing and being stirred up, but I never imagined that such a deadly conspiracy was being formed, (and that) by citizens.

Now whatever the situation is, and whichever way your minds incline and your sentiments turn, you must decide before nightfall. You see what a great crime has been reported to you. If you think that only a few are involved, you are greatly mistaken. This evil has been spread more widely than anyone thinks; it has penetrated not only through Italy, but even across the Alps, and stealing by obscure paths has now covered many provinces. It cannot be checked in any way by endurance and procrastination; punishment must be given quickly by you in whatever way you decide.

4. I see that there are two opinions up to this point, one of Decimus Silanus, who advises that those who have attempted to destroy the state should be punished by death, and the other of Gaius (Julius) Caesar, who disapproves of the death penalty, but embraces the affliction of all other punishments. Each one insists upon the greatest severity, in accordance with his own high office and the magnitude of the events. One of them thinks that those who have attempted to deprive all of us and the Roman people of life ought not to enjoy for one instant of time the life and this air that we breathe, and he recalls that often in this state this kind of penalty has been used against depraved citizens. The other understands that death has been ordained by the immortal gods

55

not as a punishment, but as a necessity of nature and as a rest from labors and miseries. "Accordingly," (he says), "wise men have never accepted it unwillingly, brave men often gladly. But imprisonment, and that too for life, has been invented as a special punishment for foul crimes." He (Caesar) orders them to be distributed among the free towns.

This course seems to have injustice, if you wish to order it, and a difficulty, if you ask for it; but let it be enacted, if it pleases you. I shall undertake to find those who, I hope, will not think it consistent with their dignity to refuse that which you order for the sake of all. He sets a heavy penalty on the towns if anyone of these men should break from his chains; he surrounds them with grim prison regulations, worthy of the crime of these wretched men; he orders that it may never be possible for anyone, by vote of either the senate or the people, to lighten the punishment of those who have been condemned; he even takes away hope, which is the only thing which is accustomed to console men in their misery. He also orders the confiscation of their property; he leaves only life to these criminals; if he took that from them, (according to Caesar) he would have removed at the same time much suffering of the mind and body, and all the punishment for their crimes.

Therefore, in order that there would be some fear presented in life for the wicked, those men of ancient times wanted some punishments among the shades to be ordained for evildoers, because they realized that obviously if these were removed even death itself was not to be feared.

5. I now see, senators, what is to my interest. If you follow the opinion of Gaius Caesar, since he has followed the policy in the state which is regarded as democratic, perhaps I shall have to fear less the attacks of the people, since he is the author and proposer of this opinion; but if you follow that other one, I know not whether a large measure of trouble may be in store for me. But still, let the exigencies of the state outweigh any considerations of my danger.

For we have from Caesar, just as his own rank and the dignity of his ancestors demanded, a proposal as a sort of hostage of his lasting good-will toward the state. It is well known what a difference there is between the fickleness of agitators and a truly popular mind looking out for the safety of the people. I see that of those who wish to be considered democratic, now a few are absent, lest apparently, they have to express an opinion about the life of Roman citizens. He (Caesar) on the day before yesterday, gave Roman citizens into custody, and he voted for a thanksgiving in my name, and yesterday he bestowed magnificent rewards on the witnesses. Now there can be no doubt to anyone what he who has voted for custody for the defendant(s), congratulation for the investigator, and a reward for an informer has judged about the whole case and affair.

But Gaius Caesar realizes truly that the Sempronian law has been enacted for Roman citizens; moreover, (he also knows) that one cannot be a citizen in any way if he is an enemy of the state: (and) finally that the proposer of the Sempronian law himself paid the penalty of the state without the order of the people. The same one does not think that Lentulus himself, prodigal and spendthrift (as he is), can be called (one) of the popular (democratic) party, when he has so ruthlessly and bitterly plotted the ruin of the Roman people and the destruction of this city.

And so this very mild and humane man does not hesitate to consign Lentulus to eternal darkness and imprisonment, and he would decree that hereafter no one be able to achieve prominence by lightening the punishment of this man and thereby become popular to the destruction of the republic. He also adds the confiscation of property, so that all torture of the mind, together with poverty and want, may follow.

6. Therefore, if on the one hand you decide on this, you will give me an associate for the public meeting (with the people) who is dear and pleasing to the people; if you prefer the other, the opinion of Silanus, the Roman people will easily free me and you from the accusation of cruelty, and I will maintain that this policy is much more merciful. And yet, senators, what cruelty can there be in the punishment of so inhuman a crime? For I judge according to my own feelings. For may it be my lot so to enjoy the saved state with you as not to be moved by any cruelty in my mind, in showing unusual insistence in this case, but rather — for who is more gentle than I am? — by a certain special kindness and mercy.

For I seem to see this city, the light of the whole world and the fortress (*citadel*) of all the nations, suddenly engulfed in one great conflagration. I see in my mind's eye the wretched and unburied heaps of citizens in the buried fatherland; there comes before my mind the sight and madness of Cethegus reveling in your slaughter. But when I envision Lentulus ruling, just as he himself admitted he had hoped to do according to the fates, and Gabinius dressed in royal purple, and Catiline arrived with an army, then I shudder at the lamentations of the mothers of families, the flight of the girls and boys, the assault on the Vestal Virgins, and because these things seem to me pitiful and deserving of pity, therefore I shall present myself as stern and relentless against those men who have wished to bring these things about.

For I ask, if any father of a family, after his children have been killed

57

by a slave and his wife murdered, and his house burned, did not inflict the most severe punishment possible on the slaves, whether this man seems mild and merciful or most inhuman and cruel. To me at least he seems unfeeling and hardhearted, since he did not mitigate his own sorrow and torture by the sorrow and torture of the guilty one. And so in the case of these men who have wanted to murder us, our wives, and our children, who have tried to destroy our homes and the common dwelling of the state, who have done this so that they could set up the tribe of the Allobroges in the remains of this city and in the ashes of the burned nation, if we are very severe, we shall be considered merciful; but if we wish to be more lenient, then the reputation of the greatest cruelty in a matter concerning the destruction of the fatherland and citizens must be endured by us.

Unless perhaps Lucius Caesar, a most brave and patriotic man, seemed too cruel two days ago, when he said that the husband of his sister, a most charming lady, when he was present and listening, ought to be deprived of life, and that his own grandfather had been killed by order of the consul, and that his son, still a youth, having been sent by his father as an envoy, had been killed in prison. What deed of these men was similar to this, what plan was formed for destroying the whole state? (It was only that) state doles and some party strife prevailed at that time in the state.

And also at that time the grandfather of this Lentulus, a very famous man, stood armed against Gracchus. He even received a grave wound at that time, so that the welfare of the state would not suffer in any degree; this man (Lentulus) summoned the Gauls to overturn the government, he stirred up the slaves, he called Catiline, he assigned us to Cethegus to be butchered, and the killing of the other citizens to Gabinius, the burning of the city to Cassius, and the devastation and plundering of all Italy to Catiline. Of course you may well be afraid that you may have seemed to have decided something too severe in this so huge and shameless a crime; much more is it to be feared that by the lessening of the punishment we may seem cruel toward our country, rather than that by the severity of our punishment we may appear to be stern toward these most bitter public enemies.

7. But, senators, I am not able to conceal the things which I hear. Voices are being uttered which reach my ears, of those who seem to fear that I do not have enough of a garrison to carry out the measures which you vote today. All has been provided and prepared and set up, senators, not only by my very great care and diligence, but also by the much greater determination of the Roman people to retain their government at its height and to save their common fortunes.

All men of all classes, ranks, and ages are here; the Forum is full, the temples around the Forum are crowded, all the approaches to this temple and place are crowded. This is the only case known since the founding of the city in which all men feel one and the same thing, except those who, since they saw that they must perish, wished to perish with all men rather than alone. I except (*make an exception of*) these men and gladly separate (segregate) them, and I do not think that they ought to be classed as wicked citizens, but in the number of most bitter enemies.

But the rest, immortal gods! with what crowds, with what eagerness, with what courage they unite for the common safety and glory! What should I say here of the Roman knights? They concede to you the first place in rank and counsel only so far that they vie with you in love for the state; after a struggle with this body for many years, this day and this case have joined (them) in a harmonious fellowship with you. If we keep everlasting this harmony in the state which has been established in my consulship, I assure you that hereafter no civil and domestic strife will ever come to any part of the state.

I see that the tribunes of the treasury, very brave men, have come together with a like zeal for defending the state; likewise I see that all of the government clerks, whom chance has this day brought to the treasury in large numbers, have turned their attention from the allotment of duties to the common safety. The whole multitude of freeborn men is here, even the poorest; for who is there to whom these temples, the sight of the city, the possession of liberty, finally, this light itself and the common soil of the fatherland are not dear and sweet and pleasing?

8. It is worth while, senators, to note the eagerness of the freedmen who, having won a place in this state by their own merit, truly judge that this is their country, which certain ones born here, and born of high station, have judged to be not their fatherland, but a city of the enemy.

But why do I mention these men and these classes whom private fortunes and the common republic, and finally that liberty which is most sweet, excite to the defense of the common safety? There is no slave, provided only he is in a tolerable condition of slavery, who does not shudder at the audacity of these citizens, who does not want these things to stand, who does not contribute to our safety as much goodwill as he dares and is able.

Therefore, if anyone of you is disturbed by this rumor which is being circulated, that a certain agent of Lentulus is running around the shops and for a price is hoping to win over the support of the poor and the inexperienced, indeed this was begun and attempted, but no one has been found so wretched in fortune or so abandoned in desire that he

59

did not want this place of daily work and gain, his own couch and bed, and finally this peaceful course of life, to be kept safe. But much the greater part of those who are in the shops, nay more — for this should rather be said — this whole class, is most loving of peace. For the equipment of every worker, all of his gainful occupation, is sustained by intercourse of citizens and fostered by peace; if the gain of these men is diminished when the shops are closed, what, pray, would have happened if the shops had been burned?

Since these things are so, senators, the guards of the Roman people are not lacking (to you); you must see to it that you do not seem to be lacking (in concern) for the Roman people.

9. You have a consul saved from many dangers and plots and from the jaws of death, not for his own sake, but for your safety. All classes are united in purpose, heart, and voice for the saving of the state. Our country, beset with the torches and weapons of an impious conspiracy, extends its hands to you as a suppliant, she commends herself to you, the lives of all the citizens, the citadel and the Capitol, the shrines of her household gods, the everlasting fire of Vesta, the temples and shrines of all the gods, and the walls and buildings of the city. Moreover, you must decide today about your lives, the lives of your wives and children, about the fortunes of all, about your homes and firesides. You have a leader mindful of all of you, forgetful of himself, an advantage which is not always given; you have all classes, all men, the whole Roman people, a thing which we see for the first time in a political matter, feeling one and the same.

Think how one night almost destroyed the government, founded by so much toil, the liberty established by such bravery, and our fortunes increased and augmented by the kindness of the gods. Provision must be made today so that never (again) can this not only not be accomplished, but not even planned, by citizens. And I have said these things, not to excite you who are already running ahead of me in enthusiasm, but so that my voice, which should be the first in the state, may seem to be performing its consular duty.

10. Now, before I return to the sentence, let me speak a few words about myself. As great as the band of conspirators is, which you see is very great, so great (is) the multitude of personal enemies I see that I have made for myself; but I consider them base, weak, and powerless. If, however, that band, incited by the madness and crime of someone, shall have more power than your prestige and that of the state, I never will repent, senators, my deeds and my advice.

For death, which perhaps these men are threatening, has been prepared for all; no one has ever before attained such praise as you have honored me with in your decrees; for you have always decreed congratulation to others for the good management of the state (in wars of conquest), to me alone for having saved it.

Let Scipio be famous, by whose wisdom and courage Hannibal was forced to return to Africa and to leave Italy; let that other Africanus, who destroyed two cities of our greatest enemies, Carthage and Numantia, be honored with special praise; let that noble Paulus be exalted with special praise, whose triumph the once powerful and noble king Perseus adorned; let Marius be (held) in eternal glory, who twice freed Italy from siege and the fear of slavery; let Pompey be placed ahead of all of them, whose deeds and virtues are limited only by the regions and boundaries that confine the course of the sun: surely there will be room for my glory among the praises of these men, unless by chance it is a greater thing to open up provinces to which we may go than it is to take care that those who are away may have a place to which they can return as victors.

And yet in one respect the lot of an external victory is better than a domestic one, in that foreign enemies are either conquered or become slaves, or else they are accepted as friends, and so they think that they are bound by kindness; but when men belonging to the class of citizens are depraved by some madness and begin to be enemies of their country, you can neither coerce them by force nor win them by kindness when you thwart them in their desire to destroy the state. Therefore, I see that I have taken upon myself an unending struggle with wicked citizens.

I am confident that this (danger) can easily be pushed away from me and my family by your aid and that of all upright men, and by the memory of these great dangers which will always remain, not only among the people who have been saved, but in the words and thoughts of all nations. And certainly no force will ever be found so great that it will be able to break and dissolve your union with the Roman knights and the complete accord among all upright men.

11. Since these things are so, I ask of you nothing except the eternal memory of this time and my consulship, in place of the power, the army, the province which I renounced, the triumph and other insignia of distinction which I rejected that I might care for the city and you, in place of the clients and my friendly relations with the provincials which I maintain by my influence in the city with no less labor than I spend in securing them, in place of all of these things, and in return for my extraordinary efforts and this diligence in saving the state which you all see; for as long as this remains fixed in your minds, I shall think that I am guarded by a very safe wall.

But if the power of the criminals shall disappoint my expectation and win out, I commend to you my small son, who will surely have enough protection not only for his safety but also for his career, if you will but remember that he is the son of the man who saved the entire state, at his sole peril.

Therefore, decide carefully and diligently, as you have begun, about the greatest welfare of you and the Roman people, about your wives and children, about (your) altars and hearths, shrines and temples, the dwellings and homes of the entire city, the government and liberty and the whole state. You have a consul who will not hesitate to obey your decrees, support your decisions as long as he lives, and assume personal responsibility for their accomplishment.

The Speech on Pompey's Commission

1. Although your assembled presence has always seemed to me most pleasing, citizens, and this place for speaking most dignified and most full of honor for addressing the people, however, not my own wish (*disinclination*), but the planned course of my life followed from my early years, has kept me from this avenue to praise, which has always been available to any distinguished man. For since before this, on account of my age I did not dare to aspire to the dignity of this place and I decided that nothing ought to be brought to this place unless perfected by talent and elaborated by industry, I thought that all of my time ought to be given over to the needs of my friends.

Accordingly this place was not ever empty of men who would defend your cause; and my labor, entirely and solely employed in the trials of private citizens, has now gained the most generous reward from your judgment. For when, on account of the adjournment of the comitia, I was three times declared praetor first by all the centuries, I easily understood, citizens, both what you judged of me and what you would prescribe to others.

And now, since there is in me as much authority as you have wanted there to be by entrusting these honors, and as much ability in speaking as almost daily practice in speaking could bring to an industrious man from practice at the bar, certainly whatever authority is in me I shall use for the benefit of those who have given it to me, and if I can accomplish anything in speaking, I shall show it most especially to those who in their judgment have thought that the fruits of this art ought to be given (to me).

And I see that I ought to rejoice especially, because in this rôle which is unusual for me, of speaking from this place, there has been offered a cause such that in it eloquence could fail no one. For I must (am to) speak about the singular and eminent character of Gnaeus Pompey; and it is more difficult to find an end than a beginning of this speech. Therefore I must seek not so much abundance as moderation in my speaking.

2. And so that my speech may start from that point whence this whole cause is derived: a serious and dangerous war is being waged against your tributaries and allies by two very powerful kings, Mithridates and Tigranes, one of them left alone, the other — having been provoked — thinks that an opportunity is being offered him to occupy all Asia.

Letters are being brought (to Rome) every day from Asia, to Roman knights, most honorable men, whose great sums of money, occupied in collecting your revenues, are now at stake; these men, on account of the close connection which I have with that order, have brought to me the cause of the state and the dangers to their fortunes: that in Bithynia, which is now your province, several villages have been burned; the kingdom of Ariobarzanes, which is right next to your tributaries, is totally in the hands of the enemy; that Lucullus, after performing great exploits, is withdrawing from that war; that for him who may succeed him, there have not been sufficient preparations for pressing such a (serious) war; that one man is sought and demanded by all our allies and citizens as commander for the war, and this same man is alone feared by the enemy as no one else is.

You see what the case is; now consider what is to be done. First it seems to me that I must speak about the kind of war, then the size, then the choosing of a general. It is a war of such a kind that it ought to excite your minds greatly and stir you to a desire for carrying it through. (It is) a war in which the glory of the Roman people is at stake, which has been handed down to you by your ancestors, not only great in all affairs, but especially great in military matters; the safety of our allies and friends is at stake, for whom your ancestors have waged many great and serious wars; the surest and the greatest revenues of the Roman people are at stake, and if these are lost, you will look in vain

63

for both the blessings of peace and the reserves (*means*) of war; and the property of many citizens is at stake, for which you must take counsel, both for the sake of the men themselves and for the state.

3. And since you have always been seekers for glory and eager for praise more than all other nations, this stain gained in the earlier Mithridatic War must be wiped out by you, which has already penetrated deeply and become (an) old (stain) on the name of the Roman people; because he who in one day in the whole of Asia, in so many states, through one messenger and by one signal, accomplished the killing and murdering of Roman citizens, not only has up to this time received no punishment worthy of the crime, but is still ruling now twenty-three years after that time, and he rules in such a way that he is now not willing to hide himself in Pontus or the hiding places of Cappadocia, but (wishes) to emerge from his own native kingdom and carry on operations in your tributaries, that is in the light (plain view) of (all) Asia.

Now up to this time our generals have fought with this king in such a way that they have brought back from him the badges of victory, but not victory itself. Lucius Sulla celebrated (an official) triumph over Mithridates, Lucius Murena celebrated a triumph — two very brave men and the greatest of generals — but they triumphed in such a way that he (the king), though beaten and routed, still reigned. But nevertheless, praise should be given to these generals for what they accomplished, and forgiveness for what they did not accomplish, because the state (itself) recalled Sulla from that war into Italy and Sulla recalled Murena.

4. Mithridates, however, devoted all the rest of his time, not to forgetting the old war, but to preparing for a new one. Afterwards when he had built and outfitted very large fleets, and assembled very large armies from whatever peoples he could, and pretended that he was waging war against the people of the Bosphorus, his neighbors, he sent ambassadors and letters even into Spain to those leaders whom we were then fighting, so that you would be fighting a war on land and sea, and in two very widely separated and dissimilar places, with a single strategy by the two armies of the enemy; and you, torn by a double strife, would be fighting for (your very existence as a) ruling power.

However, the danger on one front, that of Sertorius and the Spanish (threat), which had much more vigor and strength, was removed by the divine wisdom and singular courage of Gnaeus Pompey; on the other front the war was administered by Lucius Lucullus, that outstanding man, in such a way that the first efforts of these affairs, great and successful, seemed as if they should be attributed not to good luck, but to

64

his virtue, whereas these latter misfortunes which have happened recently, more to his bad fortune than to his fault.

But I shall speak of Lucullus in another place, and I shall speak in such a way, citizens, that true praise may not seem to have been taken from him by my speech nor false praise added; concerning the dignity and glory of your command, since this is the beginning of my speech, see what feeling you think you should have.

5. Our ancestors often waged wars because our merchants and seafaring men were treated somewhat injuriously; now you, when so many thousands of Roman citizens have been killed by one order and at one time, how do you think you ought to feel? Because their envoys were too haughtily addressed, your fathers wanted Corinth, the light of all Asia, to be destroyed; will you allow that king to go unpunished who has killed an envoy of the Roman people of consular rank, after he was tortured with chains and beatings and all manner of suffering? They did not allow (even) the liberty of Roman citizens to be infringed; will you neglect the taking of a life? They avenged the right of an embassy when violated by a word; will you leave unavenged the killing of an ambassador with all tortures?

See to it that, just as it was very glorious for them to hand over to you the glory of our state, so it may be very disgraceful for you not to be able to keep that which you have received and to protect it.

What? how do you think you should feel because the safety of our allies has been placed in the greatest danger and hazard? King Ariobarzanes, an ally and friend of the Roman people, has been driven from his kingdom; (those) two kings are threatening all of Asia, (kings) not only very hostile to you, but also to your allies and friends; moreover, all states in all of Asia and Greece are forced to await your help, on account of the magnitude of the danger; nor do they dare to demand a certain general from you, especially since you have sent out another, and they do not think that they can do this (i.e., ask for the "certain general") without very great danger.

They see and realize the same thing which you do, that there is one man in whom there are all the highest qualities, and that he is nearby, for which reason they miss him all the more keenly; at his mere arrival and name, although he came (out) for the maritime (*pirate*) war, still they realize that the attacks of the (other) enemy have been checked and slowed down.

Since it is not permitted to these people to speak freely, they ask you silently that you think them worthy also, just like the allies of other provinces, of having their safety entrusted to such a man; and this even more so, because we are sending other men into the province with

65

command, of such nature that even if they protect them from the enemy, still the arrival of these people in the cities of the allies is not very different from a hostile capture; they heard of him (this "certain general") before, now they see him present, a man of such temperance, such kindness, such humanity, that they seem to be the most fortunate among whom he stays for the longest time.

6. Therefore, if our ancestors, (even) when provoked with no injury (to themselves), waged war for their allies with Antiochus, Philip, the Aetolians, and the Carthaginians, with what great zeal is it proper for you, provoked by injuries, to defend the safety of your allies, along with the dignity of your own sovereignty, especially since it is now a question of your greatest revenues? For the revenues from the other provinces, citizens, are only so great (*only enough*) that we can scarcely be content with them for defending the provinces themselves; but Asia is so fertile and productive that it easily excels all other lands in the fertility of its soil, and the variety of its fruits, and great size of its pastures, and by the multitude of things which may be exported.

Accordingly, this province must be defended by you. citizens, not only from calamity but also from the fear of calamity, if you wish to retain the advantage in war and the dignity of peace. For in other matters, when a calamity comes, then a loss is received; but in revenue matters, not only the arrival of disaster, but the very fear itself brings disaster. For when the forces of the enemy are not far away, even if no attack is made, still the flocks are abandoned, agriculture is deserted, and the navigation of merchants grows still.

Thus, not from port tax, nor from tithes, nor from the pasture tax, can any revenue be saved; in this respect often the fruits of a whole year are lost by the mere rumor of danger and the fear of war. How, then, do you think those people feel, who either pay the taxes to us, or collect the taxes and contract for them, when two kings with very large forces are close at hand? when one attack of cavalry may in a very short time wipe out the taxes of a whole year? when the tax collectors think that the very large companies of slaves which they have in the forest pastures, in the fields, and in the ports and customhouses are there in very great danger. Or do you think that you can enjoy these things, unless you keep those who are thus useful to you, not only free from disaster, but also from the fear of disaster?

7. And that must indeed not be neglected by you, which I had proposed for myself as the last thing to be mentioned, when I was intending to speak about the kind of war, which pertains to the property of many citizens; a plan must carefully be made by you, citizens, for this, according to your wisdom. For the collectors, very honorable and wealthy citizens, have transferred their means and their wealth into that province; the fortunes and property of these same men ought to be of (for) concern to you. For if we have always considered the revenues to be the sinews of the state, we shall certainly say that that class who collect them are the support of the other classes.

Next, active and industrious men from other classes are partly carrying on business themselves in Asia, whom you should look out for in their absence, and partly have their large holdings (capital) invested in that province. It is therefore the part of humanity to keep the large number of these citizens from disaster, and the part of wisdom to perceive that disaster of (so) many citizens cannot be separated from a disaster to the state.

For it makes little difference that we later recover by victory the (right to) revenues, after the (present) collectors have been ruined; for there will not be means for the same people to undertake tax contracts, on account of their disaster, nor will there be the desire in others to do so, on account of fear. Then, too, we, trained in disaster, ought to remember that which the same Asia and the same Mithridates taught us at the beginning of the Asiatic War. For then when many people in Asia lost very great fortunes, we know that here at Rome credit collapsed, with the payment of debts being hindered.

For in one (and the same) state many people cannot lose their property and fortunes, without drawing many more into the same calamity; keep the republic from a danger like this; and, believe me, that which you yourselves see, this system of credit and money which is used at Rome and here in the Forum is closely bound up with and clings to those Asiatic investments; those cannot collapse without these falling, weakened by the same fall.

Therefore see to it whether you should have any doubt that we ought to press on (take all pains) with this war, in which the glory of your name, the safety of allies, the greatest revenues, and the fortunes of very many citizens, joined with the whole state, are at stake (being maintained).

8. Since I have spoken about the kind of war, I shall now say a few words about its size. For this can be said, the kind of war is (one) so unavoidable that it must be waged, but it is not so great that it needs to be feared. And in this, great care must be taken lest those things which must be most carefully provided by you seem to you (something) to be made light of.

Accordingly, that all may know that I grant to Lucius Lucullus as much praise as is due to a hero (brave man) and a wise man and a great general, I say that at his arrival the very, very great forces of Mithridates were equipped and supplied with all things, and that the town of the Cyzicenians, the most celebrated in Asia and most friendly to us, had been besieged by the king himself with a very large multitude, and had been assaulted most violently, and this town Lucullus freed from the most extreme dangers of siege through his valor, perseverance, and planning.

By the selfsame general a large and well-equipped navy which, inflamed with eagerness and hatred, was being rushed to Italy to the Sertorian leaders, was defeated and sunk; besides this, large forces of the enemy were defeated in many battles; and Pontus, which had previously been closed to the Roman people from every approach, was opened up to our legions; that Sinope and Amisus, towns in which there were palaces of the king adorned and filled with all things, and very many other towns of Pontus and Cappadocia, were captured by his mere approach and arrival; that the king, deprived of the kingdom of his father and grandfather, went off as a suppliant to other kings and to other nations; and that all of these things were accomplished with the allies of the Roman people (remaining) safe and the revenues undiminished.

I think that this is sufficient praise, citizens, and such that you may understand that Lucullus has been praised from this place in a similar way by none of the people who are opposing this law and cause.

9. It will perhaps be asked now how, since this is the case, the rest of the war can be great. Learn this, citizens, for this seems to be asked not without reason. In the first place, Mithridates fled from his kingdom in the same way that Medea is said to have fled from the same Pontus; they say that she in her flight scattered the limbs of her brother in those places where her parent would be following her, so that the collecting of these scattered limbs, and the sorrow of her father, would delay his speed of following.

Thus did the fleeing Mithridates leave in Pontus all that abundance of gold and silver, and all the very beautiful things which he had received from his ancestors and which he himself had collected into his own kingdom — things plundered from all of Asia in the earlier war. While our men were too attentively gathering up all these things, the king slipped out of their hands; thus grief delayed him (Medea's father) in his eagerness in following, and joy delayed these men. Tigranes, the king of the Armenians, received him in his fear and flight, and strengthened him when despairing of his affairs, and raised him when afflicted, and revived him when ruined.

After Lucullus came into his kingdom with his army, more tribes were stirred up against our general. Fear was thrown into those nations which the Roman people had never thought of attacking in war or trying to do so; there was also a strong and forceful impression, which had spread through the minds of foreign peoples, that our army had been led into their lands for the sake of plundering a very wealthy and holy shrine.

Thus many great nations were aroused by a certain new terror and fear. Our army, moreover, although it had captured a city in the kingdom of Tigranes and had fought some successful battles, was nevertheless moved by the too great distance of these places and a longing to see their (own) people. I shall say no more here; for this was the end result, that a speedy return was sought by our soldiers from those places rather than a further advance.

Mithridates, moreover, both strengthened himself and his own army by the service of those who had retreated to him from his kingdom and was assisted by the large arrival of auxiliary troops of many kings and nations. For we have learned that this is accustomed to be the case, that the afflicted fortunes of kings easily entice the help of many on account of pity, and especially of those who either are kings or live in a kingdom, so that the name of king seems to them great and holy.

Accordingly, he was able to accomplish as much when defeated as he never would have dared to hope for when he was safe. For when he had returned to his own kingdom, he was not content with that which had happened to him beyond his hope, that he should ever again touch that soil after he had been driven out, but he even made an attack on our brilliant and victorious army. Allow me, citizens, to pass over that disaster of ours, just as poets do who write about the affairs of Rome, (a disaster) which was so great that a messenger from the battle did not report it to the ears of the general, but rumor through (of) common talk. Here in this calamity and most serious disaster of the war, Lucius Lucullus, who perhaps might have been able to bring some remedy to these losses in some way, forced by the order of you (here at home) who thought that the length of the long command should be limited by old-time precedent, dismissed a part of the soldiers, who had completed their term of enlistment, and handed over a part to Glabrio.

I pass over many things advisedly; but you may yourselves learn of them by inference, how great you think that war is, which most powerful kings unite in, agitated nations renew, whole countries are undertaking, (and) our new commander is now taking over, with the former army defeated.

10. I seemed to have said enough to show that the war is necessary by its very nature and dangerous because of its size; it remains for me to speak about the selecting of a general and putting him in command of such great affairs. Would that you had, citizens, such a supply of brave and honest men that this deliberation would be difficult for you as to who you think especially ought to be put in charge of such important affairs and such a great war.

Certainly now since Pompey is the only one who has surpassed the glory not only of those men who are now living but even the memory of early times in respect to his character, what thing is there which can bring doubt to the mind of anyone in this case? For I think this, that in a very great general there ought to be these four qualities: knowledge of military affairs, courage, authority, and good fortune.

Who then ever was or should have been more experienced in military matters than this man? — (a man) who from his school days and boyhood training proceeded to the army of his father and training in war, in a very great war against very fierce enemies; and at the end of his boyhood, he was himself a soldier in the army of a very distinguished general; (and) on entering young manhood, he himself was the commander of a very large army, who fought with enemy hosts more often than anyone else disputed with a personal enemy, waged more wars than others read about, completed conquest of more provinces than others aspired to (reach as a governor); whose youth was schooled for a knowledge of military matters not by the teachings of others, but by (holding) his own commands, not by misfortunes of war but by victories, not by (earning) a soldier's pay but by (a commanding general's) triumphs.

What kind of a war can there be in which the good fortune of the state has not given him some training? The civil, African, Transalpine, Spanish, slave, naval, and various other kinds of both wars and enemies, not only waged by him but also won, show that there is nothing laid down in military practice which could escape the knowledge of this man.

11. Now what words can match the virtue of Gnaeus Pompey? What is there which anyone can say either worthy of him or new to you or not heard before by everyone? For these are not the only virtues of a (good) general which are commonly valued — exertion in his tasks, fortitude in dangers, diligence in action, speed in carrying (things) out, and strategy in looking ahead; (and) these things are as great in this man as they have not been in all other generals whom we have either seen or heard of.

Italy is a witness, which that victorious Sulla himself has admitted was liberated by the courage and help of this man; Sicily is a witness, which when it was surrounded on all sides by many dangers he delivered, not by the terror of war, but by the speed of his planning; Africa is a witness, which when it was oppressed by large forces of the enemy overflowed with the blood of those very same forces; Gaul is a witness, through which a route to Spain was opened up for our legions by the slaughter of (those same) Gauls; Spain is a witness, which quite often has seen very many enemies overcome and prostrated by this man; Italy is a witness again and again, which, when it was oppressed by the disgraceful and dangerous slave war, asked for help from this man when he was far away, (a war) which was weakened and lessened by the expectation of this man and was finished and buried by his arrival; now in truth, there are as witnesses all shores and all foreign peoples and nations of the earth, and finally all seas, both collectively and individually, (and) all bays and harbors.

For what place in the whole sea through these recent years ever had such a firm garrison that it was safe, or was so remote that it lay hidden? Who ever set sail without committing himself to the dangers of death or slavery, since he was sailing either in winter or on a sea swarming with pirates? Who ever would have thought that this great war, so base, so long-standing, so widely scattered and spread around, could have been finished by all our generals in one year or by one general in all years? What province have you kept free from the pirates through these years? what revenue has been safe for you? what ally have you protected? whom have you protected with your fleets? how many islands do you think have been abandoned, how many cities of our allies have been left through fear or captured by the pirates?

12. But why do I speak of things far away? It was once characteristic of the Roman people to wage wars far away from home and by the bulwarks of national power to protect the fortunes of (distant) allies, not their (*our*) own houses.

Shall I tell you that during recent years the sea was closed off to our allies, when even your own armies never crossed over from Brundisium except in extreme winter? Shall I complain that those men were captured who came to you from foreign nations, when even envoys of the Roman people were being ransomed? Shall I remark that the sea was not safe for your merchants, when twelve axes (two praetors) fell into the power of the pirates? Need I mention that Cnidus or Colophon or Samos, very noble cities, and countless others were captured when you know that your own harbors and those harbors from which you draw life and breath were in the power of the pirates?

Or do you not know that the port of Caieta, very celebrated and filled with ships, was plundered by pirates with our praetor looking on, or that from Misenum the children of that very man who before had waged war with the pirates were carried away by the pirates?

71

Or why should I complain about the disaster at Ostia, that stain and disgrace to our state, when with you yourselves almost (near enough for) viewing it that fleet over which a consul of the Roman people was put in command was captured and sunk by pirates?

By the immortal gods! was the incredible and divine courage of one man able to bring so much light to the state in so short a time that you, who only recently saw the fleet of the enemy before the mouth of the Tiber, now hear that there is no ship of the pirates (*enemy*) inside the opening of the Ocean (*Straits of Gibraltar*)? Accordingly, although you see yourselves how quickly these things have happened, they still ought not to be passed over by me in speaking. For who ever has been able to go to so many places or finish so many travels in so short a time, either with a desire of transacting business or seeking after gain, as quickly as the attacking fleet of such great force, with Pompey as general, sailed?—(a man) who on a sea not yet at the season for sailing went to Sicily, explored Africa, came into Sardinia with his fleet, and fortified these three great sources of the grain supply of the state with very firm garrisons and fleets.

Then when he had returned to Italy, after the two Spains and Transalpine Gaul had been strengthened with garrisons and ships, and with ships also having been sent to the coast of the Illyrian Sea and Achaia and all of Greece, he himself annexed Cilicia to the rule of the Roman people on the 49th day after he had set out from Brundisium; all who were pirates everywhere were in part captured and killed, in part surrendered themselves to the authority and power of this one man.

Also he did not take away the hope of surrender from the Cretans, when they had sent to him even into Pamphylia envoys and intercessors, and he ordered from them hostages.

Thus this war which was so great, so scattered far and wide, in which all nations and peoples were being oppressed, Gnaeus Pompey prepared for in the depths of winter, initiated in the early spring, and finished in (*by*) midsummer.

13. This is the divine and unbelievable talent of this commander! How great and how many are the other qualities which I began to mention a little while ago! For not only must excellence in fighting be sought after in a great and accomplished general, but there are many other excellent qualities which are the handmaids and companions of this talent. And first, how much honesty ought generals to have, then how much self-control in all things, how much faith, how much approachableness, how much genius, and how much humanity! — which of these qualities are in Gnaeus Pompey let us consider.

For they are all very great, fellow citizens, but they can be learned and understood more (*better*) by a comparison with others than by themselves. For what general can we think of in any number in whose army the office of centurion may be, or has been, sold? What can this (*such a*) man think about the state in a great or lofty manner, who divides among officials money taken from the treasury for carrying on a war, on account of his eagerness to have a province, or who on account of greed leaves it invested at Rome?

Your muttering, citizens, indicates that you seem to (*apparently*) recognize people that have done these things; I mention no names; therefore no one can be angry with me unless he wants first to admit his own guilt. And who does not know what great defeats our armies have suffered wherever they have gone, on account of this greed of the generals?

Recall the journeys which during these recent years our commanders have made in Italy through the fields and towns of Roman citizens, then you will settle more easily what you may judge is being done among foreign nations. Do you think that through these years more cities of the enemy have been destroyed by the arms of your soldiers, or states of (our) allies by their being quartered (on them) for the winter? For no general can control an army who cannot control himself, nor does he want to be severe in judging (others), who does not want others to be severe in judging him.

Are we then surprised that this man so excels others, whose legions have come into Asia in such a way that not only (not) a hand of (*in*) so great an army, but not even a footprint, is said to have injured any peaceful person? And letters and reports are coming daily telling of how his soldiers are wintering; not only is force not being used on anyone to bring about expense for (*in connection with the*) soldiery, but nothing even is allowed for (*of*) wanting to do it. Our ancestors wanted there to be a refuge from the winter, not (a harbor for) greediness, in the houses of their allies and friends.

14. Come now, consider how great is his self-control in other matters. Whence do you think was found that speed so great and such incredible (distances) travelled?

For it was not some extraordinary power of his oarsmen, nor a certain unheard-of skill in navigating, nor some new winds that carried him so quickly into the farthest lands, but (rather) those things which are accustomed to delay others did not delay him; greed did not call him away from his planned course for the sake of some booty; nor lust to (take his) pleasure, nor pleasant scenery to enjoy it, nor the nobility of a city to become acquainted with it, and finally not even (did) work itself (hold him up by making him feel the need) for rest; lastly, he did

73

not think that the statues and paintings and other ornaments of Greek towns, which others thought should be plundered, should even be visited.

Accordingly, all in these places now regard Pompey not as someone sent out from Rome, but as sent down from heaven; now at last they begin to believe that there may once have been Roman men of this (kind of) self-restraint, a thing which indeed seemed to foreign nations incredible and falsely handed down to their memory; now the splendor of your power begins to bring some light to these peoples; now they realize that their ancestors not without reason, then when we had magistrates of such self-control, preferred to be servants of the Roman people (rather) than (themselves) to rule others.

For now, indeed, the approach(es) of private men to him is so easy, the complaints about the injuries of others are said to be so free, that he who excels the chiefs in dignity seems on a level with the most humble in affability. For you have often learned from this very place, citizens, how much power he has in wisdom, gravity, and fluency in speaking, in which there exists a certain dignity befitting a commander.

Indeed, how great do you think his loyalty is estimated among his allies, which all our enemies of all races judge to be most sacred? For he is a man of so much humanity that it is difficult to say whether the enemy when fighting fear his valor, or when defeated love his mercy, more. And will anyone doubt that this war so great should be entrusted to him, who seems to have been born by a certain divine plan for the purpose of completing all the wars within our memory?

15. And since authority is very important also in carrying on wars and in military command, certainly no one can doubt that in this respect this man is the most powerful. Who is ignorant of the fact that what enemies (and) allies think about our generals has a very important bearing on the administering of wars, when we know that men in such great affairs are moved, no less by opinion and by reputation than by good reason, to scorn or fear or hate or love?

What name in the whole world, then, was ever more famous, whose deeds are equal (to his)? — about what man, a thing which adds greatly to authority, have you yourselves made such great and outstanding judgments? Or do you think that there is any land so far away and deserted that the story of that day has not reached there, when the whole Roman people, in a packed Forum, with the temples all filled, from which this place can be seen, all demanded for themselves Pompey as the commander for the common war of all nations (against the pirates)?

Accordingly, so that I may say no more (*be brief*) and not establish by the examples of others how much authority has influence in war, examples of all the outstanding exploits are to be taken from this same Pompey: on the day when he was placed in command of the maritime war by you, so great a cheapness in the cost of grain followed after very great scarcity and high cost, by the mere hope and reputation of this man, as scarcely a long-lasting peace with great fertility of the fields could have brought about.

Moreover (*Now*), after the disaster sustained in Pontus, from that battle about which I reminded you unwillingly a little while ago, when our allies were afraid, the wealth and spirits of our enemies had increased, and the province did not have a sufficiently strong garrison, you would have lost Asia, fellow citizens, if the good fortune of the Roman people had not brought Pompey into these regions providentially at this time. For his arrival both checked Mithridates, inflamed with unaccustomed victory, and delayed Tigranes, threatening Asia with great forces. And will anyone doubt what he will accomplish with his valor, who has already accomplished so much by his authority? or how easily he will save our allies and revenues with his command and army, who has already protected them by his mere name and reputation?

16. But come, does not this thing itself show how great is the authority of this same man among the enemies of the Roman people, the fact that they all surrendered to him in such a short time from such far distant and diverse places! that envoys of the Cretans, when (another) general of ours and an army was on their island, came to Pompey in the farthest regions and said that all of the states of the Cretans wanted to surrender themselves to him! What? — did not that very Mithridates send an ambassador to the same Pompey even into Spain: he whom Pompey always judged to be an envoy, but those to whom it was always annoying that he was sent especially to him (Pompey), preferred to consider a spy rather than an ambassador. You can therefore decide, citizens, how much you think that this authority, increased by many later exploits and by your very great opinions (of him), will avail among these kings and foreign nations.

It remains for me to say a few things timidly about his good fortune, which no one ought to talk of about himself, but which we can remember and mention about another, just as it is right for men to talk about the power of the gods. For I think this, that commands have been given and armies entrusted to Maximus, Marcellus, Scipio, Marius, and other great generals, not only on account of their ability, but more often on account of their good fortune.

For to certain very great men there has certainly been divinely added a certain good fortune to their grandeur and glory for successfully

75

carrying out great exploits. But about the good fortune of this man about whom we are now speaking, I shall use this moderation in speaking, in order not to say that fortune was placed in his power, but so that we may seem to have remembered past things and hope for the future, lest my speech seem to be arrogant or displeasing to the immortal gods.

Accordingly, I am not going to tell you what great things he has done at home and in war, on land and sea, and with what success; that not only have the citizens assented to all his wishes, and the allies obeyed them, and the enemy submitted, but also the winds and storms have been favorable; I shall say this very briefly, that no one was ever so immodest (*conceited*) as (even) secretly to dare to wish for so many and such great things as the gods have bestowed on Pompey. But (*In this*) you ought to wish and hope, citizens, that this may be his own perpetually, both for the sake of the common safety and the state and for the man himself.

Therefore, since the war is so unavoidable that it cannot be neglected, and so great that it must be administered most carefully, and since you are able to put in charge of it a man in whom there is the highest knowledge of war, extraordinary virtue, most distinguished authority, and outstanding good fortune, do you doubt, fellow citizens, that you should make use of this great good, which has been given and offered to you by the immortal gods, for saving and glorifying the republic?

17. But if Pompey were a private citizen here at Rome at this time, still he should be chosen and sent to so great a war; now, since this opportunity is also added to other great advantages, that he is present in these places, that he has an army, that he can at once receive more from those who have them, why should we wait? or why do we not, with the immortal gods guiding us, entrust this war with kings to the same man to whom other wars have been entrusted, with the greatest welfare of the state?

But a very famous and patriotic man, and one honored with your very considerable favors, Quintus Catulus, and also a man endowed with the highest ornaments of honor, fortune, virtue, and genius, Quintus Hortensius, disagree with this opinion; I admit that the influence of these men has been and ought to be very important on many occasions; but in this case, although you know that the influences of the bravest and most illustrious men are contrary, still, leaving out the authorities, we can inquire into the truth from the very case itself; and this all the more easily, because these very men concede that all the things which I have said up to this time are true, that the war is unavoidable and great, and that Pompey possesses all of the very important qualifications.

What then does Hortensius say? That Pompey is the most worthy, if everything is to be assigned to one man, but that everything should not be put in the hands of one man. This argument is now out of date, refuted more by fact than by words. For you said the very same thing, Quintus Hortensius, gravely and eloquently, according to your very great fluency and singular ability in speaking, in the senate against the brave man, Aulus Gabinius, when he proposed the law about appointing one general for the war against the pirates, and from this very place (as well) you also spoke many words against that law.

What, now? — by the immortal gods! If your influence among the Roman people had prevailed over the safety and true cause of the Roman people, would we today be holding this glory, and our national power over the whole world? Or did this seem to you to be national power, when ambassadors of the Roman people, quaestors, and praetors were being captured, when we were being cut off from grain supplies, both private and public, from all the provinces, when the seas were closed to us so that we were not able to transact any business, private or public, across the sea?

18. What state ever was there before — I do not speak of the Athenians, (a state) which is said once to have held a sufficiently wide part of the sea, nor of the Carthaginians, who were very strong in their fleet and in maritime matters, nor of the Rhodians, whose naval training and glory has remained even to our memory — what state ever before was so feeble or what island so small, that it could not defend its own ports and fields and some part of the region along the sea coast by itself?

But, by Hercules, for some successive years before the Gabinian law, the Roman people whose name remained invincible in naval battles even to our memory, lacked the great and much the most important part not only of its usefulness, but (worse still) of its dignity and power. We whose ancestors with their fleet defeated King Antiochus and Perses and the Carthaginians in all the naval engagements, men most skilled in maritime matters and very well equipped — we were in no measure able to be equal to (*a match for*) the pirates. We, who before kept not only Italy safe, but were able to keep safe all our allies in the most remote places, by the authority of our national power, then (*a time*) when the island of Delos, so far from us, situated in the Aegean Sea, where all assembled with their cargoes and loads, filled with riches, small and without a wall (nevertheless) it feared nothing, now we were deprived not only of our provinces and the seacoasts of Italy, and our ports, but even of the Appian Way.

In those days weren't the magistrates of the Roman people ashamed to ascend into this place, when our ancestors left it to us adorned with naval spoils and the trophies of fleets?

19. The Roman people thought that you, Quintus Hortensius, and the others who were of the same opinion, were speaking in good faith those things which you thought; but still, in a matter affecting the common safety, this same Roman people preferred to obey their own painful feelings (rather) than your authority. Accordingly one law, one man, one year not only freed us from that misery and disgrace, but also brought it about that we once again might truly be seen to rule over all tribes and nations on land and sea.

From this it seems to me even more unworthy that there was opposition — shall I say to Gabinius, or to Pompey, or (that which is truer) to both? — so that Gabinius would not be appointed as lieutenant to Pompey, asking for it and requesting it. Is not he who requests a lieutenant for such a great war fit to obtain whomever he wants, when others have taken out whomever they wished for the purpose of pillaging (our) allies and plundering the provinces? or should not he, by whose law safety and dignity has been restored to the Roman people and to all nations, be a sharer in the glory of that army and general which was set up by his counsel and (personal) peril?

But Falcidius, Metellus, Caecilius Latiniensis, Lentulus, all of whom I name for the sake of honor, after they had been tribunes of the people, in the following year were able to be lieutenant generals; (but) are they so diligent in the case of this Gabinius, who ought to be in this war by special right, which (*when the command*) was set up by the Gabinian Law, under this commander-in-chief and in this army which he himself constituted through you?

I hope that the consuls will refer to the senate about the choosing of a lieutenant general. If they are hesitant or reluctant, I declare that I myself will bring it up; and not anyone's hostile edict will deter me, relying on you, Romans, from defending your right and favor; and I will not listen to anything except the veto (of the tribunes), concerning which I think these same men will consider over and over again what is permissible. In my opinion, citizens, Gabinius alone is the man to be enrolled as associate to Pompey for the maritime war and its exploits; because the one gave the war to be undertaken by your vote to one man; the other finished it when it was received and undertaken.

20. It remains, as it appears, that I should say something about the authority and opinion of Quintus Catulus. When he asked you, should you put everything in the hands of Pompey (then) in whom would you put your hope if anything should happen to him, he received the great (*fine*) reward of his excellence and dignity, when you all almost with one voice said that you would place your hopes in him. For he

(Catulus) is such a man that there is nothing so great or so difficult that he cannot both guide it by his counsel and defend it by his integrity and accomplish it by his valor.

But in this particular case, I violently disagree with him, because the less certain and the less lasting is the life of a man, so much the more ought the state enjoy the life and talents of an illustrious man while it is allowed by the immortal gods. But (then) you say, "Let nothing new be done, contrary to the examples and customs of our ancestors."

I shall not say in this place that our ancestors always in peace obeyed custom and in war utility, that they always adapted considerations of new plans to new circumstances of the times; I will not mention the two very great wars, Punic and Spanish, that were carried on by one commander, and that two very powerful cities, Carthage and Numantia, which were greatly threatening this government, were destroyed by the same Scipio; I will not remind you that more recently it seemed best to you and your ancestors that the hope of the nation's sovereignty should be placed in Marius alone, and that the same man should conduct the war with Jugurtha, with the Cimbrians, and with the Teutons: even in the case of Pompey, in (regard to) whom Catulus wishes nothing new (*no new measure*) to be adopted, remember how many new things have (already) been adopted with the fullest approval of Catulus.

21. What was so unprecedented as for a young man, (only) a private citizen, to raise an army in a difficult time of the republic? He did it. Or to be in charge of it? He was in charge. Or to manage the war most admirably under his own generalship? He managed it. What was so contrary to custom as for a command and army to be assigned to a very young man, whose age was far from that required (to qualify him) for senatorial grade, and for Sicily and Africa to be assigned to him, and the administration of the war in that province? In these provinces (*fields of operation*) he was a man of singular honesty, dignity, and courage; he finished successfully a very great war in Africa and brought back a victorious army.

What is so unheard of as for a Roman knight to celebrate a triumph? The Roman people not only saw this thing, but thought that it ought to be viewed and celebrated with the greatest enthusiasm of everyone. What was so unusual as for a Roman knight to be sent to a very great and dangerous war as a proconsul, when there were (on hand) two most illustrious and brave consuls? He was sent.

At this time when there was someone in the senate who said that a private citizen ought not to be sent as a proconsul, Lucius Philippus is said to have remarked that in his opinion he was not being sent "for a consul," but for both consuls. Such great hope of managing well the affairs of state was placed in him that the function of two consuls was entrusted to the valor of one youth.

What was so exceptional as that he be made consul, released from the laws by a decree of the senate, before he was legally entitled to hold any other office? what so incredible as that a Roman knight should a *second* time celebrate a triumph (and that) by the vote of the senate? Whatever new things have been decreed in the cases of all other men (together) are not so numerous as these which we see in the case of this one man. And these precedents so numerous, so great, and so novel have all been carried out in the case of this same man with the authority of Catulus and the other very distinguished men of like worthiness.

22. Therefore let them see to it that it not be unfair and intolerable that (*to have*) their judgment about the worthiness of Pompey (has) always (been) approved by you, and that your judgment and the authority of the Roman people about this same man be not approved (by them), especially since the Roman people can by its own right defend its judgment in the case of this man against all those who disagree, because when these same people were objecting before, you chose him alone from all the rest to be placed in charge of the war with the pirates.

If you did this rashly and took counsel too little for the state, then rightly they are trying to overrule your endeavors; but if you yourselves saw more deeply into the interests of the state, and if you over the objections of these same men brought dignity to this empire and safety to the world, let these men admit finally that they and the others should obey the authority of the whole Roman people.

And in this war in Asia, not only that military talent which is eminent in Pompey, but other great and many (*numerous*) qualities of the mind are also needed. It is difficult for our general to be engaged in Asia, Cilicia, Syria, and the kingdoms of the interior nations, so that he thinks about nothing except the enemy and renown.

Then, too, if there are any more moderate in their modesty and self-control, nevertheless no one thinks that they are so, on account of the large number of greedy men. It is difficult to say, citizens, how much we are hated among foreign nations because of the lawlessness and the injuries of those men whom we have sent out there with command during recent years. What shrine do you think has been sacred to our magistrates in these lands, what state holy, or what house sufficiently shut up or defended? Rich and opulent cities are sought for, against which a pretext for waging war may be found, on account of the desire for plundering.

I would gladly discuss these things openly with Quintus Catulus and

Quintus Hortensius, most eminent and illustrious men; for they know the injuries of (to) our allies, they see their calamities, they hear their complaints. Do you think that you are sending an army for your allies against enemies, or with a pretense of (*that they are*) enemies against your allies and friends? What state is there in Asia which can satisfy the mind and spirit, not only of a commander, or lieutenant, but even of a single tribune of the soldiers?

23. Therefore, even if you have someone who after the standards (*legions*) have been collected seems to be able to defeat the kings' armies, still, unless he be one who can restrain himself from the money of (our) allies, and his hands, eyes, and mind from their wives and children, and from the ornaments of temples and towns, and from their gold and royal treasures, he will not be a suitable man to be sent out to an Asiatic (war) and a royal war (*war with kings*). Do you think that any state has been made peace with, which (*if it*) is rich, or that there is any rich state which may seem to these commanders to be subdued?

The seacoast sought out Pompey, citizens, not only on account of his military glory, but also on account of the self-control of his mind. For they saw that except for a few, our generals were enriching themselves every year by public money, and that we did not appear to be gaining them anything else in the name of our fleets except that by receiving losses they were afflicted with a greater disgrace.

Now, evidently, those people who do not think that all power ought to be conferred on one man, do not know with what greed men set out into the provinces, with what bribery and what commitments; so that we may see that Pompey is great not only because of his own virtues, but also from a comparison with the faults of others. Therefore, do not doubt that you should (*do not hesitate to*) entrust everything to this one man, who is the only one to be found in recent years whom our allies are happy to see come into their cities with an army.

But if you think that this bill ought to be strengthened by supporters, you have a man most skilled in all wars and greatest events as a supporter, Publius Servilius, whose deeds have been so great on land and sea that when you are thinking about a war, no one deserves to be a weightier authority with you; you have Gaius Corio, endowed with your greatest favors, a man of the highest genius and wisdom, who has accomplished great things; there is Gnaeus Lentulus, in whom you all know, by reason of your most splendid honors, there is the greatest wisdom and influence; and there is Gaius Cassius, of singular integrity, courage and perseverance. See from this that with the backing of these men, we are seen (as quite) able to (give an) answer (to) the argument of those who disagree (with you and me).

24. Since this is the case, Gaius Manilius, first I praise and greatly approve of that law, purpose, and opinion of yours; then I urge you to remain (firm) in this opinion with the support of the Roman people, and not to fear the violence or threats of anyone. First I think that there is in you enough courage and perseverance; then, since we see here such a great crowd with (equally) great support (as the first time) which for the second time we see (shown) in the matter of putting this man in a command, what is there which we can doubt, either about the matter itself or the power of accomplishing it? As for me, whatever I have of zeal, counsel, industry, (and) talent, whatever I can do by this favor of the Roman people and by this power as a praetor, and whatever I can do by my authority, faith, and firmness, I promise and offer all this to you and the Roman people for (successfully) finishing this matter. And I call to witness all the gods, and those especially who preside over this place and temple, and who see most easily into the minds of those who are in public office, that I am not doing this at the request of anyone, nor because I think that I can gain the favor of Pompey for me through this cause, nor because I seek from the generosity of anyone either protection for myself in dangers or the means of acquiring honors, because we shall easily repel dangers, being protected by our innocence, as a man ought to, and we shall gain public office, not from any one man nor from this place, but by that same hard-working manner of life of ours (*mine*), if your wish will have it so.

Therefore, whatever I have taken on in this case, all this I assert has been undertaken for the sake of the state, and so far am I from seeming to have been seeking anyone's favor, that I also realize that I have taken on many enemies, partly secret, partly open, not necessary to me and not without use to you. But I have decided that I, invested with this honor (and) experiencing your (so) many favors, citizens, ought to prefer your wishes and the dignity of the state and (*along with*) the safety of the provinces and allies, to any advantages or considerations of my own.

The Speech for Archias

1. Whatever talent there is in me, judges, and I know how small this is, whatever practice in speaking, and I do not deny that I am (but) moderately experienced, and whatever theoretical mastery I have gained from the study of the best arts and from instruction, to which I confess I have not been inattentive at any time of my life, (*Archias*) here deserves to claim from me by his own right the fruit of all of these things. For as long as my mind can look back into the space of the past time, and recall the earliest memory of my boyhood, going back as far as that, I see that this man stood out as the prime mover for choosing and pursuing a course of these studies. And if this voice of mine, trained by the encouragement and teachings of this man, has ever been of any help to anyone, certainly to this (man of all men) I ought to bring help and safety, as far as it lies in my power, from whom I have received that by which I can help the rest (of my clients) and save other (men). And lest it seem strange to anyone that this is being said by me, because there is in this man some other faculty of genius (poetry), and not this talent and training in speaking, not even I have been ever completely devoted to this one study. For all the arts which pertain to humanity have a certain common bond and are held together as if by some affinity among themselves.

2. But lest it seem strange to any one of you that in a legal trial and a public court, when the case is being tried before a praetor of the Roman people, most upright man, and before the most strict judges (*jury*), in such a great throng and assembly of men, that I use this kind of speaking which is different not only from the custom of (*at*) trials but also from public speaking (in general), I ask that in this particular case you give me this indulgence, suited to this defendant, and not, I hope, annoying to you, so that you may allow me, while speaking in behalf of this very great poet, in this gathering of very educated men, before an enlightened jury such as this, and finally, with such a praetor presiding at the trial, to speak a little more freely of the study of the liberal arts and letters, and in the case of a personality of this kind, who has been drawn into legal actions and trials very little on account of his retirement and devotion to his studies, to use a certain (*some*) almost novel and unusual kind of speaking.

And if I feel that this is being granted and allowed me by you, I will surely bring it about that you will think that this Aulus Licinius not only ought not to be separated from the number of citizens, since he is already one, but that even if he were not one, he should have been enrolled.

3. For when Archias first outgrew his boyhood and those studies by which the boyish age is accustomed to be trained, he devoted himself to the study of writing, first at Antioch — for he was born there of an illustrious family — once a populous and rich city, and well filled with

the most scholarly men and learned studies: and he quickly had the good fortune to excel all in the glory of his talents. Later, in other parts of Asia and all of Greece, his arrivals were so celebrated that the expectation of seeing the man exceeded the reports of his ability, and the arrival and (consequent) admiration for the man himself exceeded the expectation.

Italy was at that time full of Greek arts and learning, and these studies were then both cultivated more strongly in Latium than now in these same towns, and here at Rome they were not neglected on account of the peaceful condition of the state. And so the people of Tarentum, Regium, and Naples presented this man with citizenship and other gifts, and all who were able to judge anything about his talents thought him worthy of their acquaintance and hospitality.

As a result of this widespread publicity given his fame, when he was (already) well known to men at a distance, he came to Rome during the consulship of Marius and Catulus. He first found those consuls of whom one was able to provide him with very great things to write about, and the other not only great achievements, but also enthusiasm and attentive ears. At once the Luculli, when Archias was still a young man, took him into their home. And it was not only because of his talents and literary ability, but also his character and virtue, that the same house which first favored his youth, also was most familiar to him in his old age.

At that time he was pleasing to Quintus Metellus of Numidian (fame) and to his son Pius, he was heard by Marcus Aemilius, he lived with Quintus Catulus, both father and son, and he was esteemed by Lucius Crassus. Since he held closely bound to him by intimate association the Luculli and Drusus, and the Octavii and Cato and the whole family of the Hortensii, he was most highly honored; because not only did those people esteem him who wanted to learn something or hear him, but also any who by chance pretended that they did.

4. Meanwhile, after a fairly long lapse of time, when he had set out for Sicily with Marcus Lucullus, and departed from that province with the same Lucullus, he came to Heraclea. Since this state enjoyed most favorable treaty relations (with Rome), he expressed a desire to become enrolled as a citizen in that state, and since he was considered worthy of it not only because of himself, but also because of the influence of the Luculli and their favor, he gained his request from the Heracleans.

Citizenship was granted according to the law of Silvanus and Carbo:

"To those who had been enrolled among the confederated cities; if then when the law was passed, they had a residence in Italy; and if they registered before the praetor within sixty days."

84

Since he had a residence at Rome now for many years, he registered before the praetor Quintus Metellus, his very close friend. If we are to say nothing more than about his citizenship and the law, I have no more to say; the case is completed. For which one of these can be denied, Gratius? Will you say that he was not enrolled at Heraclea? A man is present here, of the highest authority, religion, and integrity, Lucius Lucullus, who says that he does not think, but he knows, that he did not hear, but he saw, that he was not merely present, but that he enacted it. There are also present envoys of the Heracleans, very noble men, here for the sake of this trial with instructions and public testimony, who say that he was enrolled as a Heraclean.

Or do you ask for the public records of the Heracleans, which we all know were destroyed in the war with Italian (allies), when the registry was burned. It is ridiculous to say nothing about those things which we have, and to ask for what we cannot have, to be silent about the memory of men and to demand the memory of letters (*documents*), and when you have the word of a most upright man and the oath of a very honest free town, to reject those things which can in no way be falsified and to ask for records, which you yourself say are accustomed to be falsified. Or that he did not have a residence at Rome, he who for so many years before citizenship was granted placed all of his affairs and fortunes at Rome? Or that he did not register? Nay, indeed, he registered in those tablets which alone, out of that profession and college of praetors, maintains the authority of public records.

5. For although the records of Appius were said to have been kept rather carelessly, and of Gabinius that the levity as long as he was safe, and after his conviction the calamity, had destroyed all confidence in the records, Metellus, most upright and scrupulous of all men, was so careful that he came even to the praetor Lucius Lentulus and said that he was disturbed by the erasing of one name.

In these records, then, you see no erasure on the name of Aulus Licinius. Since these things are so, judges, what do you doubt about his citizenship, especially when he has also been enrolled in some other states? For when men in Greece (*Magna Graecia*, i.e., southern Italy) were granting citizenship freely to many mediocre men with either no skill or very little, I suppose that the people of Regium, Locri, Naples, or Tarentum would have been unwilling to grant to him, endowed with the highest talent and ability, that which they were accustomed to give even to theatrical artists! What? — when others not only after citizenship was granted, but also after the Papian Law, had crept into the records of these towns by some means, will this man, who did not even use those in which he was enrolled because he always wished to be a

Heraclean, be rejected?

You ask for our (own Roman) census. Certainly; for it is not known to you that at the last taking of the census, this man was with the most illustrious general Lucius Lucullus, with the army; that in the previous census he was with the same man as quaestor in Asia; and that in the first one, that of Julius and Crassus, no (real) part of the people was counted. But since the census does not prove the right of citizenship, but only indicates that he who was counted was acting like a citizen, in those times he whom you are charging that not even in his own judgment he had any share in the rights of Roman citizens, he often made a will under our laws, and accepted inheritances of Roman citizens, and his name was turned over to the treasury among (other) beneficiaries by Lucius Lucullus, the proconsul.

6. Seek proofs, if you can; for he will never be convicted either in his own opinion or that of his friends.

You ask us, Gratius, why we are so greatly pleased with this man. Because he supplies us that with which both the mind is refreshed from the din of the Forum, and the ears, fatigued from the noises of the court, may find rest. Or do you think that we can supply ourselves with what we say daily on such a variety of things, unless we cultivate our minds by study, or that the mind can endure so much strain (and struggle), unless we relax it by the same study? I confess that I am completely given over to these pursuits.

Others may be ashamed if they have so buried themselves in their books that they can bring forth nothing to the common good or present nothing for public view or light; but why should I be ashamed, who have lived for so many years, judges, in such a way that my own leisure has not ever called me away from the needs or advantage of anyone, nor has my rest kept me away, nor pleasure called me back, nor finally has sleep delayed me? Therefore, who, pray, can blame me, or who can justly censure me, if I spend as much time in the pursuit of these studies as others spend transacting their affairs, celebrating festival days of games, and other pleasures of mind and body for that rest, or as some assign to themselves at all-night banquets, or finally to games of dice or ball?

And this should be granted to me all the more, because from these studies my oratorical po'er also grows, which, however great it is, has never been denied (*wanting*) to the needs of my friends. If this may seem trivial to anyone, at least I know from what source I draw those things which are the most important. For if I had not persuaded myself from my youth, by the teachings of many people and by many books, that nothing ought to be greatly desired in life except praise and honor, and that in attaining these all tortures (*agonies*) of the body and all dangers of death and exile should be considered of small importance, I never would have exposed myself for your safety to so many and such great struggles and to those daily attacks of profligate men.

But all books are full, all the voices of wise men are full, antiquity is full of examples; and these would all be lying in darkness, unless the light of literature was added. How many images of the bravest men, portrayed not only for gazing at but also for imitating, have the Greek and Latin writers left to us! I, keeping these always before me in governing the state, used to strengthen my spirit and mind by the thought of these excellent men.

7. Someone will ask: "What of this? — those very men whose virtues have been expressed in writings, were they trained by this same learning which you are now extolling by your praises?" It is difficult to say this about them all, but it is clear nevertheless what my answer will be. I admit that there have been many men of excellent mind and virtue without any training, and by some almost divine gift of nature, they have stood out as discreet and important men: I even add that more often has nature without learning been of value to attain praise and virtue than learning without any natural talent. But I maintain also that when there is added to an outstanding and illustrious nature a certain method and systematic training, then some unusual and noble excellence is likely to emerge.

From this group of men whom our fathers knew (*saw*) are Scipio Africanus, that divine man, and also Gaius Laelius, Lucius Furius, both most discreet and self-disciplined men, and also in those times, that most brave and learned man, Cato the Elder; and they surely never would have devoted themselves to a study of these things, if they were not being helped by literature in understanding and cultivating virtue. But even if this (so) great advantage were not shown, and if from these studies pleasure alone was sought, still I believe you would judge that this relationship of the mind is most refined and befitting a gentleman. For other things are not of all times, ages, and places; but these studies nourish youth (and) delight old age, adorn prosperity (and) offer a refuge and comfort in adversity; they please us at home (and) are not in the way out of doors; they are with us at night, they travel with us, they go to the country with us. But even if we ourselves were not able to achieve these things or enjoy them with our own senses, still we ought to admire them when we see them in others.

8. Who of us was so rude and insensible in mind that he was not moved recently by the death of Roscius? Although he died an old man, still on account of his excellent skill and artistic grace he seemed as if

he ought not to have died at all. So he by the mere motions of the body won from all of us such great love; shall we (then) overlook an unbelievable activity of the mind and quickness of mental talents? How often have I seen this man Archias, judges — for I shall use your kindness, since you are attending me so carefully in this novel kind of (public) speaking — how often have I seen him, when he had not written down a single word, speak extemporaneously a great number of verses about those things which were then going on! — and when he was called back, say the same thing with changed words and sentences!

Indeed, the things which he wrote out carefully and thoughtfully, I have seen so approved that he seemed to gain even the glory of ancient writers! Shall I not then love this man, admire him, and think that he should be defended in every way? And we have learned from great and most scholarly men that the studies of other things are based on the teachings and the arts; that a poet has power because of his very nature, and he is aroused by a strength of mind and inspired by a certain almost divine spirit. Therefore, that Ennius of ours rightly calls poets "sacred," because they seem to have been entrusted to us by some gift and prize of the gods.

Let the name of poet, then, judges, be holy among you, most cultivated (of) men, a name which not a barbarian has ever violated. Rocks and deserts reply to their voices, and wild beasts often are turned aside by their song and stand still; should not we, trained in the best things, be moved by the voice of poets? The Colophonians say that Homer was a citizen of their state, the Chians claim him as theirs, the Salaminians say the same, and the Smyrnians claim that he is theirs, and they have dedicated a shrine for him in their town; very many others besides fight and contend among themselves (over this question).

9. These people, then, seek out (*claim as their own*) a foreigner, because he was a poet, even after his death; shall we reject this living man, who is one of ours both by his own wish and by our laws, especially since Archias has devoted all his genius and talent to the celebration of the glory and praise of the Roman people? For in his youth, he touched upon the war with the Cimbri, and he was pleasing to that Gaius Marius himself, who seemed rather austere for literary efforts like these; and yet there is not anyone so unfriendly to the Muses that he does not gladly allow the eternal heralding of his efforts to be entrusted to verse.

They say that that Themistocles, the greatest man of Athens, when it was asked of him whose voice he would most gladly hear, said: "(The voice) of that man by whom his (*Themistocles's*) own excellence was best proclaimed." And so that (same) Marius also especially loved Lucius Plotius, by whose genius he thought (*judged*) that those things which he had done were being celebrated; now the Mithridatic war, great and difficult and carried on in many a diverse land and sea, has been fully written up by this man (Archias); these books bring honor to Lucius Lucullus, a very brave and famous man, but also to the name of the Roman people.

For the Roman people, under the command of Lucullus, opened up the Pontus, formerly walled off both by the wealth of kings and by the very nature of this region; the army of the Roman people, under this same commander, with a not very large band, routed the countless forces of Armenians; there is glory for the Roman people that the very friendly city of the Cyzicenians, by the wisdom of this same man, was saved and protected from every attack of the king and from the open jaws of the whole war; it will always be referred to our glory, and we will gain honor from the fact that when Lucullus was fighting, the fleet of the enemy was sunk and its leaders killed, in that incredible naval battle off Tenedos; ours are the trophies, ours the monuments, ours the triumphs; the fame of the Roman people is celebrated by those through whose genius these things are being written.

Our Ennius was dear to the elder Africanus, and so he is even thought to have been portrayed in marble on the sepulcher of the Scipios. Not only is that man who is praised, but also the name of the Roman people, surely honored by these same praises. Cato, the great-grandfather of the present one, is extolled to the skies; great honor is (thereby) added to the history of the Roman people. Finally, the Maximi, Marcelli, and Fulvii are all distinguished not without the common honor of all of us.

10. Therefore, our ancestors received into their state the man who had done these things (Ennius), who was a man of Rudiae; shall we throw out this Heraclean, who is sought by many states and legally enrolled by our laws, from our state?

For if anyone thinks that there is less glory to be gained from Greek verses than from Latin, he is greatly mistaken, because the Greek ones are read in almost all nations and the Latin ones are bound by the Latin limits, which are certainly small. Therefore, if these things which we have done are bounded by the lines of the (whole) world, we ought to wish that where the weapons of our armies reach, our fame and glory will penetrate to the same place, because these things are full of honor not only to the very (*particular*) peoples about whom it is being written, but also, surely, because to those who are fighting for life and the sake of glory this is the greatest incentive for taking risks and for their hardships.

How many writers of his accomplishments is that Alexander the

Great said to have had with him! And he, furthermore, when he stood at the tomb of Achilles near Sigeum, said, "Oh fortunate young man, who found Homer as the herald of your valor!" And truly so. For if the *Iliad* had not existed, that same tomb which covered his body would also have buried his name. What, did not this Great of ours (Pompey), who equaled his fortune with his courage, present with citizenship Theophanes of Mytilene, the writer of his own affairs; and those brave men of ours, (though) but simple (and) soldiers, as if moved by a certain sweetness of glory, approved with a great cheer, as if they were sharers of the same praise? Accordingly, I suppose if Archias had not been (already) a Roman citizen by our laws, he could not have brought it about that he would be presented with citizenship by some general.

Though Sulla gave it to Spaniards and Gauls, I suppose he would have rejected this man if he asked for it; (him) whom we saw in a gathering in the Forum, when a bad poet from among the people had presented him with a little book which he had written for him in epigrams (with no merit except) the alternate verses were a little longer, at once order a reward to be given to him from those things which he was then selling, but on the condition that he would not write anything afterwards. Would not he who thought the industry of a bad poet still worthy of some reward have sought out the talents and ability in writing and richness (in expression) of this man (Archias)?

What? — could he not have gained his request from Quintus Metellus Pius, his very close friend, who presented many with citizenship, or from the Luculli, through his own efforts? — he who so wanted to have (things) written about his exploits, that he even gave ear to poets born at Corduba, who sounded rather dull and barbarous.

11. For this must not be disguised, which cannot be suppressed, but must be brought before us: we are all drawn by a desire for praise, and every good man is greatly influenced by glory. Those philosophers themselves also in those very books which they write about scorning glory, inscribe their own name; in regard to this very matter in which they despise praise and renown, they want themselves to be mentioned and named. Indeed, Decimus Brutus, a great man and general, adorned the approaches of his temples and monuments with the songs of his most intimate friend Accius. And also that Fulvius who fought with the Aetolians, with Ennius as his companion, did not hesitate to consecrate to the Muses the spoils of war. Therefore, in a city in which generals almost in (scarcely out of) arms have revered the name of poets and the shrines of the Muses, judges clad in togas ought not to be averse to the honor of the Muses and safety of poets.

And so that you may do this more willingly, judges, I shall now declare myself to you, and confess to you (about) my own certain love for glory, perhaps too keen, but still honorable. For he has touched upon in his verses and made a beginning about the things which in my consulship I carried on together with you, for the safety of the city and the nation, and for the lives of the citizens, and for the whole commonwealth. When I heard these verses, because it seemed a great and pleasing work, I encouraged him to complete it. For virtue desires no other reward for its labors and perils than that of praise and glory: if this is taken away, judges, what is there which makes us exercise ourselves in hardships in this span of life, so short.

Surely if the mind cherished no anticipation for the future, and if it ended its thought with the same limits by which the duration of (earthly) life is circumscribed, it would not exert itself with such great toils, nor would it torment itself with so many cares and wakeful nights, nor would it fight so often for life itself. There resides now in every good man a certain virtue which night and day excites the mind by the stimulus of glory, and warns it that the memory of our name must not be let go with the time of (the end of) life, but must be made equal to (*co-extensive with*) all posterity.

12. Or do we indeed all appear to be of such small minds, we who are engaged in the republic (*affairs of state*) and in these dangers and labors of life, that when we have drawn no tranquil or peaceful breath even to the extreme end of life, we should think that all things are going to die with us? Many great men have carefully left behind them statues and images, representations not of their minds but of their bodies; ought we not to prefer much more to leave behind the expression of our virtues and thoughts, expressed and elaborated (*perfectly portrayed*) by the greatest geniuses?

I indeed thought that all the things which I was doing, then while doing them, I was scattering and spreading to the eternal memory of the (whole) world. Whether this (memory) will be absent from my (conscious) perception after death or, as the wisest men have thought, it will (still) concern some part of me, now indeed I am delighted certainly with the thought and hope that it will.

Therefore, judges, save this man of such a sense of honor, whom you see is approved not only by the dignity but also by the veneration of his friends; a man of as much talent as can be imagined, because you see him sought by (*desired in*) the opinions of the greatest (of) men, in a cause of this (such a) kind that it is approved by the favor of the law, by the authority of a free town, by the evidence of Lucullus, and the records of Metellus.

Since this is the case, we ask you, judges, if there deserves to be any commendation not only human but also divine in such great talents, that you receive him into your trust, (he) who has always honored you, your ancestors, and the affairs of the Roman people, and who promises that he will give eternal proof of our recent domestic perils, and yours, and who is from that number which is always held to be holy among all people, in such a way that he will seem to be relieved by your kindness rather than (*and not*) harmed by any bitterness.

I trust that these things that according to my custom I have said briefly and simply about the case have been approved by all, judges; the things which I have said not according to the usual custom of the bar and judicial practice, both about the genius of this man and about these studies in general, I hope have been received by you in good part, judges; I certainly know that they have been well received by him who presides at this trial.

Fourth Verrine Book

1. I come now to that (fellow's), as he himself calls it, studious pursuit; his friends, sickness and insanity; the Sicilians, robbery; I do not know by what name I should call it; I will merely lay the case before you, weigh it yourselves by its (actual) mass, not by its name. Learn, judges, first the nature of the thing; then you will perhaps not ask very many questions about the name by which it should be called.

I state that in all of Sicily, a province so rich and so old, with so many wealthy towns and families, that there was not any silver vessel, any Corinthian or Delian bronze, not any gem or jewel, nothing made of gold or ivory, nor any statue of bronze, marble, or ivory, nay, not a picture on either wood or tapestry, that he did not seek out, look over, and carry off whatever pleased him.

I seem to be saying a great (deal): but listen carefully to the way in which I will prove it. For I do not include all this for the sake of exaggerating or enlarging upon his crime, but when I say that that man left nothing of this kind in the whole province, know that I speak the plain truth, and not in the manner of a prosecutor. Or to be even clearer: he has left nothing in the house of a single man, not even his hosts, nor in public places, nor in shrines even; nothing at the house of a Sicilian, or a Roman citizen, in short, nothing which came before his eyes and mind, whether it was private or public, profane or sacred. Where then shall I begin better than in that city which was always first for you, Verres, in love and enjoyment, or from what number better than those (who are) your (special) praisers? For it will be seen more easily what you were like among those who hate and accuse and prosecute you, when you are shown to have plundered among your own people of Messina in a very perverse way.

2. Gaius Heius is a Mamertine, perhaps the wealthiest in that state in all respects; all those of you who have been to Messina will easily grant to me this (fact). For his house at Messina is perhaps the finest, and certainly the best known, and always has been very open to our countrymen. Before the arrival of that man, this house was so ornate that it was also an ornament to the city. For Messina itself, which is in its location very beautiful with its walls and harbor, has now been emptied and stripped of those things which Verres delights in.

There was at the house of Heius a sacred chapel of much dignity, handed down to him by his ancestors and very old, in which there were four very beautiful statues of the greatest artistry and merit, which could give pleasure not only to that man of genius and intelligence, but even to any one of us, whom he calls laymen (in art matters). One was a marble Cupid of Praxiteles — of course I learned the names of (these) artists while I was making my investigation of the defendant. This same artist, I believe, made a Cupid of the same kind at Thespiae, the reason people go to visit Thespiae, for there is no other reason. And that Lucius Mummius, when he carried off the (statues of the) Muses, which are now near the Temple of Good Fortune in Rome, did not take away that Cupid of marble, because it was sacred.

3. But to return to the chapel of Heius, there was that marble statue of Cupid of which I have spoken, (and) on the other side was a beautifully made bronze Hercules; this is said to be the work of Myron, and I am sure that it is (*of that opinion: in fact, sure*). Before these two statues were also small altars, which could signify to anyone the sanctity of the shrine. There were besides, two other bronze statues, not very large, but especially beautiful, in the shape and dress of maidens, who in the manner of Athenian maidens were holding certain sacred objects which were placed on their heads, with their hands uplifted. These are called Canephoroe; but their sculptor — who? who (was it)? you prompt me correctly — they say he was Polyclitus.

When anyone of us came to Messina, he was accustomed to go to see these; they were open to everyone to look at every day; the house was no more an ornament to its master than to the whole city. Gaius Claudius, whose aedileship we all know was most magnificent, used this statue of Cupid for the time (while aedile) that he had the Forum decorated to the glory of the immortal gods and the Roman people, since he was the guest of Heius and a patron of the people of Messina, but just as he used their great kindness in order to borrow it, so he was (himself) careful to return (it).

Distinguished men used to act in this way a little while ago, judges, but why should I say "a little while ago"? For very recently we have seen men decorate the Forum and the basilicas not with the spoils of the provinces, but with art objects of their friends, with the loans of friends, that is, not thefts taken by guilty men; moreover, they returned these statues and treasures to each owner. These things were not carried off from the cities of friends and allies for a four-day festival, through the pretense of (needing things while) aediles, and then taken home to their own villas. But all of these statues which I have told you about, Verres removed from the chapel of Heius; he left not one of these, nor anything else except one very old wooden one, of Good Fortune, I think; he did not wish to have this in his house.

4. By the faith of gods and men! what do we have here? — what is the pretext here? what shamelessness of that (fellow)? These statues which I speak of, before they were carried away by him, no one ever came to Messina with power (*as an official of Rome*), who did not go to see them. So many praetors, so many consuls there have been in Sicily both in peace and also in time of war, so many men of both kinds — I shall not talk of the upright, innocent, and conscientious — but so many greedy, wicked, daring men, not one of whom seemed to himself so bold, so powerful, or so notorious that he would dare to ask for, or carry away, or even touch a single thing from that shrine. Shall Verres take away whatever is most beautiful everywhere? Will no one else be allowed to have anything? Shall his house alone contain (the ornaments of) so many wealthy houses? Has not one of these earlier men taken anything, just so that this man could steal them? Did Claudius Pulcher bring them back, just so that Verres could take them away?

14. But now, by Hercules, judges, I shall tell you about this. I remember that my friend and host, Pamphilus of Lilybaeum, a noble man, told me that when he (Verres) had taken away from him, through his power of praetor, a jug made by Boethus, a beautiful and large work, and he indeed had returned home sad and disturbed, because the jug of this type, which had been left to him by his father and ancestors and which he was accustomed to use on festival days and at the arrival

94

of guests, had been stolen from him.

"When I was sitting sadly at home," he said, "a venerian slave came up to me; he ordered me to take to the praetor at once my embossed cups.

"I was dismayed," he said, "I had two; I ordered them both to be brought out, lest anything worse happen to me, and to be carried to the praetor's house in company with me.

"When I came there, the praetor was resting; (but) those brothers from Cibrya were walking about. When they saw me, they said, 'Where are the cups, Pamphilus?'

"I showed them sadly; they praised them. I began to moan that I would have nothing of any value, if the cups were also taken from me.

"Then when they saw that I was disturbed, they said, 'What are you willing to give us, so that those (cups) will not be taken from you?' To cut it short," he told me, "they demanded a thousand sesterces; I said that I would pay it.

"Meanwhile the praetor called and asked for the cups." Then they began to say to the praetor that they had thought, from what they had heard, that Pamphilus's cups were of some value; (but) they were rubbish, not fit for Verres to keep among his silver. Verres said that it seemed the same to him. And so Pamphilus carried home (again) his very fine cups.

24. And lest by chance you think that the man wanted to pile up this large collection of art objects without a reason — see how much importance he attached to you, or what the Roman people might think of him, or for laws and trials, or Sicilian witnesses — after he had collected such a large number of objects that not even one thing was left to anyone else, he set up a very large shop in the palace at Syracuse.

He openly ordered to be assembled here all artists, engravers, and metal workers (from the city) and he had a great many others, his own (slaves): he shut them all up, a huge crowd of fellows. For eight continuous months, work was not lacking for them, although not a single vase was made except in gold. Then those (carved figures) which he had taken off of the dishes and incense burners he fastened onto the gold cups so skillfully and attached them so cleverly to the gold goblets, that you would say that they had always been there; the praetor himself, moreover, who says that there was peace in Sicily because of his vigilance, used to sit in this shop for a great part of the day in his gray tunic and Greek mantle.

27. I come now to a matter that is not a theft, not avarice, not greed, but a crime of the sort that all wickedness seems to me to be contained and inherent in it, a crime in which the immortal gods have been vio-

95

lated, the reputation and prestige of the name of the Roman people has been lessened, hospitality has been violated and betrayed, and because of the crime of this one man, all very friendly kings and nations, and those who are in their command and power, have been alienated from us.

For you know that the two princes of Syria, the sons of King Antiochus, were here at Rome recently; they had come here not because of the kingdom of Syria, for they held this with no argument, as they had received it from their father and ancestors; but they thought that the kingdom of Egypt (also) belonged to them and their mother Selene. After they, excluded from the senate, were not able to accomplish what they wanted on account of the conditions in the state, they set out for Syria, to their native lands. One of them, who is called Antiochus, wanted to make the journey through Sicily; accordingly, he came to Syracuse when Verres was governor.

Here Verres thought that an inheritance ("*windfall*") had come to him, because that man had come into his power and hands, who he had heard and suspected had with him many valuable treasures. He sent to the man (*prince*) rather large supplies for his domestic use: whatever oil and wine seemed necessary, and also from his own tithes (*dues in produce*), what seemed to be enough wheat. Then he invited the prince himself to dinner. He furnished the dining room lavishly and magnificently; he set out what he had in abundance, many (and) very beautiful silver vessels — for he had not yet made the ones of gold; he took care that the whole banquet should be laid out and furnished with everything.

What need I say more? The prince went home thinking that (dinner) abundantly embellished and himself received with the greatest honor.

He himself then invited the governor to dinner; he laid out all of his wealth, much silverware, not a few gold cups, which as is the royal custom especially in Syria were inlaid with the most brilliant gems. There was a wine utensil, a ladle hollowed out of a single very large gem, with a golden handle; about this you have heard Quintus Minucius speak, a sufficiently impressive witness, I think. Verres picked up each vessel in his hands, praised them, admired them. The prince rejoiced that his banquet was so acceptable and pleasing to the praetor of the Roman people.

After they had all gone home, Verres thought of nothing else, as the later events prove, except how he might send the prince out of the province stripped and robbed of his possessions. He sent to ask for the most beautiful objects which he had seen at his house; he said that he wanted to show them to his engravers: the prince, who did not

96

know (the real Verres), without any suspicion gave them most willingly. He also sent to ask for the ladle carved out of a precious stone; he said that he wanted to examine this more carefully. This also was sent to him.

28. Now, judges, hear the rest, about which (both) you yourselves have heard before and the Roman people will not hear now for the first time, and it has been spread even to the farthest lands and among foreign nations. These two princes whom I have been been speaking of, when they had brought to Rome a candelabrum made of the most beautiful artistry out of the rarest jewels, in order to put it up in the Capitol, because they found the temple not yet completed, and they were not able to put it in place and did not want to expose to common view or show it off, so that it would appear more magnificent when it was put in the sanctuary of the most high Jupiter at the proper time, and more outstanding when its beauty came to the eyes of men fresh and unimpaired, decided to carry it with them back to Syria, so that when they heard that the statue of Jupiter Optimus Maximus had been dedicated, they would send envoys to bring this excellent and very beautiful gift to the Capitol with other things.

The matter came to the ears of the praetor in some way or other; for the prince had wanted it to be kept secret, not because he feared or suspected anything, but so that many would not see it with their eyes before the Roman people (saw it).

The defendant asked the prince, and pleaded with him with many words, that he send it to him; he said that he wanted to look at it and that he would not give the others a chance to see it. Antiochus, who had a boyish and princely mind, suspected nothing about the wickedness of that fellow; he ordered his men to take it wrapped up to the governor's house as secretly as possible. After they brought it there and set it up with the wrappings taken off, he began to cry out that it was worthy of the kingdom of Syria, worthy of a royal gift, worthy of the Capitol. And indeed it had all the splendor which it should have, made with such brilliant and beautiful jewels; (it had such) variety of workmanship that the artistry seemed to vie with the materials, (and) such size that it could be easily understood that it had not been prepared for a man, but that it had been made for decorating a most magnificent temple.

When he seemed to have looked enough, they lifted it to return it. Verres said that he wanted to see it again and again; that he was not yet satiated; he ordered them to go away and leave the candelabrum (behind). Thus, they returned empty-handed to Antiochus.

29. At first the prince had no fears, he suspected nothing; one day passed, (then) another, (then) many; it was not returned. Then he sent word, asking him if it seemed (proper) to send it back. (Verres) ordered him to come back later. It began to seem strange to him; he sent again; it was not returned. He called in person on that fellow (and) asked him to give it back. Learn, now, the extraordinary "face" and impudence of the man. That which he knew, which he had heard from the king himself, was to be put up in the Capitol and which he saw was being kept for Jupiter Optimus Maximus and the Roman people, he began to ask and demand most vehemently that it be given to him.

When he (the prince) said that he was prevented both by the sanctity of Capitoline Jupiter and the respect of men, because many nations were witnesses of the masterpiece and present, the defendant began to threaten the man most fiercely. When (Verres) saw that he was affected no more by his threats than by prayers, he suddenly ordered the man to get out of the province before night; he said that he had found out that pirates were coming to Sicily from his kingdom.

The prince, in a very great crowd in the forum at Syracuse (lest anyone think that I am making up an obscure charge, by chance, and inventing something which nobody knows about), in the forum, I say, at Syracuse, weeping and calling on the gods to witness, began to cry out that the candelabrum made of jewels, which he was going to send to the Capitol and which he had wanted to be a lasting token of his alliance and friendship with the Roman people in the very beautiful temple, that (candelabrum) Verres had stolen from him; regarding the other works of gold and precious gems that were taken from him to Verres's house, he was not concerned, but that it was an outrage and a scandal that this one had been taken. Although it had been consecrated before in the minds of his brother and himself, nevertheless, right then in that assembly of Roman citizens, he gave, donated, hallowed, and consecrated it to Jupiter Optimus Maximus and called upon Jupiter himself to be a witness of his wish and religious purpose.

43. What? Did you not steal from the most sacred shrine of Aesculapius at Agrigentum, another memorial of Scipio, a very beautiful statue of Apollo, on whose thigh was inscribed the name of Myron in small silver letters? When he had done this, judges, by stealth, when he had summoned for this nefarious crime and theft certain evil men as leaders and helpers, the state (city) was gravely disturbed. At one (and the same) time the people of Agrigentum felt the loss of the kindness of Africanus, their domestic religious object, the ornament of the city, the proof of victory, and testimony of their friendship with Rome.

Accordingly, instructions were given by those who were the chiefs in that state (*city*), and the quaestors and aediles were directed to maintain watches near the sacred shrines at night. For Verres at Agrigentum did not dare to demand openly or carry away what pleased him — I suppose on account of the great numbers in that town and their courage, and because very many Roman citizens, brave and honorable men, live and carry on business with the townsfolk in a very friendly manner.

Among the Agrigentines, there is a temple to Hercules not far from the forum, especially venerated and sacred among those people. There is a statue there of Hercules himself of bronze, (and) I cannot easily say that I have ever seen anything more beautiful than this — although I do not understand so much about these things, as I (simply) have looked at many of them — so much so, judges, that its mouth and chin are a little rubbed away because in their prayers and veneration people have been accustomed not only to worship it but to kiss it. On this temple, when the defendant was at Agrigentum, suddenly in the dead of night an attack of armed slaves and a rush was made, with Timarchides as captain.

The watches and guards of the shrine raised a cry; when they (Verres's band) at first tried to oppose them and defend (themselves), they were repulsed, having been beaten up with clubs and cudgels. Later, when the bolts were wrenched off, and the doors were broken open, they tried to pull down the statue and pry it loose with crowbars.

Meanwhile news spread through the whole town, from the cries of the guards, that the native gods were being attacked, not by the unexpected arrival of an enemy, nor the sudden attack of pirates, but that a band of well-equipped and armed fugitives had come right from the governor's house. No one at Agrigentum was so worn out by age or so feeble in strength that he did not rise up that night, awakened by the messenger, and snatch whatever weapon chance offered to him. And so there was a rush to the temple in a short time from the whole city. For more than an hour by then many men had been working to pry the statue from its pedestal; it, meanwhile, gave way on no side, although some were trying to move it by putting levers underneath, and others to pull it towards them with ropes tied to all the limbs.

But suddenly the people of Agrigentum rushed in; there was a great throwing of stones; those illustrious night-soldiers of that general took to flight. They did, however, take away two very small statues, so that they would not have to report back to that robber of temples entirely empty-handed. Never are the Sicilians so badly off that they cannot say something in jest and opportunely, just as at this time, they said that among the labors of Hercules this very monstrous "boar" ought to be reckoned no less than that Erymanthian boar.

48. There is an ancient belief, judges, which is established from the most ancient Greek letters and monuments, that the whole island of Sicily is consecrated to Ceres and Libera. Other peoples think this same thing, and the Sicilians are so convinced of it that it seems to be implanted in their minds and inborn.

For they think that these goddesses were born in these places, and that produce was first found in the earth here, and that Libera, whom they also called Proserpina, was carried away from a grove near Henna, a place which because it is situated in the middle of the island is called the navel of Sicily. When Ceres went to search for her and seek her out, it is said that she lighted torches from the fires that break out from the top of Etna; while she carried these before her, she wandered all over the earth.

Henna, moreover, where they say that these things that I am discussing took place, is on a very high and lofty place, on the top of which there is a plain of level field and perennial springs, truly the whole (plain) is cut off from every approach and (is) steep (on all sides), around which are very many lakes and woods, and very beautiful flowers at every season of the year, so that the place itself seems to indicate that the virgin was carried off from here, a story which we have heard from boyhood.

There is also a certain cave here, facing north, extremely deep, where they say that Father Pluto suddenly appeared with his chariot, seized and carried away the maiden with him from that place, and suddenly went underground not far from Syracuse; and a lake suddenly appeared in that place, where even up to this time, the people of Syracuse celebrate annual festivities with a very great throng of men and women.

49. Because of the long standing of this belief, that the footprints and cradle of these divinities are found in these places, there is a certain remarkable devotion to Ceres at Henna, both privately and publicly. For numerous portents often indicate her power and presence there; her present help has been brought to many people in very difficult circumstances, so that this island seems to be not only loved but also guarded and watched over by her.

Not only the Sicilians, but other races and peoples also have great reverence for Ceres of Henna. And if the sacred rites of the Athenians, to whom Ceres is said to have come and brought fruits in her wandering, are sought out with the greatest eagerness, what must be the feelings of those among whom it is well known she was born and (where she) came upon fruits.

Therefore, even among our fathers, at a most critical and difficult time of the state, when after Tiberius Gracchus had been killed and fear of great dangers was indicated by the omens, the Sibylline Books were consulted by the consuls Mucius and Calpurnius; it was found by them that the most ancient Ceres must be appeased. Then from the most distinguished body of decemvirs, priests of the Roman people set out even to Henna, although there was in our own city a very beautiful and magnificent temple of Ceres. Such was the prestige and reverence for her cult, that when they went here, they seemed to set out, not (simply) for a temple of Ceres, but Ceres herself.

I shall not weary you further; for I have long been worried that my speech may be too different from that used in law courts and the everyday practice of (public) speaking. I can say only this: that this very Ceres (i.e., the statue), the most ancient and most sacred Ceres, the foremost of all sacred cults which there are among all nations and tribes, was stolen by Gaius Verres from her very own temple and home. Any of you who have gone to Henna have seen the marble statue of Ceres and, in the other temple, the statue of Libera. They are very large and beautiful works, but not very old. But there was also a bronze one of moderate size and exceptional workmanship, and very old, showing her with torches, much the oldest of all the statues which are in her shrine. (Even) it Verres stole.

And yet he was not content with this. Before the temple of Ceres, in an open and uncovered place, there are two statues, one of Ceres, and the other of Triptolemus, both very beautiful and very large. Their beauty was a cause of danger to them, (but) their size a protection, because pulling them down and carrying them off seemed very difficult. In the right hand of the Ceres stood a fairly large statuette of Victory, exquisitely made; this the defendant had torn away from the statue of Ceres and carried off.

52. I shall now relate to you about the plundering of one of the most beautiful and wealthy of all cities, Syracuse, and I shall tell you about it so that I may finally bring to a conclusion and end this whole division of my speech. There is almost no one of you who has not often heard how Syracuse was captured by Marcus Marcellus, and sometimes read it also in the history books.

Compare the peace of this man with the war of that, the victory of that general with the arrival of this governor, the filthy gang of Verres with the undefeated army of Marcellus, the lawlessness of this man with the restraint of that; you will say that Syracuse was founded by this man who captured it, and captured by this man who received it all built.

For I leave out those things which will be said and have been said by me in different places: that the forum of the Syracusans, which was kept free from bloodshed at the entrance of Marcellus, when Verres came in overflowed with the blood of innocent Sicilians; that the port of the Syracusans, which was in those days closed to our fleets and that of the Carthaginians, has been opened up by this governor to a pirate ship and Cilician pirates; I say nothing about violence used upon freeborn persons and the raping of married women, which acts were not committed then when the city was captured, not by wartime passions, nor by license of soldiers, nor in the practice of wars and the rights of victors; I omit, I say, all these things which have been perpetrated by that fellow for three years: learn now of things closely related to these things about which I have spoken before.

You have often heard that the city of Syracuse is the largest and most beautiful of all the Greek cities. It really is, judges, just as is said. For it is both well fortified in situation and beautiful to behold from any approach, either by land or sea, and it has harbors almost enclosed in the buildings and embrace of the city; although these have different approaches far apart, they flow together and are joined at the end. Where they meet, the part of the city which is called "the Island," cut off by a narrow strip of sea, is joined and held to the mainland by a bridge.

53. This city is so large that it is said to consist of four very large cities; one part of it is that which I have called "the Island," which, girt by two ports, is thrust out into the mouth and entrance of each port; in this part was the palace of King Hiero, which the praetors are accustomed to use. There are several sacred temples on it, but two which far surpass the others, one of Diana, and the other of Minerva, which was very rich in treasures before the arrival of Verres. At one end of this island there is a fountain of fresh water, named Arethusa, of incredible size, very full of fish, which would be entirely covered by water from the sea unless it were cut off from the sea by a wall and pier of stones.

There is a second (part of) the city, of which the name is Achradina; in this there is a very large forum, some beautiful colonnades, a most ornate town hall, a very large senate house, and a magnificent temple of Olympian Jupiter, and other sections of the city, which is held together by one wide, continuous street and many cross streets, divided by numerous private dwellings.

There is a third (part of the) city, which is named Tycha, because in that section there was an ancient temple of Fortune; in this section, there is a large athletic ground and several sacred temples, and this part of the city is crowded and most densely populated.

Then the fourth (part) is called Neapolis, because it was built last;

102

on the highest part of this is a very large theater, besides two very fine temples, one of Ceres and the other of Libera, and a large and very beautiful statue of Apollo Temenites; if that fellow had been able to carry this, he would not have hesitated to take it away.

54. Now to go back to Marcellus, lest all these things seem to have been said by me without reason. When he had captured this lovely city with his strong forces, he did not think that it added to the glory of the Roman people to blot out and extinguish this beauty, particularly as there was no danger apparent. Accordingly, he spared all the buildings, public and private, sacred and secular, just as if he had come with his army not to attack but to defend them.

In respect to the ornaments of the city, he had consideration for victory, and also for humanity; he thought it was proper for the victor to carry back to Rome many things which could serve as an ornament to that city; but it was the duty of a humane man not to rob a city completely, especially one which he wanted to save. In this division of art works the victory of Marcellus sought for the Roman people no more than his humanity saved for the Syracusans. We see the things that were taken to Rome near the Temples of Honor and Virtue, and in other places. He put nothing in his own house, nothing in his gardens, nothing in his country house; he felt that if he did not take ornaments of the city into his own house, his house would be an ornament to the city.

Besides, he left at Syracuse many beautiful things; he did not violate, did not touch, a single god. Compare now Verres, not as you would compare a man with a man, lest some injury be done to a dead man, but as you would compare peace with war, law(s) with force, the forum and the decisions of the court with the sword and arms, the arrival (of a governor) with his retinue and the victory of a general with his army.

55. There is on "the Island," about which I have spoken before, a temple of Minerva; this Marcellus did not touch, (but) left filled and embellished; this has now been so plundered and robbed by this fellow that it seems to have been despoiled not by some enemy, who still would respect its sanctity and the rights of custom even in war, but rather by some barbarous pirates.

A cavalry battle of King Agathocles was painted on the walls of this temple; furthermore, the inner walls of the temple were covered with these paintings. There was nothing more noble than this picture, nothing at Syracuse which was more worth seeing. Marcellus, although he had made everything unconsecrated by his victory, still, hindered by his scruples, did not touch these panels; the defendant, although on account of the long-lasting peace and the loyalty of the people of Syracuse he had received them as sacred and religious, took away all of these paintings; he left the walls bare and unsightly, which had been adorned for so many centuries (and) had escaped so many wars.

Also, Marcellus, who had made a vow that if he captured Syracuse he would dedicate two temples at Rome, was unwilling to decorate that which he was about to build with those things which he had captured: Verres, who makes his vows not to Honor and Virtue, as Marcellus (did), but to Venus and Cupid, tried to rob the temple of Minerva. He (Marcellus) did not want the gods to be honored with spoils of other gods; but this man transferred ornaments from the temple of virgin Minerva into the house of a prostitute.

He also removed from the same temple twenty-seven other very beautiful paintings, in which were the portraits of the kings and tyrants of Syracuse, which gave delight not only on account of the skill of the painters, but also because of the memory of these men and a notion of their appearance. And see how much more hateful was this tyrant to the people of Syracuse, than any of the earlier ones, (the fact) that they nevertheless did adorn temples of the immortal gods; while this (Verres) carried away the monuments and decorations.

56. And now what shall I tell you about the doors of this temple? People who have not seen them will think, I fear, that I am unduly coloring or exaggerating all these things, a thing which no one should suspect, since there are so many distinguished men, especially from the number of the judges themselves, who have been to Syracuse and seen these things, who would be aware of any reckless and false statements of mine. I can state this honestly, judges, that there have never been any more magnificent doors, made more perfectly from gold and ivory, ever on any temple. It is incredible to say how many Greek men have left writings about the beauty of these doors.

Perhaps they extol and praise them too much; so be it; nevertheless, judges, it is more honorable to our state for our general in war to have left, than for a praetor in peacetime to have carried off, those things which seemed to him attractive. On the doors were carved in ivory various scenes (*subjects*), very painstakingly made; he took pains to remove them all. He took off and carried away a beautifully made head of the Gorgon, encircled with snakes, and he showed that he was influenced not only by the workmanship, but also by the cost and money value; for he also did not hesitate to take away all the golden knobs from these doors, which were many and heavy. And so he left the doors of a kind that now seemed to be made only for opening and shutting, when they had formerly been a great adornment for the temple. Did you not even take in your greed, Verres, the bamboo apears also — I saw that you were all influenced greatly by the mention of these when the witness was speaking — in which there was nothing of art or beauty, but only incredible size, about which it is enough to hear, too much to see more than once?

57. For the Sappho which was taken from the town hall may give you some just excuse, so that it might almost seem that it should be overlooked and forgiven. For who could have a better claim to this very well-made work (*masterpiece*) by Silanion, so well finished and so carefully carved, than a man so elegant and erudite (as you), Verres, whether he be a private citizen or a man of the people? Doubtless nothing can be said against this.

For each one of us, who is not so fortunate as he is nor can we be so fastidious, if we wish to see anything of this sort, may go to the Temple of Felicity, or the monument of Catulus, or the colonnade of Metellus, or may give effort to gain admission to the villa at Tusculum (belonging to) one of the defendant's friends; let him look at the decorated Forum, if that fellow has loaned any of his (art treasures) to aediles: but let Verres have these things in his own house, let Verres have his house full, and his country houses filled with the art treasures of (*taken from*) shrines and towns.

Will you, judges, endure the "hobbies" and delights of this day laborer who was born and educated and made by nature in such a way, both in mind and body, that he seems much better fitted to carry (on his back) than to carry away (as a connoisseur) these statues? For it cannot be truly stated how great a loss this stealing of the Sappho has left (in Syracuse). For not only was it beautifully carved itself, but it had a very noble Greek epigram cut in the base, which that (so) scholarly and Greek-reading gentleman, who understands so much about all of these things (and) alone appreciates, would certainly not have left behind, if he could have read one Greek letter. For now what was written on the empty base points out what it was and indicates that it has been stolen.

What? — did you not take out of the temple of Aesculapius a statue of Apollo, sacred and venerated, which on account of its beauty everyone was accustomed to visit, and on account of its religious worth, to worship? Was not a statue of Aristaeus also openly removed from the temple of Liber by your order? Did you not also take from the temple of Jupiter a very sacred statue of Jupiter Imperator, beautifully made, which they call Urios? What? — you did not hesitate, did you, to take from the temple of Libera an excellent head of a wild boar, which we were all accustomed to go to see? And that Apollo (which) was worshiped, together with Aesculapius, in annual sacrifices by these people; (the statue of) Aristaeus, who is said to have been the discoverer of olive oil, had been consecrated among the others along with Father Bacchus in that same temple.

58. As for the Jupiter Imperator, however, with how much honor do you think he was worshiped in his own temple? You may judge, if you wish to remember what great veneration was felt for the statue of the same shape and design, captured (*taken*) from Macedonia, that Titus Flamininus put up in the Capitol.

For there were reported to be three very excellent statues of Jupiter of the same kind in the whole world; one (was) the Macedonian one, which we see in the Capitol; a second in the narrow straits of the Black Sea (*the Bosporus*); (and) the third which before the praetorship of Verres was at Syracuse. The first one Flamininus took out of its (original) temple to put up in the Capitol, that is the earthly dwelling place of Jupiter. The one that is at the entrance to the Black Sea has been kept whole and inviolate up to this day, although so many wars have broken out in this region, and so many others a long way off have been drawn into that (same) sea.

This third one, which was at Syracuse, which Marcellus had seen when he was there with his victorious army and had refrained from taking because of its sanctity, which the citizens and residents of Syracuse were accustomed to worship and visitors also not only go to see but also to worship, this statue Verres took out of Jupiter's (own) temple! To go back once more to Marcellus, judges, know this: more gods have been lost by the Syracusans at the arrival of the defendant than men were lost in the victory of Marcellus. In fact, he (Marcellus) is said to have searched for that man of the greatest learning and genius, Archimedes, (and) when he heard that he had been killed, he was deeply distressed; but this fellow (Verres) sought out all the things which he was searching for, not to protect, but to carry away.

59. I will now pass over those misdeeds that may seem less important, (the fact) that Delphic tables of marble, beautifully made bronze bowls, a vast amount of Corinthian vases, he carried off from all of the sacred temples at Syracuse. And so, judges, those men who are accustomed to conduct visitors to see those things which they have come to visit — those (men) who are called guides — and to point out each object, now have a very different (matter for) explanation. For whereas they used to point out what each piece was in each place, now they just explain what was taken away everywhere.

What then? — do you think that these people feel only a slight sorrow? It is not true, judges; first, because they are all moved by a deep sense of religious feeling, and they think that they ought to keep and worship the native gods which they have received from their ancestors. Then, too, all of these ornaments, masterpieces, statues, and paintings especially delight men of Greek background; thus, we can appreciate from their complaints that those things seem very bitter to them which perchance seem to us trivial and (a matter) to treat lightly.

You may believe me (in this), judges — although I know that you yourselves certainly hear the same things — while (our) allies and foreign nations in recent years have received many disasters and injuries, the Greeks feel distress at nothing more than the plundering of this sort of their temples and shrines. Verres may say that he bought them, as he is continually saying, but believe me, judges, in this: not any state in all of Asia and Greece ever sold of its own free will any statue, any painting, or any ornament of its city; unless perhaps you think that since the trials at Rome have ceased to be strict (*severely just*), Greek men have begun to sell those things which they not only did not ever sell when the trials were honest, but they even would buy: or unless you think that, while there was no sale (*traffic in*) of such things by (*with*) Greek men to Crassus, Scaevola, and Claudius, very (fine and) influential men, whose aedileships we saw embellished (with borrowed statues), opportunity (to buy Greek art) is available to those made aediles since courts have become lax.

60. You should know that this false and pretended buying is even more bitter to these states than if he secretly stole (art treasures) or openly seized and carried them away. For they think that it is the greatest disgrace to have it put in the public records that their state was influenced by a price, and a small price at that, to have sold and sent from the country those things which they have received from their ancestors. For Greek people enjoy in a wonderful way these things which we Romans seem to scorn.

Accordingly, our ancestors readily allowed them to keep these things as far as possible: among our allies, so that they would be as much as possible (a matter of) pride and enjoyment to our empire, (and) among those whom they made subjects and tributaries they left these things so that they, to whom these things were (so) enjoyable that seemed to us unimportant, would have some comfort and consolation for their subjected state.

What do you think that the people of Regium, who are now Roman citizens, would want to ask to let the marble Venus be taken away from them? or the Tarentines, to lose their famous Europa on the bull? or the Satyr in their temple of Vesta, or their other works of art? or the Thespians, for their statue of Cupid, which is the only reason for people

107

to go to see Thespiae? or the people of Cnidus for their marble Venus, or the people of Cos for their painted Venus? or the Ephesians for their Alexander, or the Cyzicenians for their Ajax or their Medea, or the Rhodians for their Ialysus? or the Athenians for their marble Iacchus, or the picture of Paralus, or their bronze heifer by Myron? It would be long and not necessary to mention all the things which people think should be visited in all of Asia and Greece; but that is why I tell you these things, because I want you to know that these (Sicilian) people, from whose towns these things have been taken, feel a certain extraordinary pain.

Letters of Cicero

1.

MARCUS TULLIUS CICERO, SON OF MARCUS, EXTENDS GREETINGS TO GENERAL GNAEUS POMPEIUS MAGNUS, SON OF GNAEUS.

If you and the army are in good health, it is well; I, for my part, am in good health. Like everyone else, I was delighted beyond belief by the letter you sent through official channels, for in it you extended that hope of peace which I have continually been promising (relying on you alone) to everyone. But I want you to know one thing: those former enemies of yours who are now your friends have been dealt a mighty blow, thrown down from the height of their hopes, and laid low by your letter.

As far as I am concerned, however, I want you to know that I was pleased with the letter you sent to me, however little indication it offered of any affection for me; for nothing ordinarily gives me so much pleasure as the knowledge that I have been of service, and if no adequate return is made to my services, I am entirely satisfied to let the balance of service rendered remain on my side. There is one thing of which I am certain: even if my most enthusiastic efforts on your behalf have failed to make you my friend, political necessity will bring us together and make us allies.

And, that you may know what it was I missed in your letter, I shall write frankly, as is demanded both by my own nature and by our friendship. There are certain deeds of mine for which I hoped you would congratulate me in your letter, both for the sake of our relationship and for the good of the state; but I suppose you left such congratulation out for fear of hurting someone's feelings.

But I do want you to know that what I have done for the state has won universal approbation, as the whole world bears witness; when you come, you will realize that mine were deeds of such great discretion and courage that you will welcome an alliance, both in politics and friendship, between yourself, a much greater man than Africanus, and me, who am only a little less great than Laelius.

2.

MARCUS, TO HIS BROTHER QUINTUS.

Now I shall tell you what you especially want to hear. We have lost our grip on constitutional government, to the extent that Cato, who, though he is a young man and lacking in judgment, is after all a Roman citizen and a Cato, scarcely escaped with his life, because he was trying to arraign Gabinius for bribery and, since the praetors could not be approached for several days, he took the platform to address the people and called Pompey a self-appointed dictator. He was almost killed. From this you may see what the state of the nation is.

As for my case, it seems that there will be no lack of supporters; they volunteer their services, put themselves at my disposal, make promises, all to a surprising degree. For my part, not only are my hopes very high, but my confidence is higher still: my hopes, that is, that I shall win out, my confidence that even in the present state of politics I need not fear even an unpleasant incident. In any case, this is the situation: even if he prosecutes, all Italy will run to my aid, so that I shall come off with an enhanced reputation; but if, on the other hand, he resorts to force, I hope to be able to resist force with force, with the support not only of my friends but of outsiders as well.

Everyone is promising not only his own support but that of his friends, clients, freedmen, slaves, even money. My former band of loyalists is on fire with enthusiasm and affection for me. Anyone who up to now has been more or less against us or a rather lukewarm supporter is now joining our party out of hatred for those "kings." Pompey is making all sorts of promises, Caesar too; I believe them, but not enough to relax any of my own preparations. The plebeian tribunes-elect are on my side; the consuls appear quite well-disposed: we have for praetors good friends of mine and energetic patriots, Domitius, Nigidius, Memmius, Lentulus; the others are good men, too, but these especially so. Therefore see that you keep up your courage and your hopes. I shall continue to inform you regularly about the details of daily events.

109

3.

As I was departing from Brundisium, I wrote you why I had not departed for Epirus, the fact that Achaia next door is full of my most violent enemies, and when I was leaving there it was hard to find proper points of departure. Besides, when I was at Dyrrachium two messages were brought to me, one that my brother was coming from Ephesus to Athens, the other that he was coming through Macedonia. So I sent word to him to Athens to come from there to Thessalonica. I myself set forth and reached Thessalonica on the 23rd of May. I had no certain knowledge of his route except that he had left Ephesus sometime before.

Now I am greatly fearful of what goes on at Rome; although you write in one letter that on May 15th it was rumored that a more severe bill was sought, in the other you wrote that the terms were milder. But the last letter was written the day before the other, and so I'm all the more disturbed. Thus, not only does my sadness daily torture me and wear me out, but also there is this added worry which scarcely lets me live.

But sailing has been very difficult, and he, not knowing where I was, possibly has sought another way. For Phaetho his freedman did not see him. Driven back from Ilium by unfavorable winds to Macedonia he met me at Pella. I am aware how fearful I must be of everything to come and I don't know what to write and I fear everything, and there appears to be no misery so great that it has not fallen to my ill luck. Indeed, persecuted with my great tribulations already and with this added fear to increase my woes, I remain at Thessalonica in the greatest indecision nor do I dare anything.

The recollection of my own troubles and fear for my brother hinder me in writing. Look after all my affairs at home and take charge of them. Terentia thanks you profusely. I sent you a copy of a letter which I wrote to Pompey. Written May 29th at Thessalonica.

4.

From the letters of many and from everybody's conversation I am informed that your bravery and endurance are unbelievable and that no effort of mind or body wears you out. Oh, wretched me! That you with all your courage, faithfulness, honesty, and kindness should have fallen on such troubles because of me! And that our little Tullia should have such cause for grief from a father who was such a source of pleasure to her! And what shall I say about Cicero? — who as soon as he began to understand (anything) felt the bitterest grief and misery.

If I thought that these things were "all fate's doing," as you write, I should bear them more easily; but I am guilty of all of them, I who thought that I was loved by all of those who hated me and did not cultivate those who made overtures to me. But if I had followed my own counsels and had not heeded so much the talk of misguided or insincere friends, we would be now most happy.

As it is, since our friends bid us take hope, I shall take care that my ill health does not fail (to support) your efforts. I know what a great matter it is and how much easier it would have been to remain at home than to return; but nevertheless, if we have all the tribunes of the people on our side, if Lentulus is as zealous as he seems, and if indeed Pompey and Caesar are for us, we must not despair.

Regarding the slaves, we shall act in the manner which you write that our friends recommend. As for this place, the plague has now already gone by, but as long as it lasted, it did not touch me. Plancius, a most obliging fellow, wants me to stay with him and keeps me here. I should prefer to be in a more deserted spot in Epirus where neither Piso nor his soldiery would come, but so far Plancius has kept me here. He hopes it will be possible to go to Italy (in company) with me. If ever I see that day and clasp you in my arms and we are all recovered from this, I shall feel that I have received enough return for your devotion and mine.

Nothing could be greater than Piso's kindness, goodness, and love to all of us. Would that he might get some pleasure from it! Some cause for pride I see he will have. On the score of my brother Quintus I did not reproach you, but since there are so few of you, I wished that you might be as close as possible. Those whom you wished me to thank I have (thanked) and have written that you told me about them.

As for your writing me, my (dear) Terentia, that you are about to sell a row of houses, what, I beseech you from the depths of my misery, what will become of you? And if the same ill fortune continues to oppress me, what will become of my poor son? I can write no more; such is the force of my tears. Nor shall I reduce you to the same state of weeping. I write only this: If only our friends remain loyal, money will not be lacking; if not, you will be able to effect nothing by your expenditures. In the name of our pitiable misfortunes, see that we do not utterly ruin our son; for if only he has some little (income) to stave off want, all he needs is average ability and average good luck for all the rest to follow. Take care of yourself and send me couriers to let me know what is happening and what you are doing. The time of waiting for a letter to arrive is now quite short. Give my love to little Tullia and Cicero. Farewell. Written at Dyrrachium on November 25th.

P.S. I came to Dyrrachium because it is a free state and kindly disposed to me and very near Italy; but if the frequent coming and going is a nuisance to me, I shall go elsewhere and let you know about it.

5.

MARCUS (SENDS) GREETINGS TO HIS BROTHER QUINTUS.

I sent you a letter before, in which I wrote saying that our Tullia had been betrothed to Crassipes on the fourth of April and I gave a full account of all public and private matters.

As I was about to go on a journey, I gave the betrothal feast on April 6th. That best of boys, your Quintus, my dear nephew, could not attend this party because he was somewhat indisposed. On the 7th of April I visited Quintus and saw that he was fully recovered. He and I had a long and very friendly talk about the squabbles of our womenfolk. You ask, what? — nothing could have been more amusing. Pomponia furthermore even complained about you; but this we shall discuss in person.

When I left the boy, I went to your building lot. Many carpenters were pushing the work ahead. I encouraged Longilius, the contractor. He gave me his word that he wished to please us. The house will be splendid; for more of an idea of it can be formed now than we gathered from the plans. My own is likewise going up fast.

I am writing this letter before dawn on April 8th and am en route to spend tonight with Titus Titius at his estate near Anagnia; but tomorrow I intend to be in Laterium, and then when I've been five days at my place in Arpinum, to go to the villa at Pompeii, and returning to look in at the one at Cumae in order, since Milo's trial has been appointed for May 7th, to be in Rome the day before and see you as I hope on that day, my dearest, sweetest brother. It seems a good idea to hold up the construction work at Arcanum against your arrival. Take care of yourself, my brother, and return as soon as possible.

6.

MARCUS TO HIS BROTHER, QUINTUS, GREETINGS.

So far I have received two letters, one of them at the very moment of my departure, the other written at Ariminum, (but) the many (other)

112

letters which you say you have written I have not received. Except for the fact that I am away from you, for the rest I enjoy myself quite comfortably at my villas at Cumae and in Pompeii and intend to stay in them until June 1st.

I am writing that work which I named *Politiká*, truly a slow and laborious task; but if it comes out to my satisfaction, it will be work well spent; if not, I shall throw it into that sea in full view of which I write and shall take up other subjects, for I cannot be idle.

I shall follow your instructions carefully both as regards winning over certain people and not estranging others. Indeed, it will be my greatest care to see your son, my nephew Cicero, at least once a day, but to look into his studies as often as possible and, unless he disdains me, I shall even offer myself as his instructor, in which I've had some practice in the leisure of these days in helping along my own Cicero, junior.

You will indeed act as you write you will (and even if you did not so write, I know that you are carrying out these things most diligently) to set in order my instructions, follow them out, and bring them to a conclusion. When I come to Rome, I shall not let any courier of Caesar go without giving him letters for you.

During these days (I ask your pardon) there has been no one to whom I could give a letter before this same Marcus Orfius, a Roman knight, and my friend not only in his own right but because he comes from the town of Atella, which, as you know, is under my protection. And so I commend him to you all the more warmly as a man distinguished at home and influential even abroad. See that by your generosity you bring him under your obligation. He is a military tribune in your army. You will see that he is a pleasant and attentive man. I especially ask you to show the greatest affection to Trebatius.

7.

CICERO, TO (HIS FRIEND) TREBATIUS.

Because of your letter I have thanked my brother Quintus and can at last praise you highly, in that you now seem to have arrived at some settled purpose. For I was greatly disturbed by your letters in the first months, because (I say it with all due respect) you seemed to me sometimes light-minded out of your longing for the capital and its life, now idle, at times timid in the soldier's work, and furthermore often (and this is most unlike you) even a bit presumptuous.

113

Therefore, so long as I thought that I would go into a province, I trust you remember what I of my own accord offered you. After I abandoned that idea, when I saw that I was treated most honorably and was especially esteemed by Caesar and when I recognized the man's unbelievable generosity and remarkable good faith, thus I commended you to him and introduced you with all the seriousness and care possible. This charge he accepted in the same spirit and has often indicated to me in his letters and shown you in word and deed that he was strongly influenced by my recommendation.

Now that you have found this man, if you think that I have any sense or any good wishes in your cause, don't let him go: and, if sometimes something may perchance offend you, when he seems to you rather dilatory out of preoccupation or difficulty, endure it and wait for the outcome, which I will guarantee you pleasant and honorable.

I must not exhort you with more words. Only let me remind you there never was a greater opportunity to secure the friendship of a very great and generous man nor of getting a very rich province nor of making the most of your time of life; and if you miss it, you will never find it again. "This," as you lawyers are accustomed to write in your briefs, "is also the opinion of Quintus Cornelius."

I rejoice that you did not go to Britain, because you were spared the hardship and I shall not have to hear all (the tales you would have to tell about it). I wish you would write me where you expect to pass the winter, with what prospects, and under what conditions.

8.

MARCUS (EXTENDS) GREETINGS TO HIS BROTHER QUINTUS.

I have nothing to reply to your previous letter, which is full of vexation and complaints; also you say that you had given one in the same vein to Labienus the day before, and he has not yet arrived. Indeed your more recent letter dispelled all my worry.

Only I admonish and exhort you in the midst of all your troubles and hardships and homesickness to remember the purpose we had in view when you went. For we pursue no small or ordinary advantages.

For what was it we thought we ought to buy at the price of our separation? We are looking for the strongest bulwark in the good will of a very great and powerful man for the general maintenance of our position.

Also I warn you not to put into my letter that which if divulged would cause us annoyance. There are many things which I prefer not to know rather than to be aware of (but) with some risk. I shall write more to you with undisturbed mind, when, as I hope, my Cicero gets well. I wish that you would let me know to whom I ought to give the letter which I shall send you next, whether to Caesar's couriers, that he may forward them to you straight off, or to Labienus's. For I don't know where those Nervii of yours are or how far away.

I took great pleasure from the courage and dignity which you said in your letter Caesar had shown in the midst of his great suffering. Regarding the poem addressed to him that you bid me finish, in spite of distractions of work and far more of my thoughts, nevertheless since from the letter I sent to you, Caesar knows that I have started something, I shall return to my undertaking and finish it in the business-free days of the thanksgiving.

9.

CICERO, GREETINGS TO ATTICUS.

Before I settle down in some place don't expect long letters from me or always written in my own handwriting. When I have time, I guarantee both. Now I am on the march by a very hot and dusty road. I wrote from Ephesus day before yesterday; this letter I've written at Tralles. I expect to be in my province on the first of August.

Meanwhile these pieces of news which I wished to hear were reported to me: first that the Parthians are peaceful, then that the contracts with the revenue collectors have been signed, and finally that the mutiny of the soldiers has been put down by Appius and payment to them made in full to the 15th of July.

Asia received me wonderfully. My arrival didn't cost any one even the tiniest expense. I hope that all my staff are looking out for my good reputation. Nevertheless I am fearful, but hope for the best. All my retinue except your friend Tullius have come. I have it in mind to set out directly to the army, spend the remaining summer months on military matters, and devote the winter to dispensing justice.

I wish, since you know that I am no less devoted to public affairs than you, that you would write me everything that's happening and about to happen. You can do me no greater favor; excepting however what would be the greatest service to me, your carrying out the various commissions I gave you.

This is a letter full of haste and dust. The ones to come will be more detailed.

10.

I am greatly delighted you have gotten the reward of your devotion to your family, your patriotism, and your most distinguished and excellent consulship, in the election of Gaius Marcellus to the consulship. I have no doubt what the sentiments are of those about you; we, indeed, far away and sent by you into the outermost realms, I swear are lauding you to the skies with the truest and most deserved praise. For although I have regarded you with especial affection since boyhood and you have always wished, and thought me to be, of very great influence in every direction, in particular has my affection for you become the more keen and ardent for this accomplishment of yours, or rather the Roman people's regard for you; and I feel the greatest joy when I hear from the wisest and best men that I am like you in all my words, deeds, studies, and pursuits or that you are like me.

And truly if you add this one other to those outstanding accomplishments of your consulship, namely that someone (be appointed to) succeed me as soon as possible or no time be added to the term you set me in accordance with law and the senate's decree, I shall think that I have achieved everything through you. Take care of your health, and esteem and protect me in my absence.

The announcements that have been made to me about the Parthians, because I thought that just now I should not report on them officially, for that reason in spite of our friendship I did not write you of, lest, since I had written to a consul, I should seem to have written a public dispatch.

11.

Just see how letters to me are not delivered; for I can't be led to believe that you wrote none after you were elected aedile, especially since it was a matter for such great congratulation! But yet know for certain that I have received no letter of yours since that famous election which elated me with joy. By the same token I fear that the same may be happening to my letters. Indeed I never wrote a single letter home without writing another one to you, for there is no one more agreeable or dearer to me than yourself. But to return to the matter in hand.

116

As you hoped it would be, so it is; for you would wish, you say, that I should have only enough trouble to provide for just a little triumph, that you fear the Parthians because you distrust our troops. Anyway, this is the way it turned out; for when war with Parthia was declared, relying on certain passes and the nature of the mountains I led the army to Amanus, sufficiently supported by auxiliaries and with some authority as a result of my name among those who did not know me. For there is much talk of this sort in these parts: "Is this the man who the city — ? whom the senate —?" You know the rest.

When I came to Amanus, a mountain range which I hold jointly with Bibulus, the watershed marking the boundary of each command, our friend Cassius had successfully driven back the enemy from Antioch, which caused me great pleasure, and Bibulus had taken over the province. Meanwhile, with all my forces I had harassed the Amanians, our everlasting foes. Many were killed or captured and the rest scattered. The fortified strongholds were surprised by our unexpected advance (and) were taken and burned. And so because of this substantial victory I was hailed as "imperator" at Issus where, as I have often heard from you, Clitarchus informed you that Darius was defeated by Alexander. I then led my army to the most unsettled section of Cilicia.

There for the last twenty-five days with earthworks, sheds, and towers I have been attacking a very strongly held town, Pindenissus, with such resources and great pains that nothing is lacking to my supreme glory except the name of the town. But if, as I hope, I take it, then indeed I shall send public dispatches. I write this to you at present to give you hope of attaining what you wished.

But to return to the Parthians, this summer has seen this quite successful outcome. The next summer is what causes me great anxiety. Therefore, my dear Rufus, see to it that someone succeeds me as soon as possible. If this will be, as you write and as I think, too difficult, then see that my time of office is not extended, which is an easy matter.

Concerning politics, as I have written you before, I wait (to hear) of present doings but even more so of future (doings). Therefore, I earnestly beseech you describe everything to me as carefully as possible.

12.

GENERAL MARCUS CICERO EXTENDS GREETINGS TO CURULE AEDILE MARCUS CAELIUS.

I am indeed concerned about conditions in the city; news of such riotous assemblies and such a disturbed festival of Minerva was brought to me (for I have not yet heard more recent news); but yet nothing is of more concern to me than that I cannot laugh with you if there be anything to laugh at in all these troubles. For of course there are many things to laugh at, but I dare not write them down. I do feel badly about this, that I have not yet had any letter from you about these matters. And so, although when you read this I shall have completed my term of office, nevertheless I should wish for a letter from you to meet me on the way, to bring me up-to-date on all matters of state, so that I don't come home an utter stranger. And nobody else can do this better than you.

Stay in the city, my dear Rufus, I repeat it, stay in the city and live in its bright light. All absence abroad, as I have been aware from young manhood, is dark and dreary for those whose activity can be clearly visible in Rome. Since I knew this so well, would that I had persisted in my feeling! By heaven, I would not compare all the profits of a province with one little stroll or a conversation of ours. I hope that I have gained a reputation for uprightness; I gained no less reputation from refusing a province than from managing one well. "(Your) hope of a triumph?" you ask. I would sufficiently triumph were I indeed not so long in want of the things dearest to me.

But, as I hope, I shall see you soon. Send me on my way home letters worthy of you.

13.

CICERO, GREETINGS TO ATTICUS.

We came to Tarsus on the fifth of June. There I found much to disturb me, a great war in Syria, many cases of brigandage in Cilicia, and the general difficulty of organizing my affairs because I have only a few days left of my year's term of office, (including) moreover, that most difficult matter, that I must leave behind according to the senate's decree someone to be in charge. No one is less appropriate to leave behind than the quaestor Mescinius. For I hear nothing about Caelius. It would seem that my brother is the most proper person to leave in command; but that entails many difficulties, our separation, the danger of war, the villainy of the soldiery, and a hundred others. What a thoroughly nasty situation! But let luck take care of these matters, for we haven't much opportunity to plan.

When you have come safely to Rome, as I hope, you will see, as you are accustomed, to all the things which you know concern me, in particular my Tullia, about whose marriage I have written my wishes to

Terentia since you were in Greece; next, concerning my recognition (*honor*). For as you are away, I fear that sufficiently vigorous action has not been taken in the senate about my letter. I cannot write down all my fears; do you cause your letter to fly to me. I have written this hastily on the march with the army. You will (please) give my greetings to Pilia and to Caecilia, that most beautiful of girls.

14.

TULLIUS SENDS GREETINGS TO HIS (WIFE) TERENTIA.

If you and Tullia, the light of my life, are well, I and my dearest son Cicero are, also. We arrived at Athens on the 14th of October, after experiencing very contrary winds and a slow and uncomfortable passage. There as we disembarked was Acastus to meet us with letters on the twenty-first day after he started, very good going indeed. I got a letter from you in which I learned that you feared that some of your earlier letters had not been delivered to me.

All have been delivered. You have given all the news most scrupulously, and that pleased me very much. Nor was I surprised at the shortness of this letter which Acastus delivered, since right now you are expecting me, or rather us, in person and we are indeed eager to get home to you as soon as possible, although I realize the sort of political situation we are coming back to. For I know from the letters of many friends which Acastus brought that things are shaping up towards war so that I cannot, when I arrive, hide my feelings.

But since one must submit to fortune, I shall take pains to come there the more speedily so as to consider the whole situation more readily. I wish, as far as it is consistent with your health, that you would come down as far as you can to meet us.

We, the gods willing, hope to arrive in Italy about the 13th of November. Do you and Tullia, my dearest and most beloved Terentia, take care of your health. Farewell. Athens, Oct. 16th.

15.

I, TULLIUS, MY SON CICERO, AND MY BROTHER AND HIS SON SEND MOST CORDIAL GREETINGS TO TIRO.

I thought I could bear missing you a little more easily, but clearly I cannot and, although it is of great importance to my (hope of a) triumph to get to the city as quickly as possible, yet I think I've been at

119

fault in leaving you; but because your wish seemed to be that you definitely were unwilling to sail unless you were in better health, I approved your advice and I still do if you are still of the same mind; if on the other hand, after you have taken nourishment and it seems that you can follow me, that will be for you to decide.

I sent Mario to you with the idea of his returning to me as quickly as possible or, if you should still remain behind, of his coming back at once to me. But be sure of this, that if it can be done consistently with your health I should like nothing better than to have you with me; if, however, you feel that for the sake of convalescing you must delay a bit at Patrae, I want nothing more than your good health. If you sail at once, you will overtake us at Leucas; but if you wish to become stronger, see to it carefully that you have proper companions, good weather, and a suitable ship.

Particularly, my dear Tiro, don't, if you love me, let Mario's arrival and my letter force you to move. If you do what best suits your health, you will best obey my wishes. Consider these matters in the light of your own good sense. I myself long for your presence that I may show you the more affection. My love urges me to see you well; my longing, as soon as possible. Rather, therefore, let it be the former. Take care to get as strong as possible. Of all your innumerable kindnesses to me this will be the most pleasing. November 3rd.

16.

TULLIUS SENDS HIS LOVE TO TERENTIA AND TO HIS DAUGHTER TULLIA, HIS TWO DARLINGS, AND CICERO (JUNIOR) TO THE BEST OF MOTHERS AND THE SWEETEST OF SISTERS.

If you are well, so are we. Now, not only I but you must decide what you ought to do. If Caesar intends to come to Rome in an orderly way, you may well stay at home for the present; but if the man senselessly intends to hand the city over to plunder and burning, I fear that even Dolabella cannot be of sufficient use to us. Also I fear this, that we may be cut off so that you cannot leave when you want to.

There remains the question which you yourselves can best answer, whether ladies of your sort are in Rome. For if there are not, one must consider whether you can be there with propriety. Indeed whatever the situation now is, provided that we can hold these places, you can very well stay with me or on one of our estates. For also in a short time the outbreak of famine in the city must be feared. About these matters I wish you would consult with Pomponius, with Camillus, or with anyone you see fit: in short be of good courage.

Labienus has improved the situation, and even Piso is of aid to the cause, because he left the city and convicted his son-in-law (i.e., Caesar) of criminal conduct.

You, my dearest souls, write to me as often as you can both about what you are doing and what is happening there. Quintus and his son and Rufus send your their greetings. Farewell. June 23rd, Minturnae.

17.

TULLIUS SENDS GREETINGS TO HIS TIRO.

In what peril is my safety and that of all respectable men and of the state you may know from the fact that we have left our homes and our fatherland itself, either to be plundered or burned. The situation has reached the point where, unless some god or some chance come to our aid, we cannot be saved. Indeed as I came to the city, I did not cease to think, say, and do all which tended to peace. But a strange frenzy possessed not only the wicked but even those usually regarded as virtuous, so that they desired to fight, in spite of my protesting that nothing was more wretched than civil war.

Thus when Caesar was seized with a sort of madness, and forgetful of his family name and high offices took Ariminum, Pisaurum, Ancona, and Arretium, we left the city, how wisely or how manfully it is of no use to argue. Indeed you see in what situation we are.

For we are drafting great numbers of men and think that he is afraid that if he begins to attack the city, he may lose the two Gauls, both of which are hostile to him except for the Transpadani, and he has in his rear the six legions from Spain and great forces of auxiliaries under Afranius and Petreius. It appears likely that, if he commits some folly, he can be defeated provided only the city be saved.

He has received a very great blow because Titus Labienus, who had the highest office in his army, refuses to take part in his nefarious doings. He left him and is now on our side, and many others are said to be about to do the same.

Up to this point I have been in charge of the coast south of Formiae. I wished to take on no bigger job than this so that my letters and exhortations to peace would have more effect with Caesar. But if there is to be war, I foresee that I shall be in command of a camp and certain legions. I have the further trouble of our Dolabella's being on Caesar's side. I wanted you to know these things, but take care that they don't disturb you and retard your getting well.

Since you have not been able to be with me during the time when I

121

most needed your services and fidelity, take care not to hurry or make the mistake of sailing when you are ill or the weather bad. I shall never think that you have come too late, if you arrive well. So far I have seen no one who saw you later than Marcus Volusius, from whom I received your letter. And I don't wonder at this; for I don't imagine that my letters have reached you during such wintry weather. But take care to get well! And once you feel well, when the season is proper for sailing, then sail!

My boy Cicero is at our house at Formiae. Terentia and Tullia are at Rome. Look after your health. January 27th, Capua.

18.

CICERO (SENDS) GREETINGS TO ATTICUS.

After I sent you my letter, a letter was delivered to me from Pompey; most of it had to do with events in Picenum, which (he said) Vibullius had written to him about, and about Domitius's levy, all of which you know, nor was the news so cheerful in this letter as in the one Philotimus had written me.

I should have sent you that letter, but my brother's slave is just now setting out in a great hurry. Therefore, I shall send it to you tomorrow. But at the end of Pompey's letter, written in his own hand, he said, "I think you ought to come to Luceria. You won't be safer anywhere (else)."

I took that to mean that he regards these towns and this coast as lost, nor did I wonder that he who had abandoned the head did not spare the other members of the body. I replied to him at once and sent a reliable man from my attendants, informing him that I was not looking for a place where I might be safest; and if he wished me to come to Luceria either for his sake or that of the state I would come; I pleaded with him not to give up the coast if he wished to be supplied with grain from the provinces.

I saw that I wrote this to no effect; but as I expressed my feeling about holding on to the city then, so I now do the same as to not giving up Italy.

For I see how it is being arranged, that all the troops be concentrated at Luceria and yet not even this place be regarded as the final stand, but that even from there, if we are hard pressed, flight be prepared.

Don't wonder, therefore, if unwillingly I stoop to join that side in which no plan of gaining peace or victory has been sought, but always disgraceful and disastrous flights. I must go to meet whatever lot

122

fortune brings with those who are called loyal rather than to seem to disagree with the loyal (citizens).

19.

GENERAL MARCUS CICERO SENDS HIS GREETINGS TO PROCONSUL GNAEUS POMPEY.

When I sent the letter which was delivered to you at Canusium, I had no suspicion that you, in the interests of the state, intended to cross the sea, and I had great hopes that in Italy we could either make peace (which seems to me by far the most expedient course) or defend the republic with honor. In the meantime, although my letter has not reached you yet, from the instructions which you had given Decimus Laelius for the consuls I was informed of your plans and did not wait for a letter from you to be delivered to me, but straightway with my brother Quintus and our children I started off to you in Apulia.

When I reached Teanum Sidicinum, Gaius Messius, a friend of yours, and a great many others said that Caesar was taking the road to Capua and on that very day would stay at Aesernia. Of course I was much disturbed because, if that were so, not only did I think that our road was cut off but that I myself was certainly caught. So then I proceeded to Cales to stay in that particular place until certain news from Aesernia about the rumor I had heard should be reported.

When I was at Cales, a copy of a letter of yours was delivered to me which you had sent to the consul Lentulus. This stated that you had received a letter (of which you had enclosed a copy) from Lucius Domitius; and you wrote that it was of the greatest importance to the state to assemble at the earliest opportunity all our troops, and commanded Lentulus to leave just enough to garrison Capua. On reading this dispatch I was of the same opinion as all the rest that you were on your way to Corfinium, where since Caesar was encamped before the town, I didn't think the road was safe for me.

When we were at the height of expectancy, we heard at the same time what had happened at Corfinium and that you had begun the march to Brundisium; although my brother and I did not doubt that we should hasten to Brundisium, we were advised by many who kept coming from Samnium and Apulia to be on guard against being captured by Caesar, for he had set out for the same places where we were heading and would arrive at his destination even more quickly than we could.

That being the case, neither I, nor my brother, nor any of our friends thought we ought to run the risk of letting our rashness injure not only ourselves but also the common welfare, especially since we did not doubt that, even if it were a safe road for us to travel, we could not now catch up with you.

Meanwhile I got your letter, written at Canusium on the 20th of February, in which you urged us to come the more quickly to Brundisium. As I received this on February 27th, I don't doubt that by now you have reached Brundisium and I see that our road is completely shut off and we no less captured than those who were at Corfinium. For I don't think that only they are captured who have fallen amongst enemy bands, but no less those also who — shut off from a district — are caught in a position between their own garrisons and enemy forces.

20.

CICERO (SENDS) GREETINGS TO ATTICUS.

Although I have nothing to write, yet in order not to let a day pass without a letter, I've written this one. It was announced that Caesar would stop at Sinuessa on the 27th of April. I got a letter from him on March 26th in which he says he is hoping for my "influence," not as in former letters my "assistance." When I praised in a letter the mercy he showed at Corfinium, he wrote back as follows:

GENERAL CAESAR TO GENERAL CICERO, GREETINGS.

You quite rightly imagine that nothing could be more alien to my character than cruelty (for I am so well known to you). Not only do I take great pleasure from the fact itself, but also I rejoice beyond measure that my action is approved by you. Nor am I disturbed by the fact that those whom I let go are said to have departed only to make war on me again. For I much prefer that I stick to my principles and they to theirs. I wish you would come to me in the city so that I may employ your wisdom and your influence in all matters as I used to. Know that no one gives me more pleasure than your Dolabella. For this, in fact, I shall be grateful to him; for he can do no other than arrange it. So great is his thoughtfulness, feeling, and kindness for me.

21.

CICERO SENDS GREETINGS TO ATTICUS.

I feel that you are concerned not only about your fate in common with us all, but especially about me and my unhappiness. Indeed this grief of mine not only is not diminished when it allies your sorrow to it, but is even increased. To be sure with your natural good sense you understand with what comfort I can be particularly consoled. For you approve of my decision and say that there was nothing else to be done at such a time. You also add (although this has less weight with me than your judgment, nevertheless it is not light) that all the rest also, those at least who carry any weight, approve of my action.

If I thought so also, I should grieve the less. "Trust me," you say. I do indeed trust you, but I know how eager you are to alleviate my grief. I've never regretted having left the camp. There was so much cruelty on their side, so many alliances with barbarous nations that the proscriptions had been planned wholesale, not on an individual basis, so that already everyone had decided that the property of all the capitalist class like yourself should constitute the spoils of their victory.

My Tullia's illness and her bodily weakness (greatly) agitates me. I know how great a concern she is to you, and that is a great comfort to me. I was never in the slightest doubt as to Pompey's fate. For so great despair of his cause had taken hold of the minds of all kings and peoples that I thought it would end up this way for him wherever he had gone. But I cannot fail to grieve for his fall, for I knew him to be an upright and a virtuous and an eminent man.

I hear that my brother Quintus has set out for Asia to sue for pardon. Of his son I have heard nothing. But inquire of Diochares, Caesar's freedman, whom I have not seen and who brought those dispatches you mentioned from Alexandria. He is said to have seen Quintus on his way to, or possibly already in, Asia.

I await a letter from you as the occasion demands. Please see that it is delivered to me as quickly as possible. November 27th.

22.

MARCUS CICERO SENDS GREETINGS TO SERVIUS SULPICIUS.

The purpose which, you write, you followed in not refusing this appointment in Achaia, not only would I have approved of under any circumstances, but I approved it the more when I read your recent letter. For all the reasons which you give are very proper and worthy of your position and your wisdom.

As to the fact that you think that your situation has fallen out differently from the way you thought it would, I don't agree with you there at all; but because there is such great disorder and confusion in matters generally and such an overthrow and ruin of all things because of this

125

most abominable war that whatever situation each one finds himself in seems the most wretched, and each one seems the most wretched individual to himself, for this reason you repent your decision and we, who remained at home, seem happy to you; but on the other hand to us, while you do not appear completely free of troubles, yet in contrast to ourselves you give the appearance of happiness.

And in this one regard your situation is better than ours, in that you dare to write of your grievances. We can't even do that safely, and that is no fault of the victor, than whom no one could be more restrained, but of the victory itself, which in civil wars is always immoderate.

I have the advantage of you in one matter, that is that I learned about your colleague Marcellus's pardon a little before you did, and even more, I swear it, that I saw the way in which that matter was handled. For just think after all these sufferings of ours, that is after questions of constitutional rights began to be put to the arbitration of arms, no other act has been performed with our old self-respect. For Caesar himself, although he found fault with Marcellus's "bitterness" (for thus he called it) and praised to the skies your fair-mindedness and wisdom, suddenly — contrary to expectation — said that he would not refuse the senate's request in regard to Marcellus, not even in spite of its being a bad omen (for himself).

Moreover the senate acted in this way, that when Lucius Piso had brought up the question of Marcellus and Gaius Marcellus had thrown himself at Caesar's feet, the whole body rose and approached Caesar in supplication. Don't ask to hear more; so fair did that day seem to me that I thought I saw another spectacle, that of the republic being restored to life as it were.

Thus, when all before me had been asked to state their vote and had expressed their thanks to Caesar, all, that is, except Volcacius (he said if he'd been in Caesar's position, that he would not act so), I, when asked, changed my mind; for I had determined, not, I beg you to believe, out of sloth, but feeling the lack of our former self-respect, to remain silent forever.

This resolution of mine broke down before Caesar's magnanimity and the loyalty of the senate. Therefore, in a few words I gave my thanks to Caesar, and now I fear that I have deprived myself in all other affairs of that honorable leisure which was the one solace of my misfortunes.

Yet however, since I have escaped giving offense to him, who might have thought that I did not regard this as a constitutional government, if I never spoke, I shall do this in moderation — or even less than that — to serve his wishes and my own pursuits as well. For although from my

126

childhood every skill and liberal study and especially philosophy charmed me, yet this last study becomes a more serious pursuit with me every day, partly, I believe, because of the inclination of my time of life to wisdom and partly because of the faults of the age in which we live, so that there is nothing else that can so free the mind of its troubles. From this pursuit I know from your letters that you are drawn away by the duties of your office, but nevertheless the nights will be of some assistance to you now.

Sallust's "Catiline's War"

5. Lucius Catiline, born of a noble family, was endowed with great vigor of mind and body, but by nature he was evil and depraved. From his youth civil war, murder, pillage, and political discord were dear to his heart, and in them he trained his youth.

His frame was able to endure hunger, cold, and sleeplessness beyond belief. His spirit was bold, crafty, and treacherous; he was the pretender and concealer of anything at all; he was covetous of the possessions of others, and lavish of his own, violent in his passions, and possessed of some eloquence and very little common sense. His insatiable spirit ever sought the extravagant, the incredible, and the gigantic.

After the tyranny (*dictatorship*) of Lucius Sulla, this man had been possessed with the greatest desire of getting control of the government, with little regard for the manner by which he could achieve it, so long as he made himself the supreme authority. Every day his fierce spirit was more and more goaded on by his poverty and his consciousness of his guilt, both of which he had increased by those qualities which I mentioned above. Besides, he was spurred on by the corrupt morals of the state, (a condition) which two evils, both of the worst sort and mutually exclusive, namely extravagance and avarice, were aggravating.

23. Now in the conspiracy was one Quintus Curius, born of an illustrious family, but involved in every dishonor and crime, whom the censors had removed from the senate because of his immorality. This man was as empty-headed as he was reckless; he did not keep secret

127

what he had heard, nor did he hide his own crimes; in short, neither in speaking nor in doing did he exhibit any concern.

He had an affair of long standing with Fulvia, a woman of good family. When he became less acceptable to her because in his poverty he was not able to give her such lavish gifts, suddenly he began with the greatest boastfulness to promise her oceans (of money) and mountains (of gold) and sometimes to threaten her with the sword if she were not subservient to him and finally behaved more wildly than he had been accustomed. But Fulvia, when she learned the reason for Curius's unwonted behavior, thought that so grave a danger to the republic ought not to be concealed but, without mentioning her authority, told a number of people what she had heard from various sources.

It was this rumor especially which aroused the enthusiasm of the citizens to entrust the consulship to Marcus Tullius Cicero. For before this time many of the nobility burned with ill will and felt that the consulship was, as it were, defiled if some "new man," however distinguished, should get possession of it. But when danger approached, ill will and haughtiness were secondary considerations.

24. Therefore, when the elections were held, Marcus Tullius and Gaius Antonius were announced as consuls. This outcome at first had thrown consternation into his (*Catiline's*) associates in the conspiracy. However, his (*Catiline's*) frenzy did not abate, but from day to day he devised more schemes; he assembled arms in suitable places throughout Italy, and money which he had borrowed on his own security or that of his friends he sent to Faesulae to a certain Manlius, who afterwards was a leader in carrying on the war.

26. Although he had made these preparations, Catiline nevertheless sought the consulship for the following year, hoping if he were consul-elect to do easily what he wished (along) with Antonius. But he was not idle in the meantime and in every way devised plots against Cicero. Nor was the latter, however, lacking in guile or shrewdness for taking care (for his safety). For in the beginning of his consulship by lavish promises made through Fulvia he had brought it about that Quintus Curius, whom I mentioned a little before, betrayed Catiline's plans to him. Furthermore he had prevailed upon his colleague Antonius, by agreeing to resign his province (Macedonia), not to harbor designs against the state; and he had surrounded himself secretly with a guard of friends and clients.

29. When these matters were announced to Cicero he, influenced by the twofold danger since he could no longer defend the city from these plots by personal precautions nor had found out with sufficient accuracy how great an army Manlius had and what were its intentions, referred the matter to the senate, already greatly disquieted by popular rumor. Therefore, as is the usual custom in a dangerous emergency, the senate decreed that the consuls "see to it that the republic take no harm."

In accordance with Roman custom, that power is the greatest which is entrusted to a Roman magistrate, allowing him to raise an army, to wage war, to control by every means allies and citizens alike, and to exercise the highest military and judicial authority at home and in the field; otherwise, the consul has none of these powers without the express command of the people.

30. After a few days Lucius Saenius, a senator, read aloud in the senate a letter which he said had been brought to him from Faesulae stating that Gaius Manlius had taken up arms with a large force on October 27th. At the same time, as is customary in such matters, some reported the appearance of signs and wonders, others told of meetings being held and arms carried and of slave uprisings at Capua and in Apulia.

Therefore by a decree of the senate, Quintus Marcius Rex was sent to Faesulae and Quintus Metellus Creticus into Apulia and the district around it — both men were generals in command of troops at the gates of the city and were being prevented from celebrating triumphs by the intrigues of a few men who made a business of selling whatever was honorable or dishonorable — but the praetors Quintus Pompeius Rufus and Quintus Metellus Celer were sent, the one to Capua and the other to Picenum, and were allowed in view of the emergency and the danger to raise an army.

In addition, if any one gave information about this conspiracy which had been formed against the state, they decreed for a slave's reward, his freedom and a hundred thousand sesterces, and for a free man's, immunity from complicity in this matter and two hundred thousand sesterces; likewise, decrees were passed that the troops of gladiators should be distributed about in Capua and the other municipal towns in proportion to the resources of each, and that throughout the entire city of Rome night watches should be maintained, which the minor magistrates were in charge of.

31. The citizen body was deeply moved by these measures, and the aspect of the city was revolutionized. Instead of the great gaiety and frivolity which lasting peace had begotten, suddenly melancholy seized upon all: people began to rush about, to show alarm, and to put little faith in any place of refuge or any human being; they were neither at peace nor at war, and each judged the common danger in accordance with his own fear.

Also the women, who were not accustomed to fear war because of the

129

greatness of their country, would beat their breasts and stretch their suppliant hands to heaven and lament the condition of their little ones and would persistently ask what was going on and be fearful of everything. And laying aside all pride and frivolity, they despaired for themselves and their country.

But Catiline's pitiless spirit continued to promote the same attempts, although defenses were being prepared and he himself had been accused under the Lex Plautia by Lucius Paulus. At last, in order to mislead or to clear himself, as if he had been irritated by a quarrel, he came into the senate.

Then Marcus Tullius, the consul, either fearing his presence or in rage, delivered a brilliant speech and one serviceable to the state, which afterwards he wrote out and published. But when he sat down, Catiline, being ready to conceal everything, with downcast eyes and the voice of supplication, began to beg the seantors not to believe thoughtlessly all they heard about him. He said that such was his birth and such the conduct of his life that he had the best of prospects; and he besought them not to think that he, a patrician, whose personal benefits as well as those of his ancestors to the common people of Rome were very many, needed the ruin of the state, while Marcus Tullius, a resident alien at Rome, was attempting to save it.

When he was about to add further insults, all howled him down and cried out "enemy" and "parricide." Then Catiline in fury cried, "Seeing plainly that I have been entrapped and am being driven headlong by my enemies, I shall put out my own fire by general destruction."

32. Then he flung himself out of the senate house (and went) home. There, going over in his mind the many aspects of the situation, because his plots against the consul were not making headway and because he knew the city was protected from arson by the night watch, he believed that the best thing to do was to increase his army and before legions might be enrolled to seize many places in advance which might be of use in the war. And so he set out in the dead of night with a few followers for the camp of Manlius.

But he commanded Cethegus, Lentulus, and the others, whose boldness he knew was ready, by any means possible, to strengthen the resources of their party, to nurture their plot against the consul, and to prepare slaughter, fire, and all other deeds of war, saying that he would shortly come to the city with a great army.

51. "Fathers of the senate, all men who take counsel about critical questions ought to be free of hatred, affection, anger, and mercy. The mind cannot easily discern the truth when those passions obstruct the view, nor has anyone ever obeyed at the same time both his passions and his best interests. When you exert your intelligence, it prevails; if passion possesses us, it becomes our master, and the mind has no force. I might mention many occasions, senators, when kings and peoples, impelled by anger or pity, have made errors of judgment.

"But I prefer to mention those acts of our ancestors performed duly and in order, in opposition to their impulses.

"As for Decimus Silanus, a brave and gallant man, I am sure that what he has said he said out of patriotism and that he has not shown either favor or enmity in so serious a crisis; (so well do) I know this gentleman's character and self-restraint. Indeed his motion does not seem cruel to me — for what could be cruel enough for such men? — but inconsistent with our national policy. For surely either fear or a sense of the great wrong done drove you, a consul-elect, to propose a new kind of punishment.

"It is needless to talk of fear when, thanks to the particular diligence of that most distinguished man, the consul, there is so great protection from our forces under arms. I, for my part, as far as the punishment is concerned, can say that (which is the fact) death is a cessation of woe, not a punishment; it dissolves all mortal ills; it leaves no room for sorrow or joy.

"But, in the name of the immortal gods, why did you not add to your motion that first they be punished with the lash? Was it because the Lex Porcia forbids it? But there are other laws too which provide that citizens even though condemned should not lose their lives and should be permitted to go into exile.

"Or was it because it is more severe to be scourged than to be killed? But what is too cruel or too severe for men convicted of such a heinous crime? But if it is because scourging is too light a punishment, how is it consistent to obey the exact letter of the law in a minor degree when you have neglected it in a major?

"But, some one will urge, who will complain of a decree directed against murderers of their country? Time, I answer, the passing of the days, fortune, whose caprice governs peoples. Whatever happens will justly befall those men; but do you, senators, consider what effect your decision will have on others. All bad precedents have arisen from good causes. But when the government has fallen into the hands of men inexperienced in it or less honorable, that new precedent is transferred from those that are worthy and suitable to those that are unworthy and unsuitable.

"Now, while I do not fear such actions in the case of Marcus Tullius nor in the present situation, yet in a large state there are many diverse individualities. It is possible at another time and with another consul, who likewise has an army at his disposal, that something false may be believed as true. When, following this precedent, by decree of the senate the consul has drawn the sword, who will set him a limit or restrain him?

"Is it my opinion then that they should be discharged and Catiline's army increased? By no means! But I make this motion that their property be confiscated, and that they themselves be kept in chains in the municipal towns which are strongest in resources; nor that any one of them afterwards (ever be able to) refer his case to the senate or bring it before the people. Who does other, let the senate judge that he is about to act contrary to the state and the welfare of all."

52. After Caesar finished speaking, the rest by a single word signified their assent to one or another of the different motions. But Marcus Porcius Cato, having been asked his opinion, made a speech somewhat of this sort.

"Far different is my feeling, fathers of the senate, when I reflect upon our dangerous situation and when I consider the proposals of some. They seem to me to have concentrated their discussion on the punishment of those who prepared war against their country, their parents, their hearths and altars; on the contrary, the situation suggests that we be on our guard against them rather than to take counsel as to what decision we should make in the case of the conspirators.

"For all other wrongdoing you may prosecute after it has been done; in this case, unless you take precautions that it not happen, when it has taken place, then in vain you would appeal to law. For when the city has been taken, there is nothing left for the vanquished. But, in the name of the immortal gods, I appeal to you who have always held your houses, villas, statues, and pictures dearer than the republic; if you wish to keep those possessions of yours, of whatever sort they are, to which your heart clings, and if you wish to have peace for the enjoyment of your pleasures, bestir yourselves at last and apply yourselves to the problems of your government. It is not a question of revenues nor of the wrongs of our allies; our liberty and the very breath of life is at stake.

"In a well-ordered speech Gaius Caesar a moment before in this very house spoke on life and death, presumably believing false those things which are told about the lower regions, that the wicked, traveling by a different road from the good, inhabit foul, savage, drear, and frightening places. And so he has proposed that their property be confiscated, and they themselves be kept in custody in the municipal towns, evidently fearing that, if they are kept in Rome, they will be rescued by force either by their fellow conspirators or by a hired mob; as if indeed there were evil and wicked men only in this city and not throughout the whole of Italy, or boldness were not more powerful there where the power to repel it is less.

"Therefore, surely this advice is to no purpose, if he fears danger from those men; but if amid the universal alarm he alone is not afraid, it is the more important for me to be fearful on your behalf and mine. For that reason, when you make your decision concerning Publius Lentulus and the others, be assured that you are passing judgment on Catiline's army and all the conspirators. The more energetically you carry out these matters, the weaker their resolution will be; if they see you hesitate but for a moment, presently all will be upon you with untamed fury.

"And so I make this motion, inasmuch as the state has fallen into the gravest peril through the dastardly plotting of infamous citizens, and inasmuch as they have been convicted by the evidence of Titus Volturcius and the envoys of the Allobroges and have confessed that they have prepared murder, arson, and other foul and merciless acts of violence against their fellow citizens and their country, (I make this motion, I say) that punishment be inflicted upon those who have confessed just as upon persons caught in the act of committing capital crimes, in the manner of our ancestors."

53. After Cato sat down, all the ex-consuls and also most of the senate praised his sentiments and moral courage to the skies. And in upbraiding terms they called one another cowards. Cato was considered great and noble; and the decree of the senate was passed just as he had proposed.

54. Indeed, in family, age, and eloquence they were almost equal; they possessed equal greatness of spirit and fame, but this latter quality was of a differing kind in each. Caesar was considered great because of the benefits he conferred and his generosity, Cato because of the uprightness of his life. Caesar achieved fame through his clemency and mercy; austerity lent dignity to Cato. Caesar by giving, assisting, and pardoning, Cato by never giving a bribe, achieved fame. In the one was a refuge for the miserable, in the other a source of ruin for the wicked. The affability of Caesar and the firmness of Cato were praised.

Finally, Caesar had made up his mind to work and be vigilant and, occupied with the affairs of his friends, to neglect his own; to refuse nothing which was worth the giving. For himself he eagerly desired great power, an army, and a new war in which his prowess could shine forth. But Cato strove for moderation, propriety, and especially for austerity. He did not vie with the rich for riches, nor in party spirit with party zealots, but (instead) with the energetic, in worth; with those who were discreet, in moderation; and with the blameless, in self-restraint. He preferred to be virtuous rather than to seem so. Thus, the less he sought fame, the more it caught him up.

55. After, as I said, the senate voted for Cato's motion, the consul, thinking it best during the coming night to forestall any (disturbance) that might break out anew during this interval, commanded the triumvirs to prepare those things which the (death) penalty required. He himself, stationing guards about, brought Lentulus to prison; the same was done for the others by the praetors.

There is in the prison, after you climb a little (bit) to the left, a place called the Tullianum, sunk into the ground about twelve feet; it is surrounded on all sides by walls and above there is an arched ceiling formed of stone vaulting. But it is foul with filth, darkness, and stench, and its aspect is dreadful.

After Lentulus was let down into this place, the public executioners to whom the command had been given, strangled him. Thus that patrician from the famous family of the Cornelii, a man who had held the consular power, met an end of life worthy of his character and his deeds. A like punishment was inflicted on Cethegus, Statilius, Gabinius, and Ceparius.

60. When Petreius, after making all preparations, gave the signal with the trumpet, he ordered the cohorts to advance slowly; the enemy's army did the same. After they reached a point where the light-armed infantry could engage in battle, they rushed together in bitter combat with tremendous shouts. They cast aside their javelins and fought with swords. The veterans, mindful of their former courage, pressed on fiercely in hand-to-hand combat; their enemies resisted no less bravely. The conflict raged with the greatest violence.

Meanwhile Catiline, with the light-armed troops, was engaged in the front line, brought aid to the hard pressed, summoned fresh troops to replace the wounded, and oversaw everything. He also fought hard himself, and often dealt the enemy a hard blow. He carried out the duties of both an energetic soldier and a good commander. Petreius when he saw Catiline, contrary to his expectations, exerting himself with great vigor, led the pretorian cohort against the middle of the enemy line, threw them into confusion, and killed some resisting in other places.

Then he attacked the rest from both flanks. Manlius and a man from Faesulae, fighting in the forefront, fell. Catiline, after he saw that his troops were routed and himself left with only a handful, remembering his birth and his former rank, ran into the thickest of the enemy and there still fighting was pierced through and through.

61. But when the battle was done, then indeed you might have seen how much boldness and courage there had been in Catiline's army. For almost every post which a man had occupied in the battle while he lived, that same spot he covered with his body in death.

A few, it is true, whom the pretorian cohort had routed in the center had fallen a little apart from the rest, all nevertheless showing their wounds in front.

But Catiline, far from his army, was found in the midst of enemy bodies, still breathing a little and retaining in his countenance that ferocity which he had in life.

Finally, out of the whole army, neither in battle nor in flight, was any freeborn citizen taken; so unsparing had all been of their own lives and those of the enemy alike. Nor did the army of the Roman people achieve a joyful or bloodless victory; for the bravest soldiers either died in battle or left it gravely wounded. Many also, who had gone out of camp for sight-seeing or plunder, as they turned over the bodies of the enemy, discovered a friend or a guest or a relative. There were also those who recognized their enemies. And so in varying degree the army was affected by joy, grief, mourning, and gladness.

Pliny's Letters

1.

GAIUS PLINY TO HIS (FRIEND) SEPTICIUS. GREETING.

You have often begged me to collect and publish such letters as I had written with somewhat more care. I have made the collection, not keeping the chronological order (I was not, after all, composing a history), but as each letter came into my hands. My care now is that you should not repent of your advice nor I of having followed it. For so I shall be brought to seek out those letters which still lie neglected and not to suppress any which I shall add. Farewell.

135

2.

GAIUS PLINY TO HIS (FRIEND) CORNELIUS TACITUS, GREETING.

You will laugh, and so you may. I, (yes,) that (Pliny) whom you know, have taken three wild boars, and very fine ones at that. *"You?"* you say. Yes, I; yet not in a way that made me abandon altogether my habitual laziness and leisure. I was sitting near the nets; I had at hand not hunting spear or lance, but pencil and notebook: I would give thought to some subject and note it down so that, if I came back empty-handed, my tablets would at any rate be full. There is no reason why you should despise this way of studying. It is amazing how the mind is stimulated by physical movement and exercise. Then also the woods all around and the solitude and that customary silence which one applies to hunting are great spurs to thought. Therefore, when you go hunting, you may, following my example, take along your notebook as well as a bread (*lunch*) basket and wine flask. You will find that Minerva strolls about the mountains no less than Diana. Farewell.

3.

GAIUS PLINY TO HIS (FRIEND) MINICIUS FUNDANUS, GREETING.

It is surprising how for each separate day spent in the city the account either balances or seems to balance, while for several days taken together it fails to do so. For if you should ask someone, "What did you do today?" he would reply that he had taken part in a coming-of-age ceremony, had attended a betrothal or a wedding, that one man had asked him to witness a will, another had asked him for legal support, another for advice. These activities, which are unavoidable at the time you perform them, seem pointless if you should reflect that you have performed them every single day, and seem much more so when you have retired to the country.

For then the thought comes: "How many days I have spent on such trivial matters!" And this happens to me, after I have been either reading or writing anything at my Laurentine estate, or even have been free to attend to the care of my body, since it is the foundation upon which the mind rests. I hear nothing of the sort one would be sorry to have heard, say nothing of the sort one would be sorry to have said; no one at my place attacks anybody with backbiting remarks, I for my part find fault with no one, unless it be with myself for not writing well enough; I am not worried by any hope or fear, not disturbed by any rumors: I converse only with myself and my books. What an upright and straightforward life! How sweet this leisure, and honorable, and more noble than almost any occupation! O sea and shore, you true and private *académie*, how many inspirations, how many ideas you offer! Leave, then, you also, all your hustle and bustle, your pointless dashing about, your quite absurd tasks, as soon as the opportunity presents itself, and devote yourself to studies or to leisure. For, as our friend Atilius has said with as much wisdom as wit, it is better to be at leisure than to do nothing. Farewell.

4.

GAIUS PLINY TO HIS (FRIEND) MAURICUS, GREETING.

What more pleasant charge could you have entrusted to me than to seek out a teacher for your brother's children? For thanks to you I am going back to school and almost reliving that most delightful time of life: I sit among the boys, just as I used to, and yet I also feel how much authority I have in their eyes as a result of my studies. For quite recently in a crowded hall they were loudly jesting with one another in the presence of many men of our rank: I came in and they fell silent; I would not mention the matter if it were not more to their credit than to mine, and if I did not wish you to have just hope of your nephews' being able to obtain a truly moral education. What remains (for me to do) is, when I have heard all the teachers (*who are lecturing*), to write what I think of each one and, so far, moreover, as I shall be able to accomplish it by letter, make you feel as if you had heard them personally.

For I owe you this promise (and) this interest, and I owe them also to your brother's memory, especially in such an important matter. For what is more important to you than that these children — I would call them your children, but that you love them more (as it is than if they were your own) — should prove to be worthy of him and of you, their father and their uncle? — and I would have claimed this task for myself even if you had not entrusted it to me. I am not unaware of the fact that in choosing out one teacher I must give offense, but it is right that I should bear not only their displeasure but even their enmity for the sake of your brother's sons as willingly as parents would for their own sons. Farewell.

5.

GAIUS PLINY TO HIS (FRIEND) ANNIUS SEVERUS, GREETING.

Out of a bequest which came my way I have recently bought a statue of Corinthian bronze, smallish indeed but pleasing and finely executed, so far as my taste goes, which perhaps is very poor in every (artistic) matter, and certainly is in this: but this statue, at any rate, even I appreciate.

For it is a nude, and so neither conceals any faults it may have nor fails to show its fine points: it depicts an old man, standing; bones, muscles, sinews, veins, even wrinkles look just like those of a living man, the hair is thin and receding, the forehead broad, the face shriveled, the neck lean, the arm muscles are flabby, the chest is flat, the stomach is sunken. From behind also it shows the same signs of old age, so far as one can judge from behind. The bronze itself, so far as its true color would indicate, is genuinely antique. In short, all its characteristics are such as to catch the attention of artists and delight the eye of the dilettante.

And this fact encouraged me, although a mere novice, to buy it. But I bought it, not to keep at home — for I don't yet have any Corinthian bronze at home — but to set up in my native town in some much frequented spot, preferably in the temple of Jupiter: for it seems a gift worthy of a temple, even of a god. Will you then undertake, as you always do every request I put upon you, this task and order that a base be made of whatever marble you wish, one that will leave room for my name, and my offices if you think these, too, should be put on. The statue itself I shall send to you as soon as I find someone whom it would not inconvenience, or else I shall bring it myself when I come, as you would prefer.

For I intend to run out to your place if the duties of my office ever allow. You will be glad that I promise to come, but you will frown when I add that it will be only for a few days: for these same duties which prevent me from leaving now will not allow me to be away any longer. Farewell.

6.

GAIUS PLINY TO HIS (FRIEND) CATILIUS SEVERUS, GREETING.

I shall come to dinner, but right now I make the stipulation that it be informal, that it be frugal, that it be rich only in Socratic conversations, and observe some moderation even in these. There will be those early morning calls upon which not even Cato could safely stumble, although Gaius Caesar reproaches him in such a way as to praise him. For he writes that when those whom he met discovered the identity of the drunken man they blushed, and then adds: "You would have thought, not that Cato had been caught red-handed by them, but rather they by him." Could one attribute more prestige to Cato than that even drunk he was so worthy of respect? However, as for our dinner, let a limit be set to its length as well as to its formality and its cost. For we are not the sort of people whom even enemies cannot attack without at the same time praising. Farewell.

7.

GAIUS PLINY TO HIS (FRIEND) TACITUS, GREETING.

I am glad you have arrived in the city safe and sound; and however welcome your arrival at any other time, it is especially so to me just now. I myself shall remain a few days longer at my Tusculan estate to finish up a little work I have on hand. For I fear that if I put a stop to this design when the end is already in view I shall find it hard to take it up again. In the meantime, so that my impatience may suffer no loss I shall make in this letter — my advance guard, as it were — the request which I intend to present in person.

But first let me give you the reasons for it. Quite recently, when I was in my home town, the young son of a fellow townsman of mine came to pay a call on me. I said to him, "Do you go to school?"

He replied, "Yes."

"Where?"

"At Milan."

"Why not here?" And his father — for he was present, and as a matter of fact was the one who had brought the boy — said, "Because we have no teachers here."

"Why not? — for it would be greatly to your advantage as fathers" (a number of fathers happened to be listening) "for your sons to study here rather than anywhere else. For as for their happiness, where could they better stay than in their own town; considering their morals, where could they better be kept in hand than under their parents' eyes; and with regard to thrift, where better than at home? What a small thing it would be to contribute money and hire teachers and to apply to their salaries what now you spend on lodging, travel, and what is bought away from home!

"And besides, I, though I have no children as yet, am ready for the sake of our town, as I would be for a daughter or a mother, to contribute one-third of what you decide to collect. I would even subscribe the whole amount, if I didn't fear that this gift of mine might sometime be misused for private ends, as I see happen in many places where teachers are hired at public expense. This evil can be cured by one

139

remedy alone, that the right of hiring be left solely to the parents and that on them should fall, through the requirement that they contribute money, the sacred obligation of deciding aright. For those who may be careless about other people's money will surely be careful about their own and will make it their business to see that only a worthy person gets money from me, if he is also going to get it from them.

"Therefore get together (and) come to an agreement, and pluck up greater courage from my example, for I want what I must contribute to be as much as possible. You can make no more honorable gift to your children, no more welcome one to your town. Let those who are born here be brought up here, and right from infancy let them learn to love and to keep to their native soil. And I hope that you will bring in such famous teachers that nearby towns will look here for a course of study and that other people's children will soon flock to this place just as yours now do to others!"

I thought it proper to recount this affair to you in more detail and from the very source, as it were, the better that you might know how pleased I should be if you would undertake the task I am enjoining on you. For I do enjoin and beg, in view of the importance of the matter, that from the crowd of scholars who flock to you out of admiration for your genius, you look out some teachers for us to apply to, but on condition that I do not make a binding agreement with anyone. For I am keeping the whole matter open for the parents. They are the ones who are to judge and make their choice: I claim for myself only the worry and expense.

Therefore, if anyone should turn up who has confidence in his own intellect, let him go to them, but on this condition, that he take nothing for granted but his own faith in himself. Farewell.

8.

GAIUS PLINY TO HIS (FRIEND) CALPURNIA HISPULLA, GREETING.

Since you are a model of family feeling, and since you felt for that best of men, your brother, a fondness equal to his great feeling for you, and since you love his daughter as your own and show her not only the affection of an aunt but even that which she would have had from her father, I am sure it will be a pleasure to you to know that she has turned out to be a credit to her father, to you, and to her grandfather. Both her intelligence and her housekeeping ability are of the highest: that she loves me may stand as evidence of her purity of mind. In addition to these qualities she shows an interest in literature, prompted by her affection for me. She collects my books, she reads them over and over, she even memorizes them.

How she worries when I am entering on a case, how glad she is when I have finished it! She assigns messengers to let her know what approval or applause I have aroused, and what verdict I have gained. She also sits close at hand, hidden by a curtain, whenever I give a public recital, and listens most eagerly to the applause. As a matter of fact, she also sings my poems and sets them to the cithara; and her teacher in this is not some musician, but love, who is the best schoolmaster.

For these reasons I am led to feel quite sure (*to a very certain expectation*) that our conjugal happiness (*accord*) will be a lasting one and will grow from day to day.

For she loves not my youth, which is gradually leaving me, nor my body, which is growing old, but my reputation. And nothing else could be expected of one brought up and educated by you, in that she learned from your companionship only what is holy and honorable, and even began to love me from your account of my character. For while you honored my mother as if she were your own, right from boyhood you took a hand in my training, were always praising me, and used to predict that I should become just the sort of person I now am in my wife's eyes. And so we vie with each other in thanking you, I that you gave her to me, she that you gave me to her, as if you had chosen us for each other. Farewell.

9.

GAIUS PLINY TO HIS (FRIEND) MARCELLINUS, GREETING.

It is with great sadness that I write this to you, for the younger daughter of our friend Fundanus has died, the most vivacious, amiable creature I have ever seen, and also the most worthy, not just of a longer life, but almost of immortality. She had not yet completed her fourteenth year, and already had the wisdom of age, the dignity of middle age, and yet the sweetness of girlhood, as well as maidenly modesty.

How she used to cling to her father's embrace! how lovingly, yet modestly, she used to embrace us, her father's friends! how she used to love her nurses, her tutors, her teachers, each according to his position! how diligently, how intelligently she used to do her lessons, how sparingly and discreetly she played! How mildly, patiently, and bravely she bore her last illness! She always followed the directions of her doctors, used to encourage her father and sister, and though she had lost her bodily powers she kept herself going by the strength of her spirit. This (strength) remained with her right up to the end, and was never broken by the length of her illness nor any fear of death, and consequently has left to us even more and stronger reasons to miss her and mourn her.

How very sad and bitter this death! yet crueler than the death itself was the time of it! — she had already been betrothed to an outstanding young man, the wedding day had already been set, we had already been invited. What a joy, (which) has been changed into such sorrow! I cannot find words to tell you how grievously it touched my heart when I heard that Fundanus (as grief is ever fertile in painful inventions) was giving instructions that the sum which he had meant to lay out for a trousseau, pearls, and jewels be spent on incense, ointment, and perfumes.

He, of course, is an educated man and a philosopher, as one would be who had devoted himself from his earliest years to the higher arts and studies, but now he rejects all the precepts he so often listened to and repeated, and, every other virtue repudiated, he is wholly given over to parental devotion. But you will pardon, even commend him, if you but think what he has lost. He has lost a daughter who reflected his character as well as his appearance and expressions and was an amazingly true reproduction of her father in every way.

And so, if you sent him any letters about his quite understandable grief, remember to administer your consolation not as a strong medicine, as it were reproving, but as a mild one, kindly. A long interval of time will make him admit much more readily this consolation. For just as one recently wounded first shrinks from the doctors' touch, later bears it, and eventually desires it, so one recently bereaved at first rejects and avoids consolation, but later longs for, and willingly acquiesces in, consolation tenderly given. Farewell.

10.

GAUIS PLINY TO HIS (FRIEND) VERUS, GREETING.

Thank you for undertaking the farming of the little place I gave my nurse. When I gave it to her it was worth 100,000 sesterces; then when its production went down so did its value; but now under your management it will go up again. Just keep in mind that it is not just land and trees that I entrust to your care (though these too are important), but my little gift; that this should be as productive as possible is as much to the interest of me, the donor, as of the recipient. Farewell.

11.

Never have I had more cause to complain of my business obligations, in that they did not allow me to accompany you when you set out for Campania for your health, nor, when you had left, to follow immediately in your tracks. For now, especially, I want to be with you, that I may see with my own eyes what improvement you are making in your strength and in your dear little person and whether in short you are bearing without harm the pleasures of that retreat and the plenty of that district.

Indeed, even if you were well, I should not be without anxiety in your absence; for it causes suspense and anxiety to have temporarily no knowledge of the one you cherish so ardently: really for me now the thought that you are away, alternating with the thought that you are not well, with the constant interplay of vague fears, is most frightening. For I have all sorts of fears and all sorts of fancies, and, as is natural with people who are frightened, the things I mostly picture are the things I most dread. So much the more earnestly do I beg you to humor my fear by writing to me once and even twice a day. For while I am reading your letter I shall be somewhat calmed, and I shall begin to be afraid again, directly I have finished. Farewell.

12.

You ask that I write you about my uncle's death, to enable you to hand (it) on to posterity the more accurately. Thank you; for I perceive that for his death, if it be proclaimed by you, undying fame has been set out. For, although he died in the ruin of the fairest lands, (and) as nations (and) as cities (do), he is going to live as it were forever on account of an unforgettable disaster; (and) although he himself composed (very) many (and) lasting works, nevertheless the enduring nature of your writings will add much to his continuing existence. Indeed fortunate do I think those to whom by the gift of the gods it is given either to perform things worthy of writing or to write things worthy of reading; truly, supremely fortunate those to whom both (gifts are given). In the number of these will be my uncle, on account of his own books and also (on account of) yours. Therefore the more gladly do I undertake, I even demand, (to do) what you enjoin.

He was at Misenum and personally commanded the fleet, with full authority. On the 24th of August, at about the seventh hour (*between 12 and 1 o'clock*), my mother pointed out to him that a cloud was visible, unusual both in size and in appearance. He had had a sun bath followed by a cold plunge, had eaten, and — lying on his couch — was at his books: he called for sandals (and) climbed to a place from which he could view that wonder to the best advantage.

A cloud — to those watching at a distance (it was) uncertain from which mountain (afterwards it was learned that it was Vesuvius) — was arising, the shape of which no other tree would portray (any) better than a pine. For it raised itself on high, so to speak, with a very tall trunk, and was spreading itself out with a branch-like effect, I suppose because it was carried upwards by a fresh gust of air; then, as its energy spent itself, the cloud, being without support or overcome even by its own weight, dissipated itself laterally; sometimes it was bright, sometimes it was dingy and spotted, according as it had taken up earth or cinders. This phenomenon seemed to so scholarly a man as my uncle unusual and worthy of closer acquaintance.

He ordered a Liburnican vessel (*swift yacht*) to be made ready; he offered me the opportunity (to come), if I wished to come along: I answered that I preferred to study, and as it happened he himself had given me something to write. He set out from the house: he received a note (just then) of (*from*) Tascus's (wife) Rectina (who was) terrified by the threatening danger — for his (Tascus's) villa lay right under (Vesuvius) (and) there was no other avenue of escape except by ship; she begged him (in the note) to rescue her from such a critical danger.

He changed his plan; and what he had begun to undertake with a philosophical turn of mind, he met with a hero's resolution. He launched vessels with four banks of oars (and) himself embarked, to bring assistance not only to Rectina but to many people, for that charming coast was thickly populated. He made haste to the place from which others were fleeing, and holding his course, steered straight into the danger, so free from fear that everything of that disaster, all of its phases, as he perceived them, he dictated and noted down.

Already ash was falling on the boats (and) the nearer they went, the hotter and thicker (the ash); then pumice stones and rocks blackened and scorched and cracked by fire; then (there was) a sudden ebbing (of the sea) and the shore was blocked by debris from the mountain. After hesitating a little about whether to turn back, soon to the helmsman (who was) advising that it be done (i.e., turn back), he said, "Fortune aids the brave; make for Pomponianus('s place)." He was at Stabiae, cut off by the width of the bay; for the sea floods a shore (there that is) gradually rounded and curving.

144

There, although the peril was not yet at hand, yet (was) in view, and when it spread, very close indeed, he (Pomponianus) had collected baggage on boats, (to make) sure of escape, if the contrary (*onshore*) wind fell; borne by a favorable wind, my uncle (arrived and) embraced the trembling man, comforted him, encouraged him, and in order to allay his fear by his own sense of safety, ordered that he be brought down to the bath; having bathed he lay down, (and) dined either with cheer or — what is equally magnificent — with the appearance of cheer.

Meanwhile, from Mount Vesuvius in many places very broad sheets of flame and high fires were glowing, the light and brightness of which was intensified by the night's darkness. He (my uncle) maintained, to lighten fear, that fires had been left burning by the alarm (and flight) of farmers and the deserted houses were burning in their abandonment. Then he retired and indeed rested in quite genuine slumber. For his snoring, which on account of his bodily weight was heavier and noisier (than usual), was heard by those who kept watch on the threshold.

But the court from which the apartment was entered was now so filled up and its level so raised by cinders mixed with pumice that if he had delayed longer in his bedroom, escape would have been denied (to him). Wakened, he came out, and rejoined Pomponianus and the others who had stayed awake (all night). They consulted together, whether they should stay indoors or wander in the open. For buildings swayed with frequent (and) violent shocks and, as if moved from their foundations, seemed to move to and fro, now this way, now that.

In the open air, on the other hand, they feared the fall of the pumice stones, although they were light and porous; however, the comparison of the two dangers led them to choose the latter (course). And indeed in the case of him (my uncle) reason overcame reason, but in the case of the others, fear overcame fear. They tied pillows, placed on their heads, with napkins; this was a protection against falling objects.

By now it was day elsewhere; there, night blacker and thicker than any nights (ever were); however, many torches and various kinds of light relieved (the darkness). It suited them to go out onto the shore and from near at hand to see whether the sea now permitted (escape); for thus far it continued desolate and forbidding. There, lying down on an unused sail, once and again (my uncle) asked for and drank some cold water. Then flames and the forerunner of flames, the odor of sulphur, sent the others into flight (and) aroused him.

Leaning on two servant boys he stood up, and immediately collapsed, as I myself infer, (when) some unusually gross vapor obstructed his breathing and blocked his windpipe, which was not only naturally weak and constricted, but chronically inflamed. When daylight re-

145

turned — this is the third from that on which he had last been seen (i.e., *two days later*) — his body was found unharmed, not injured, and dressed just as he had been clothed; the attitude of body was more like that of someone sleeping than someone dead.

Meanwhile, my mother and I were at Misenum. But (that has) nothing to do with history, and you did not wish to hear anything other than his (my uncle's) end. Therefore I shall put a stop (to this). Only, I shall add that I have described everything in which I had a part and heard at the time, when things are especially remembered truly. Lift out the most important things; for indeed it is one thing to write a letter, another a history; one thing to write to a friend, another to all (the public). Farewell.

13.

GAIUS PLINY TO HIS (FRIEND) SURA, GREETING.

There was at Athens a house which was large and roomy, but unhealthful and of a bad reputation. In the silence of the night a metallic sound used to be heard and, to a more attentive listener, the clanking of chains, coming at first from some distance and then near at hand: presently there would appear a ghost, an old man, utterly filthy and emaciated, with beard hanging down and bristling hair; he wore fetters on his ankles and hands, and would keep shaking them. Therefore in the fearful gloomy night the inhabitants used to lie awake through fear; sickness would follow in the train of this sleeplessness, and, as the dread grew greater, death. For even between times, though the figure had departed, the recollection of it would go on floating before the eyes, and the fear lasted longer than its cause.

And so the house was deserted and condemned to solitude and left entirely to that apparition; nevertheless, advertisements were put up, in the hope that someone who had not heard of its great drawback might wish to buy or rent it. There came to Athens the philosopher Athenodorus; he read the advertisement, and when he had heard the price, suspecting its cheapness he inquired further, and was told all; but in spite of, or rather because of, this he rented it.

When it began to grow dark, he ordered that a bed be made up for him in the front part of the house and asked for a notebook, a pencil, and a lamp; he sent all his household to the inner part of the house, while he devoted his whole attention to writing, so that his mind would not be free to imagine the appearances which he had heard of, and to frighten itself with baseless fears. At first the night was as silent as anywhere else, then the clanking of iron and the rattling of chains; he did not raise his eyes nor lay down his pencil, but concentrated his attention and closed his mind to the noises. Then the din kept increasing, kept drawing nearer, and now it sounded as if at the door, and now as if inside.

He looked up and saw a figure and recognized it as the one he had been told about. It was standing and making signs, as if beckoning, with its finger. In reply he indicated by a gesture that it should wait a moment, and turned back to his notebook and pencil.

It kept clanking its chains over his head as he wrote. He looked up and saw it making the same sign as before, and waiting no longer he took up his lamp and followed it. It went along with a laboring step, as though weighed down by its chains. When it had turned into the yard of the house, he following, it suddenly faded away and left him alone; and, finding himself alone, he plucked some grass and leaves and marked the spot. Next day he went to the magistrates and advised them to give orders for that spot to be dug up. They found a skeleton bound and wound about with chains; the body, decayed by its long stay in the earth, had left only the bare bones, corroded by the chains; they were taken up and buried at public expense. Thus was the ghost duly laid, and the house haunted no more.

14.

GAIUS PLINY TO HIS (FRIEND) CALVISIUS, GREETING.

I have spent this whole time in the most pleasant leisure, amongst my books and notebooks. "How could you," you will say, "in the city?"

The races were on, a kind of entertainment which does not attract me even slightly. They offer nothing new, nothing different, nothing which one wants to see more than once; I am so much the more amazed that so many thousand men would, like little boys, want to see over and over again the horses running and men standing up in chariots. And yet if they were attracted by the speed of the horses or the skill of the drivers, there would be some reason for it: as a matter of fact it is a mere piece of cloth that wins their enthusiasm and their love, and if the colors were exchanged right in the middle of a race, their enthusiastic backing would be transferred, and they would desert their favorite horses and drivers whom they always recognize even at a distance and whose names they keep shouting out.

So much influence, so much importance is there in one cheap tunic, I don't say in the eyes of the vulgar herd, which is cheaper than the

147

tunic itself, but in the eyes of some (people) of importance; and when I observe how insatiably they waste their time on an amusement so foolish, flat, and commonplace, I take some pleasure in taking no pleasure in it. And I am very glad to devote to literature my idleness during the days which others waste on the most idle pursuits. Farewell.

15.

GAIUS PLINY, TO THE EMPEROR TRAJAN.

It is customary for me, Sire, to refer to you all matters about which I am in doubt. For who can better set me right when in doubt or instruct me when in ignorance? I have never taken part in any trials of Christians; consequently I do not know what investigations one makes or how far one pursues them, nor what punishment one exacts or to what degree. I have been no little perplexed as to whether some distinction is to be made according to age or whether there is no difference at all between the very young and those who are more hardy, whether recantation is to be rewarded with pardon or whether anyone who has been a thorough-going Christian should get no advantage from giving it up, whether merely calling oneself a Christian is to be punished, if no crimes are committed, or whether it is the crimes that go with the name that are to receive punishment.

Here is the method I have been following in the meanwhile, in the case of those who were charged before me as being Christians: I asked them personally if they were Christians; if they said they were, I asked them a second and a third time, threatening them with punishment; if they persisted I ordered that they be executed. For I had no doubt that, whatever their confession might mean, their stubbornness and immovable obstinacy surely ought to be punished. Some others, equally mad, I designated to be remanded to Rome because they were Roman citizens.

Soon, from the very act of investigation, the charges increased in number, as is the case usually, and several variations of charge fell to my notice. An anonymous complaint, containing the names of many people, was placed before me. Those who said that they were not and had not been Christians I decided should be released after, at my dictation, they called upon the gods and worshiped a statue of you, which for this purpose I had had brought out with those of the gods, with offerings of incense and wine, and besides this cursed Christ, for it is declared that those who are really Christians cannot be compelled to do any of these things.

Others accused by an informer said they were Christians and then denied it; they had as a matter of fact been Christians, they said, but then had given it up, three years ago in some cases, longer than that in others, in a few cases as long as twenty years ago. All these, too, worshiped both your statue and the gods', and cursed Christ.

But they insisted that the sum total of their guilt and their heresy had been that they used to come together before dawn on an appointed day and sing an antiphonal hymn to Christ as if he were a god, and that they used to bind themselves by an oath, not for any crime, but that they should not commit theft, robbery, or adultery, nor break their word, nor refuse to return on demand anything entrusted to their care; after doing these things it was their custom to adjourn and meet again later to take a meal, but an ordinary and innocent one; and even this, they said, they had stopped doing after my edict in which, following your instructions, I forbade the existence of fraternities (*associations*).

And so I thought it so much the more necessary to try to find out what the truth was from two maidservants (whom they call deaconesses), even using torture. All I discovered was superstition, vile and carried to an absurd length. And so I postponed the trial and came straight to you for advice. For I thought it was worth consulting you about, especially because of the number of defendants. For many, of every age, every rank, even of both sexes, are being summoned to trial and will go on being summoned. And the contagion of this wretched superstition has spread, not only in the cities, but even to the villages and fields; yet I think that it can be arrested and cured. It is certain at any rate that the crowds have begun to return to the temples, when they were already almost deserted, and that attendance has risen at the holy rites, when they had been for some time discontinued, and that fodder for sacrificial victims is finding a sale, though before now scarcely any buyers appeared. From all this one may easily infer that the crowd of men can be reformed, if some opportunity for recantation is offered.

16.

TRAJAN TO PLINY, GREETING.

You have followed the proper procedure, my dear Secundus, in investigating the cases of those who had been denounced to you as Christians. Nor is it possible to set up for general use anything which has as it were a definite pattern. They are not to be sought out; if they are accused and convicted, they must be punished, with this proviso,

149

that anyone who says he is not a Christian and proves it by his actions, that is by worshiping our gods, may be granted pardon by reason of his recantation, however suspect he may have been in the past. But information lodged anonymously must have no place in any accusation. For it is not only the worst sort of precedent, but is also incompatible with the spirit of our time.

Deucalion and Pyrrha

The land of Phocis separates the Boeotian (Aonian) lands from the Oetian, a fertile land while it still was land, but it was at that time a broad expanse of sudden waters, a part of the sea. There high Mt. Parnassus with its two peaks sought the stars, and its peaks were above the clouds. When Deucalion and his wife had come to land here, carried in a small boat, for the sea had covered all else, they worshiped the Corycian nymphs and the gods of the mountains, and fate-revealing Themis, who kept the oracles at that time. There was not any man better than he was, nor any woman more reverent of the gods than she.

When Jupiter saw that the world was now inundated with flowing pools, and that only one man had survived from so many thousands, and that only one woman had survived also, and both were innocent and both were worshipers of the gods, he scattered the clouds and with these blown away by the north wind, he showed the lands once more to the sky, and the upper air to the lands. And the wrath of the sea did not remain; laying aside his three-pronged spear, the ruler of the sea calmed the waves and called Triton, standing above the deep, sea-blue and with his shoulders thickly overgrown with shellfish, and he ordered him to blow on his loud-resounding shell, and with this signal he recalled the seas and rivers. He (Triton) took up his hollow twisted shell, which grows from the smallest point to a broad-swelling whorl, a shell which when it receives Triton's breath in the middle of the sea, fills with its voice the shores which lie beneath both the rising and setting suns. So then, when it had touched the lips of the sea-god, wet with dripping beard, and blown upon had sounded the retreat as ordered, it was heard by all the waters of land and sea, and it held in check whatever waters heard it. The waves subsided, and the hilltops were seen to reappear; and now the sea had a shore and the rivers kept within their channels; the land rose, and the ground increased as the waves decreased; and finally after a long time, the bared tops of trees showed forth, and they still held (*still holding*) the slime left on the leaves (by the flood).

The earth was restored; after Deucalion saw that it was empty, and that deep silence covered the desolate lands, with tears gushing forth, he addressed Pyrrha in this way:

"O sister, O wife, O only surviving woman on earth, you whom a common family and race (they were cousins) and then marriage has joined to me, now these very dangers join us: we two are all the people that are left in all lands from east to west; the sea holds all others. And even this confidence in life which we have is not too sure; the clouds even now frighten my mind.

"What feeling would be yours now, poor woman, if you had been rescued without me? with whom as a comforter would you be grieving? For, believe me, if the sea possessed you, I would follow you and the sea would also possess me.

"Oh, would that by my father's skill I might be able to restore the nations, and pour life into molded earth! But now the race of mortals remains in us two alone — thus it seemed best to the gods — and we remain the only examples of the human race."

He spoke and they wept. They decided to pray to the celestial divinity and ask for help from the sacred oracles. They went side by side to Cephisus' stream, which though not yet clear, still was flowing in the well-known banks. When they had sprinkled some waters from this on their heads and clothing and offered it (*and sipped it*), they turned their steps to the shrine of the holy goddess, the rooftops of which were still discolored with foul moss, and the altars stood without fires.

When they reached the steps of the temple, each one fell prone on the ground, and trembling gave kisses to the cold rock, and they said, "If gods may be appeased by the just prayers, if the anger of the gods can be turned aside in this way, tell us, O Themis, in what way the loss of our race may be restored, and bring help, O most kind goddess, to our afflicted fortunes."

The goddess was moved and gave this oracle: "Leave the temple, and veil your heads and loosen your robes which are bound around you, and throw behind your backs the bones of your great mother." They stood amazed for a long time; then Pyrrha first broke the silence with her voice, and she refused to obey the orders of the goddess, and asked forgiveness for herself with frightened voice and was afraid to insult her mother's shades by the throwing of her bones.

Meanwhile they sought again for hidden meanings in dark prophecies, and they turned over in their minds again the prophectic oracle. Then the son of Prometheus soothed the daughter of Epimetheus with these calming words, "Either my wits fail me," he said, "or oracles are holy and never persuade people to do wrong. The earth is our great parent; I think that the stones in the body of the earth are called bones; we are ordered to throw these behind our backs."

Although Pyrrha was still moved by the interpretation of her husband, her hope was still in doubt; they were both in fact distrustful of the celestial orders. But what will be the harm in trying? They left the temple. They veiled their heads and loosened their robes, and they threw behind them the stones as they were ordered. The stones — who would believe this unless ancient tradition was the witness (for it)? — began to put aside their hardness at once, and slowly grow soft, and when soft they took on new form. Then, when they had grown larger and become milder in their nature, a certain form of human men could be seen, still not clear, but just as statues when they are begun out of marble are not sharply defined, but are very much like rough images. The part of them, moreover, which was moist and damp with the moisture of the earth, was turned into the part of the flesh; what was solid and unable to be bent, was changed into bones; and what was but now veins, remained under the same name; and in a short time, by the will of the gods, the rocks thrown by the hands of the man took on the shape of men, and 'woman' was restored by the stones thrown by the woman. Hence there came the toughness of our race and our endurance of toil, and we give proof of the origin we came from.

The Story of Phaethon

The palace of the Sun was high with lofty columns, bright with shining gold and bronze imitating flames. Shiny ivory covered the gables above, and the folding doors shone with a radiant silver light. The workmanship was even better than the material, for Vulcan had carved there the waters encircling the earth in the middle, and the world and the sky that hangs over the world. The sea holds the dark-blue gods, tuneful Triton, changing Proteus, and Aegaeon, overcoming with his strong arms two huge backs of whales, and Doris and her daughters, part of whom seem to be swimming, part sitting on a reef drying their green hair, and a part riding on a fish; there is not the same appearance for all of them, and yet they are not different, just as it ought to be with sisters. The earth bears men and cities and forests and beasts and rivers and nymphs and other deities of the country. The image of the shining sky was pictured above these things, and six signs of the zodiac on the right doors, and the same number on the left.

As soon as the son of Clymene had come to the steep path which brings you there, and had entered the home of the father (he is) not sure about, he at once turned his steps to the face of his father and stood still at a little distance; for he could not stand the light any nearer. Apollo was sitting on a throne shining with bright emeralds, clad in a purple robe. On his right and left stood Day and Month and Year and Century, and the Hours were spaced at equal distances. The new Spring was standing wreathed with a crown of flowers, and Summer unclad, with a wreathe of ripe grain; and Autumn was standing stained with trodden grapes, and glacial Winter overgrown with white locks.

The Sun himself in the midst of these things, with his eyes with which he sees all, saw his son trembling at the newness of these things and said, "What is the reason for this visit? What do you see in this palace, Phaethon my son, not to be denied by his parent?"

He replied, "O common light of the great world, Father Apollo, if you allow me the use of this name, and Clymene is not concealing her shame under a false image, grant me a pledge, Father, by which all may believe that I am your true son, and take away this doubt from my mind."

He spoke. Then his father put off his rays, shining all around his head, and ordered the boy to come nearer, and having given him an embrace, said, "You are worthy to be called my true son, and Clymene has told you the truth about your origin, and so that you may have less doubt, ask for whatever gift you wish and you may have it with me giving it. And may the Stygian swamp be witness to my promise, sworn to by gods, but unseen by my eyes."

He had scarcely finished when the boy asked for the chariot of his father and the right to drive the winged horses for one day. The father regretted his oath. Shaking his shining head three and four times, he said, "Your words have shown mine to be rash! Would that it might be permitted me not to give what I have promised. I admit this is the only thing I would refuse you, my son. But I am permitted to dissuade you. Your wish is not safe. You are asking for something too great,

153

which does not fit your strength nor your boyish years. Your lot is mortal, and what you ask for is not mortal. You in your ignorance are asking for something which is more than can be granted to the gods themselves. Though each one may do what he wishes, except for me none of them is powerful enough to stand on the fiery axle. Even the ruler of great Olympus, who throws the fierce thunderbolts with his awful right hand, cannot drive this chariot. And who do we have greater than Jove?

"The first part of the road is steep, up which horses when they are fresh in the morning can hardly make their way. It is very high in the middle of the sky, from which I myself often become afraid to look down on the sea and earth, and my heart trembles with frightening fear. The last part is very steep and needs a sure control. Even then Tethys herself, who receives me in the waters lying below, is accustomed to fear that I may be thrown headlong. Add to this that the vault of the sky is spinning around in constant motion, and it draws along the high stars and twists them with a rapid whirl. I struggle against this, and the impetus which overcomes all else does not overcome me, and I am carried against the swift revolving of the universe. Just suppose the chariot given (to you): what will you do? Will you be able to make your way against the rotating poles, so that the swift axis will not sweep you away? Perhaps you imagine that there are groves and cities of the gods there, and shrines loaded with rich gifts. No, the course is through ambushes, and shapes of wild beasts. And even though you may hold a true course and do not get carried off by some error, still you will make your way through the horns of the bull who is set against you, and the Haemonian Archer, and the face of the violent Lion, and the Scorpion, as he curves his savage arms in long sweeps, and the Crab, curving his arms in the other direction. And it is not easy for you to control the horses animated with those fires which they have in their breasts, and which they breathe out through their mouths and nostrils. They scarcely submit to me when their wild spirits are heated, and their necks rebel against the reins.

"So you, my son, beware that I do not give to you a fatal gift, and while there is still time, change your request. Do you, indeed, seek sure proof that you are born from my blood? I am giving certain proof by my anxiety, and I am proved to be your father by a father's fear. See my face, and would that you might look into my heart also and grasp there the cares of a father! Finally, look around and see all the wealth which the world possesses, and ask for any gift at all from these many and great bounties of earth and sea and sky. You will suffer no refusal. I beg off this one thing; which is not a gift but in name a punishment.

154

You are asking for a punishment for a gift, Phaethon. But why do you cling to my neck with your coaxing arms, O foolish boy? Do not doubt it, it will be given — I have sworn by the waters of the Styx — whatever you may choose. But you choose more wisely."

He finished his warning; the boy, however, rejected his advice, and pressed for his request, and burned with a desire to control the chariot. The father, therefore, having delayed as much as he could, led the boy to the high chariot, the gift of Vulcan. The axle was golden, and the pole was golden; the edge of the wheels were of curved gold, and the rows of spokes were of silver. Along the yoke, chrysolites and gems set in order reflected the clear light of Phoebus as it shone back. While the courageous Phaethon was marvelling at these things and looking at the workmanship, lo, Aurora, ever watchful, opened the purple gates at the reddening dawn, and her halls filled with rosy light. The stars fled, and Lucifer drove their ranks (before him) as he last of all went from his station in the sky. When Titan saw him (Lucifer) setting, and the earth and world growing red, and the horns of the waning moon vanishing from sight, he ordered the swift Hours to yoke the horses. The goddesses quickly did what they were ordered, and led from their stalls the horses, breathing forth fires and sated with ambrosial food, and they harnessed them with their noisy bridles. Then the father touched his son's face with a sacred ointment, and made it enduring of the rapid flames, and he put the radiant crown on his head, drawing from his heart deep sighs and aware of the sorrows to come, and he said:

"If at least you can obey these warnings of your father, spare the lashes, boy, and use the reins more strongly. They will hurry on of their own accord; the task is to restrain them in their haste. And do not take the way right through the five zones of heaven; the path runs slant-wise with a wide curve, and confined within the boundaries of three zones, it escapes the southern sky and the arch of the far north as well. Let this be your route. You will see clearly the tracks of the wheels. And so that the sky and land may have equal heat, do not go too low, and also do not go too high through the top of heaven; if you go too high, you will burn the sky, and if too low, you will burn the earth; you will go safest in the middle. And do not turn too far to the right towards the twisting Serpent, and let not your left wheel lead you to the low-lying Altar; go between the two. I entrust all else to Fortune, and may she help you and I hope that she will take better counsel for you than you do for yourself. While I speak, moist night has reached her limit on the western shore; there is now no longer delay for us. We are being summoned; the Dawn is shining with the dark-

155

ness put to flight. Take the reins in your hands — or if your heart can still be changed, take my advice, do not (take) the chariot, while you are still able and are standing on solid ground, while you are not yet in your ignorance mounted on the badly (*foolishly*) longed-for axle; allow me to give light to the world which you now see is safe."

But he with his youthful body occupied the light chariot, and standing there he rejoiced to hold the reins given over to his hands, and gave thanks to his unwilling father.

Meanwhile the swift horses of the Sun, Pyrois, Eous, Aethon, and the fourth, Phlegon, filled the air with their fire-bearing whinnying, and they beat against the bars with their feet. After Tethys, ignorant of the fate of her grandson, let these down, and a free course was given to them to the open sky, they dashed forth, and with the motion of their feet through the air, they divided the clouds in their path, and raised on their wings, they overtook the east winds that rise from the same quarter. But the weight was light, and not what the Sun's horses could recognize, and the yoke lacked its customary burden. Just as curving ships without their normal ballast roll and are borne unstably through the sea because of too much lightness, in the same way the chariot, lacking its usual weight, gave leaps into the air, and was thrown high like a chariot without a rider.

As soon as they felt this, the four-horse team ran wild and left the well-beaten track, nor did they run over the same course as before. He (Phaethon) was afraid and he did not know how to handle the reins that were given to him, nor did he know where the road was, and (even) if he had, he could not control the horses. Then the cold Bears grew hot for the first time with the rays, and they tried in vain to wet themselves in the forbidden sea; and the Serpent which lies next to the glacial pole, sluggish before from cold, and not to be feared by any, now grew hot and assumed new wrath from the fires; and they say that you, too, Boötes, fled from terror, although you were slow, and your ox-cart held you back. But when the unhappy Phaethon looked down from the highest heaven at the lands lying far, far below him, he grew pale, and suddenly his knees trembled with fear and darkness overspread his eyes from the light, so great. And now he would have preferred never to have touched the horses of his father. What should he do? Much of the sky is now behind his back, but even more is ahead; he measured both in his mind, and he looked forward to the west which he was fated not ever to reach, and sometimes he looked back to the east; dazed, he did not know what he should do; he neither let go the reins nor had he the strength to hold them, and he did not know the names of the horses. And he saw scattered all through the sky strange shapes everywhere and,

156

trembling, saw forms of vast wild beasts.

There is a place where the Scorpion curves out his arms into two bows, and with tail and arms flexed in two directions, he covers with his limbs the space of two constellations. When the boy saw this beast, dripping with the sweat of black poison, and threatening to sting him with its curved tail, out of his mind from cold fear, he let go the reins. After they felt these reins lying loose on the tops of their backs, the horses dashed off their course, and with no one restraining them, they went through the air into unknown regions, and wherever their impulse lead them, they rushed aimlessly and brushed against stars fixed high in the sky and snatched the chariot through ways far off their course; and now they aimed at the heights, and then headlong they were borne down over steep slopes to the regions nearer the earth. The Moon was amazed to see the horses of her brother run lower than her own, and the burned clouds smoking.

The earth was consumed by the fire, the highest parts first, and formed deep cracks and became arid with the moisture taken away. The fields grew white, when the trees and their leaves were consumed, and the dry crop furnished the material for its own destruction. But I am complaining of trivial things. Great cities with their walls perished, and the fires turned to ashes whole tribes with their peoples; the woods burned up with the mountains.

Then indeed Phaethon saw that the earth was ablaze on all sides, and he could not endure such great heat; (and) he drew in his mouth burning air such as comes from the depths of a furnace, and he felt the chariot growing hot under his feet; nor could he bear the ashes and sparks that were thrown out, and he was enveloped from all sides in black smoke and did not know where he was going or where he was, covered by the pitchy darkness, and was carried along at the will of the winged horses.

Men believe that at that time the peoples of Ethiopia took on a black color, with the blood drawn to the surface of their bodies; then, too, Libya became arid, with her moisture taken away by the heat. Then the nymphs with hair unkempt wept for their fountains and lakes; Boeotia sought for Dirce; Argos, Amymone; and Corinth, her Pirenian spring. Nor did the rivers who by lot were given more distant banks remain safe either; Tanais steamed in the midst of the waves, . . . : and the river birds (*swans*) which had been accustomed to throng the Maeonian banks with their songs, were burned in the middle of the Cayster. The Nile fled terrified to the ends of the world, and hid its head, which is still hidden; its seven mouths were empty and filled with dust, seven valleys without a river. All the earth was cracked

157

open, and the light penetrated through the clefts down to Tartarus, and it terrified the king of the lower world with his wife. And the sea contracted, and there was a field of dry sand where once the sea was; and the mountains which the deep sea had covered stood out and increased the number of the Cyclades. The fish sought the lowest depths, and the curved dolphins did not dare any longer to leap into the accustomed air over the surface of the sea. The bodies of sea-dogs floated lifeless, with their bellies upturned, on the top of the water. The story is that Nereus himself and Doris and her daughters lay hidden in their warm caves. Neptune tried three times to lift his arms from the water with a grim expression on his face, but three times he was not able to bear the heat of the air.

Mother Earth, however, surrounded as she was by the sea, amid the waters of the sea and the shrinking fountains on every side, which now had hidden themselves in the body of their dark mother, dry as she was, raised her oppressed face as far as the neck, put her hand to her brow, and shaking everything with a great tremor, sat down a little lower than usual, and then said these words with her sacred voice:

"If this pleases you, and I have deserved it, O king of the gods, why are your thunderbolts idle? May I be allowed, if I am to die by fire, to die by the strength of your fires, and so lighten my disaster by it being from you! Scarcely can I open my jaws to say these words," — the steam (*heat*) so oppressed her face — "see my hair singed, and in my eyes and all over my face so many ashes! Is this the reward you bring to me, is this the repayment for my fertility and services, because I endure the wounds of the hooked plow and rake, and am tormented through the whole year, and because I give leaves and kindly fodder to the cattle, fruits to the human race, and incense to you, too? But suppose I have deserved such a fate, what have the waves, what has your brother done to deserve it? Why are the seas, given to him by lot decreasing, and withdrawing farther away from the sky? But if neither regard for your brother nor for me touches you, at least have pity on your own sky. Look on both sides of you; the poles are smoking on each side. If the fire destroys these, your own halls will perish. Lo, Atlas himself is struggling and scarcely can hold the white hot axis on his shoulders. If the seas and the lands perish, and also the realm of the heavens, we are turned back into ancient chaos. Snatch from the fires whatever still remains, and take counsel for the safety of the world."

The Earth spoke these words: and she was not able to bear the heat any longer, nor say anything more, and she pulled back her face into herself and the caverns nearest to the Shades (*Underworld*). And the

158

omnipotent father, calling to witness the gods and especially the one who had given the chariot, that unless he brought help, everything would perish by a dreadful fate, climbed on high to the top of the sky, from which (place) he is accustomed to spread clouds over the wide world, and also to stir up thunderings and hurl his flashing thunderbolts. But now he had no clouds which he could spread out over the lands, nor rains which he could send down from the sky. He thundered, and balancing a thunderbolt in his right hand by his ear, he hurled it at the driver, and drove him (equally) from the chariot and from life, and so he put out the fires by means of fires. The horses were confused and jumping in different directions; they wrenched their necks from the yoke and left the reins broken. The reins lay here, the axle torn away from the pole there, on this side spokes of the broken wheels, and traces of the broken chariot were scattered far and wide. And Phaethon, with the fire ravaging his reddish hair, was rolled headlong, and carried through the air with a long trail, just as sometimes a star, although it has not fallen from a clear sky, still it could appear to have fallen. The very great Eridanus (*Po*) received him, far from his native land, in another part of the world, and bathed his smoking face. The Naiads of Hesperia lay his body, still smoking from the fires of the three-forked bolt, in a tomb, and they carved this verse in the rock:

HERE LIES PHAETHON, DRIVER OF HIS FATHER'S CHARIOT,
EVEN THOUGH HE COULD NOT CONTROL IT, HE DIED HAVING DARED GREAT
THINGS.

In the following selections, the macrons have been omitted in order to train students to read without these aids. The standard examinations of the College Entrance Examination Board do not use macrons in any passages in the examinations.

Philemon and Baucis

There is in the Phrygian hills an oak tree right next to a linden, surrounded by a low wall. Not far from here there is a marsh, formerly habitable land, and now waters filled with divers and swamp coots. Jupiter came here in mortal guise, and with his parent came Mercury, who wears winged sandals, having put aside his wings. They went to a thousand homes, seeking shelter, and a thousand homes were barred against them. Still one house received them, small indeed, and thatched with straw and marsh reeds; but a pious old woman, Baucis, and Philemon of equal age were in that cottage, married from their youthful days and grown old in that hut, and they made their poverty light by admitting it and by bearing it with contented minds. It made no difference whether you asked for masters or servants in that place; those two were the whole house, and the same two gave orders and obeyed them.

When, therefore, the gods reached that humble house, and stooping entered the low doorway, the old man, having set out a bench, ordered them to rest their limbs, and the diligent Baucis threw over the bench a rough covering. Then she moved away the warm ashes on the hearth and stirred up the fires of the day before and fed them with leaves and dried bark, and with her aged breath produced flames, and then she brought from under the roof some well-split wood and dried twigs, made them small, and laid them under the small copper kettle; then she took off the outside leaves from a cabbage which her husband had brought in from the well-watered garden; he then lifted down with a forked stick the smoky side of bacon which was hanging from the black beam, and he cut off a small part from the side, which had been preserved for a long time, and put it into the boiling water to cook. Meanwhile they made the time slip by with various conversation. A couch with soft sedge grass from the river was spread out, and the frame and feet were of willow. They covered this over with blankets which they were not accustomed to bring out except on festal days; but this, too, was cheap and old, not unworthy of the willow bed.

The gods reclined. The old woman, with her skirts tucked up, and trembling, set the table; but one of the three legs was uneven, and she made it even with a potsherd. After this had made the slope level, she wiped it, now level, with green mint. And she placed here some two-colored berries (*olives*) of the virgin Minerva, and some autumn cornel berries, soaked in the dregs of wine, and endives and radishes, and thickened cheese, and eggs cooked lightly in the warm ashes, all served in dishes made of clay. After these things, a goblet made of the same kind of silverware (i.e., clay) was put out, and cups made of beechwood, which were hollowed out, and coated on the inside with yellow wax. There was a slight wait, and the hearth gave forth its steaming foods, and the wines of no great age were brought out again, and then pushed away a little; they made room for the second course. Here were nuts and figs with dried dates, and plums and sweet apples in wide baskets, and grapes collected from their purple vines. And white honey was in the center of the table; and above all there were kindly faces added and a generous and plentiful goodwill.

Meanwhile the startled people saw that the bowl which was being emptied so often was filling itself of its own accord, and that the wine

160

was replenishing itself. With upturned hands, both Baucis and the timid Philemon utter prayers, and begged for forgiveness for their fare and lack of preparations. There was one goose, the guardian of their small place; the hosts were preparing to kill this for their godly guests; it eluded their grasp for a long time, and it tired the old people who were slow from age, and it finally seemed to fly to the gods themselves for refuge; the gods forbade them to kill it. They said, "We are gods, and this unholy neighborhood will be punished as it deserves, but you will be immune from this punishment. But you must leave your house and accompany our steps and go together to the high mountains." Both obeyed, and leaning on their sticks, they struggled to put their steps up the long grade. When they were only so far from the summit as an arrow could be shot, they looked back and saw that everything else was covered with water, and only their house remained. And while they marveled, and wept at the fate of their friends, that old house of theirs, small even for two people, was turned into a temple; columns replaced the supports; the straw turned yellow and the roof seemed golden; the gates were carved, and the ground was covered with marble. Then the son of Saturn (*Jupiter*) uttered these words with a gentle voice (*mouth*): "Now ask, just old man, and old woman worthy of a just husband, for any gift you wish." Philemon, having spoken with Baucis for a little, revealed their common decision to the gods:

"We ask to be priests and guard your temple, and since we have lived our days peacefully together, may the same hour take both of us away, so that I may never see the tomb of my wife, and also I will not have to be buried by her."

Fulfillment followed their prayers; they were made guardians of the temple, as long as life lasted; and when they had completed their years and lifetime, while by chance they were standing before the steps of the temple, and talking over the events, Baucis saw Philemon put forth leaves, and the aged Philemon saw Baucis also growing leaves. (When) already above both their faces, mutual treetops (were) growing, while it was (still) permitted, they exchanged words, "Farewell," and "O spouse," they said at one and the same time, at one and the same time shrubbery covered their (now) hidden faces. The Thymbreian native shows on this side (and) on that neighboring trunks from a twin body.

These things reliable (not untruthful) old men (nor was there [any reason] why they should wish to deceive) told me. Indeed, I have seen hanging down (and) wreathed over the branches, and I have read aloud: "The pious (*reverent*) are a concern to the gods, and those by whom they are honored (*cherished*), they (themselves) honor (*cherish*)."

161

Later Latin

AVIANUS

ABOUT TWO COMPANIONS AND A BEAR

A man was once traveling with a companion on a narrow road in unknown hills and winding valleys, safe, because whatever evil Fortune might bring, each one would be able to endure it by uniting their strength. While they continued the journey they had started with varied conversation, a she-bear came headlong in their way to meet them. One of them with an easy run, seized an oak branch, and hung his trembling weight among the green foliage; the other, without advancing a step, feigned death, and lay down, throwing himself intentionally upon the ground. The beast, eager for spoil, ran up at once, and first raised the wretched man in her curved claws; but when his limbs grew stiff with icy fear, (for the usual vital warmth had left his bones), the bear, thinking him a smelly corpse, although hungry, left him and vanished into her lair. But when they, gradually recovered, felt safe and resumed their talk, the one who had fled before, now more cheerful, said, "Tell me, if you please, what was it the bear told you while you were trembling there? She spoke much with you in secret for a long time." "Yes, indeed, she gave me much advice, but this, too, she gave me as most important, which I, poor man, must always carry out: 'Be wary of seeking the comradeship of another, lest you be caught again by a mad wild beast.'"

SULPICIUS SEVERUS

MARTIN SURPRISES HIS ENEMIES

Also, when in a certain hamlet he had destroyed a very old temple, and he tried to cut down a pine tree which was next to the shrine, then in truth a priest of that place and the rest of the crowd of pagans began to object. And while the temple was being demolished, when these same people had become quiet, with their lord ordering them, they did not allow the tree to be cut down.

He warned them zealously that there was nothing religious in the tree trunk: that they should rather follow the God that he himself was serving; that they should let the tree be cut down, because it was dedicated to a demon. Then one of them, who was bolder than the others, said, "If you have any faith in your God whom you say you worship, we ourselves will cut down the tree, and you catch it as it falls; and if your Lord is with you, as you say, you will escape."

Then he, fearlessly trusting in God, promised that he would do it. Here, all the crowd of pagans agreed to a condition of this kind, and thought the loss of the tree would be easy, if in its fall it crushed the enemy of their sacred affairs. And so, when it was cut on one side, it began to totter, he was placed bound in that place where, in the opinion of the farmers, no one doubted that the tree would fall.

Therefore, the men themselves began to cut down their pine tree with great joy and pleasure. A great crowd of admirers was standing nearby. And now little by little the pine swayed and, about to fall, threatened its ruin. The monks at a distance grew pale, and terrified as the danger approached, lost all hope and confidence, awaiting only the death of Martin. But he, waiting unafraid, trusting in God, when now the falling pine had, in falling, sounded a crash, raising his hand, he made a sign of safety (i.e., of the Cross), as it was falling and rushing down upon him.

But then — as if you thought it had been driven back by a whirlwind — it fell in a different direction, so that it almost knocked over the farmers who had been standing in a safe place. Then, in truth, the pagans, raising a cry to the sky, were amazed at the miracle, the monks wept for joy, and the name of Christ was on everyone's lips; and it is clear enough that salvation (*religion*) came to that region on that day.

THE VENERABLE BEDE

THE STORY OF CAEDMON

In the monastery of this abbess was a certain brother, remarkable for a certain particular divine grace, because he was in the habit of making poetry suitable for religion and piety; so that whatever he learned from the holy writings through interpreters, this in a short time he turned out in his own tongue, that is Anglo-Saxon, in poetical language of the greatest sweetness and humility. By his songs often were the hearts of many aroused to despise the things of earth and to seek for the heavenly life. And indeed others also after him among the Anglo-Saxon people tried to write religious poems, but none could equal him.

For he himself did not learn the art of poetry from men nor was he instructed by a man, but he received his gift assisted by the favor of heaven. Therefore, he could not make poetry of a light or uninstructive sort, but only that which had to do with religion and was proper to his religious tongue. And being in secular habit to a somewhat advanced age, he had never learned anything of poetry. Therefore, sometimes at feasts when for the sake of good fellowship it was ordered that all should sing in turn, he, when he saw the lute coming around to him, would rise from the midst of the feast and going out return home.

When one time he was doing this and on leaving the banquet hall had come to the stable of the beasts of burden, the guarding of which had fallen to him for that night, and when there at the appropriate hour he had stretched out to sleep, someone stood by him in his dream and greeting him and calling him by his name said, "Caedmon, sing something for me."

And he replied, "I can't sing; for I left the banquet for that very reason and came here because I could not sing." Again he who was speaking with him said, "But yet you have to sing for me." "What must I sing?" he asked. And the other replied, "Sing of the beginnings of creation."

When he heard this reply, immediately he began to sing in praise of God the creator, verses which he had never heard, of which this is the sense: "Now must we praise the originator of the heavenly kingdom, the power of the creator and his wisdom, and the Father's deeds of glory. How he, since he is God eternal, is the source of all miracles, who first for the sons of men created the heavens for their rooftop, and then as the omnipotent protector of human kind created the earth."

This is the sense but not the exact order of the words which he sang in his sleep; for the poetry, although most beautifully composed, cannot be translated word for word from one language to another without harm to its beauty and merit. Moreover, rising from sleep, he remembered all which he had sung as he slept; and to it soon he added in the same fashion more words of a poem worthy of God.

In the morning coming to the steward who was in charge of him, he showed what gift he had received and, brought before the abbess, he was ordered in the presence of many quite learned men to tell his dream and to recite the poem that it might be shown what or from what source was that which he related. To all it seemed that heavenly grace had been conferred upon him by God.

164

And they expounded to him a sermon of sacred story or doctrine, commanding him if he could, to turn it into the measures of verse. And he, undertaking the task, went away and returning in the morning brought back that which he was ordered, composed in the finest poetry. Therefore, soon the abbess, esteeming the grace of God in the man, told him to remove his secular garb and take up the monkish manner of life. And she took him into the monastery with all her own people and attached him to the band of monks and ordered him to be taught the course of sacred history. And all that he could learn by hearing, recollecting it in his own mind, as if he were a clean animal chewing its cud, he turned into the sweetest song and by singing the more delightfully made his teachers in turn his hearers.

Moreover he sang of the creation of the world, of the beginnings of human kind, and the whole book of Genesis, about the Israelite departure from Egypt and their entrance into the promised land, of very many other books of scripture, of our Lord's incarnation, passion, resurrection, and ascent into heaven, of the coming of the Holy Spirit, and the teaching of the apostles.

In like manner he wrote many poems about the fear of judgment to come and the dread of the punishments of Hell and the delights of the heavenly kingdom; but also (he wrote) very many other things concerning divine benefits and judgments, in all of which he tried to draw men from the love of wickedness to the true esteem and practice of good conduct; for he was a very devout man and humbly submissive to the discipline of the rule; but against those who wished to do otherwise, he was aflame with a zealous fire of great ardor. Therefore, also he brought his life to a fine end.

For as the hour of his death approached, for fourteen days he was afflicted by the oncoming of bodily weakness but of sufficient moderation that for the whole time he could talk and walk about. There was nearby a cottage, in which the more infirm and those who seemed on the point of death were customarily taken.

Therefore he asked his servant, at the approach of evening on the night he was to leave this world, that he prepare a place of rest for him in it. And he marveled why he made this request, for he did not at all seem close to death. Nevertheless he did what he had been told.

When they had taken their place there and with some joyousness of heart were talking and joking with those who had before entered into that place and when already the hour of midnight had passed, he asked if they had the eucharist therein. They replied: "What need is there of the eucharist? You do not have to die yet, who speak with us so joyously as one in good health."

165

Again he said, "Nevertheless, bring me the eucharist." When he received it in his hand he asked if all bore toward him a quiet mind and without any complaint of controversy or rancor. All replied that they were of the kindest feelings toward him and devoid of all anger, and in their turn they asked that he be of good feeling toward them.

Straightway he replied, "My sons, I bear good will toward all the servants of God." So fortifying himself with the heavenly eucharist he prepared for the entry into the other life; and he inquired how soon would be the hour when the brothers should be roused to say the lauds of the night. They replied, "It is not far off."

He said, "That is well. Therefore, let us await that hour." And crossing himself he dropped his head upon his pillow and gently falling asleep so finished his life in silence.

GREGORY THE GREAT SENDS A MISSION TO ENGLAND

They tell that on a certain day, after the recent arrival of some merchants, when much goods had been brought together into the Forum to be sold, many had flocked there to purchase, and Gregory himself among others had come and seen among other wares boys put up for sale, of fair body and charming countenance and also of remarkably beautiful hair. When he saw them, he asked from what place or what land they had been brought. And it was said that they were from the island of Britain, whose inhabitants were of such appearance.

Again he asked whether these same islanders were Christians or were involved in the errors of paganism. He was told that they were pagans. And he, drawing forth a long sigh from the depths of his soul, said, "Alas, a sorrow that the father of darkness should possess the souls of men of such shining countenance and that so fair an exterior should hold within a mind devoid of inner grace."

Again he asked what was the name of that race. He was told they were called Angli. "Good," he said, "for they have the appearance of angels, and such should be the co-heirs of the angels in heaven. What is the name of the province from which they were brought?"

They replied that these provincials were called Deiri. And he re-replied, "Good, they have been brought out of wrath and called to Christ's mercy. How is the king of that province called?"

They replied that he was called Aelli. But he playing on the name said: "Alleluia, the glory of God the creator must be sung in those places."

Going to the bishop of the apostolic see (seat) at Rome (for he had

166

not himself yet been made bishop), he asked that he send into Britain some ministers of God's word to the people of the Angli that they might be converted to Christ: (saying) that he was prepared to accomplish this work with God's help, if it should please the holy father that this be done.

Although he was not able to accomplish this, because, although the bishop wished to allow him what he had requested, nevertheless the citizens of Rome could not permit him to withdraw so far from the city, soon, when he attained the bishopric, he brought about the long desired work, sending others indeed as preachers, but himself assisting the preaching that it might bear fruit, with his exhortations and prayers.

WIDUKIND

A BRAVE SAXON

There was then in the camp a certain man of the veteran soldiers, an old man, but rugged and vigorous in his old age, who was called father of the fathers because of the quality of his good virtues, named Hathagat. He, seizing the standard which was considered sacred among them, distinguished with the image of a lion and a dragon and a flying eagle above, which showed courage and wisdom and the efficiency of these things, and portraying the firmness of mind by the agility of body, said:

"Up to now I have lived among the best Saxons, and my life has brought me almost to its last period of age, and I have never seen my Saxons flee; and how am I now forced to do what I have never learned to do? I know how to fight, but I do not know how, nor am I able, to flee; if the fates do not permit me to live any longer, at least may I be allowed to die among my friends, who are very dear to me. For example, the prostrate bodies of our friends around us are examples of our ancestral courage, of men who preferred to die rather than to be conquered, to lose their courageous hearts rather than to give ground openly to the enemy.

"But why do I have to drag out my exhortation for so long a time about the fear of death? Lo, we shall go to our axes, to so great slaughter, not to a battle; our enemies suspect nothing about the promised peace and our grave wound; today also, wearied by the battle, as they are without fear, they remain without their watches and customary guards. Therefore, let us rush upon them, unsuspecting and buried in sleep. Follow me as your leader, and I give you this hoary head of mine, if it does not happen as I say."

Therefore, aroused by his very excellent speech, they spent what was left of the day in rebuilding their strength; then at the first watch of the night, at the given signal, when a heavier sleep is accustomed to possess mortals, taking their arms, with the leader going ahead, they rushed over the walls, and finding them without guards or watches, they entered the city with a loud shout. When their enemies were awakened by this, some sought safety by flight, others wandered like drunken men through the streets and (within) the walls of the city, others fell into the hands of the Saxons, thinking that they were their citizens. Indeed, all those of advanced age they handed over to death, (but) they kept the young people for booty. And that night was filled with shouting, murder, and plunder, and there was no quiet place in the whole city, until rosy dawn arose, and showed the bloodless victory. And when centered around the king, evidently Irminfridus, there was the greatest victory, he, having been sought for, was found to have escaped with his wife and sons and a small retinue.

SHREWD METHODS OF PETTY WARFARE

Aware, however, that the count of Isilberth was a shrewd and very clever man, named Immo, he thought it was better to fight him with wisdom than with arms. But he, as he was very astute, realizing that he was bigger and better, took up arms against the leader; the leader of all troubles was most vexed at this, because he had to have as an opponent to himself one whom he thought he was still superior to. A herd of pigs taken by the shrewd Immo also increased the indignation of the leader. For when the leader's swineherds were passing before the gates of the city, Immo had a pig in front of the gate driven in and he then received all the herd of pigs through the open gates into the city.

The leader, not able to bear this insult, raising an army, besieged Immo. He, however, is said to have had many swarms of bees, and breaking these open, he directed them against the cavalry. When the bees stung the horses with their stings, they made them frenzied, so that the horsemen began to be in danger. Immo, seeing this from the wall, threatened an attack with his allies. The leader, therefore, mocked too often by tricks of this sort, broke off the siege. But he is reported to have said on departing, "With Immo agreeing with me, I have easily held all the Lotharians captive, but him alone I am not able to capture with all the Lotharians."

168

The Danes in olden times were Christians, but they still kept their idols in their pagan rites. There happened to arise a dispute over the worship of the gods at a certain banquet, with the king present, with the Danes asserting that Christ was indeed a god, but there were other gods greater than he was, in fact who would show to mortal men more powerful signs and prodigies.

In reply to them, a certain priest, now leading a religious life, a bishop named Poppa, testified that there was only one God, the Father with his only-begotten son, Jesus Christ, and the Holy Ghost, and that their images were demons, not gods. The king, Harold, however, who was said to be quick at hearing but slow at speaking, asked him if he was willing to prove his faith by himself. The priest without hesitation answered that he was willing. Then the king ordered the priest to be guarded until the next morning.

When morning came, he ordered a sword of great weight to be heated on the fire, and he ordered the priest, because of his universal (common among all believers) faith, to carry the white-hot sword. The apostle of Christ unhesitatingly seized the sword and carried it as long as the king demanded; then he showed to all his hand, unhurt, and he made again the catholic faith credible to everyone.

The king, having been converted to this belief, decided that Christ was the only God to be worshipped, and he ordered the idols to be thrown out to the subject tribes, and then bestowed deserved honors on the priests and ministers of God. But these things are also deservedly ascribed to the virtues of your father, through whose work the assembly (of Christians) and ranks of priests shone so greatly.

PETER ALPHONSUS

"A FRIEND IN NEED IS A FRIEND INDEED"

An Arab, about to die, calling to him his son, said to him, "Tell me, son, how many friends you have acquired while you have lived."

The son answered and said, "I think that I have acquired a hundred friends."

The father said, "A philosopher says, 'May you not praise your friend until you have proved him.' I was born before you, and I have acquired barely a half of one. Since, my son, you have acquired a hundred, go

169

then to test them, so that you may know who of them is the perfect friend."

The son says to him, "How do you advise me to test them?"

The father said, "Catch a calf and kill it, and put it broken in pieces into a sack, so that the sack on the outside is stained with blood, and when you come to a friend, say to him, 'My dear brother, I have killed a man by chance, and my house must be watched. He must be buried and hidden, therefore. I ask you to bury him in secret, for no one will suspect you, and thus you can save me.' "

The son did as his father ordered. The first friend to whom he came said to him, "Carry your dead man over your neck, as you have done evil; suffer your own punishment; you will not enter my house." When, moreover, he had done this to all of his friends, one by one, all answered him with the same response.

Returning to the father, he reported what he had done. And the father said, "It has happened to you as the philosopher said, 'Many are to be counted friends, but few in time of need.' Go to the half a friend that I have and see what he says to you."

He came there and said to him just what he had said to the others, and he replied, "Enter the house, this is a secret which ought not to be divulged to the neighbors." Then sending out his wife with his household, he dug a grave. When however, he saw everything prepared, he explained the matter just as it was, and thanked him. Then he reported to his father what he had done.

But the father said, "For such a friend the philosopher says, 'He is a true friend who helps you when the world fails you.' "

A STORYTELLER'S RUSE

A certain king had his own storyteller, who was accustomed to tell him five stories every night. It finally happened that the king, worried by certain cares, was not at all able to sleep, and he asked to hear more stories than usual. He told him three more than usual, however, but they were short.

The king asked for even more. He did not at all want to. For he had told him many, just as he had been ordered. The king said to him, "You have told me many, but they were short ones, but I would like to have you tell me one that can be drawn out with many words, so as to let me go to sleep."

The storyteller gave in and began, "There was a certain farmer who had a thousand soldi. He, moreover, setting out to do business, bought

170

two thousand sheep, about a dollar each. It happened, while he was returning, that a great flood of water arose. Since he was able to cross neither by fording nor by a bridge, he went away worried, seeking a way by which he might be carried across with his sheep. He finally found a small boat, and compelled by necessity, he put two sheep aboard and crossed the water."

With these words the storyteller fell asleep. The king accordingly wakened him, and urged him to finish the story which he had begun. The storyteller said this: "The flood(ed river) was big, and the boat small, and the number of sheep was innumerable. Therefore let the aforementioned farmer carry his sheep across, and then I will finish the story which I have begun."

WILLIAM FITZSTEPHEN

THE MURDER OF THOMAS A BECKET

They entered into the church itself. The monks of the church, as much terrified as amazed by such and so great an uproar, omitting the singing of vespers, when the lord archbishop entered the church, came from the choir to meet him, rejoicing and giving thanks to God that they saw him alive and received him who they had heard had been beheaded.

And when some either for joy or for fear were weeping, and some were persuading him to this course and others to that, he — not afraid to die for the freedom and cause of God's church — commanded them to go and depart from him, that they might not stand in the way of his suffering which he had foretold would come about and which he saw was at hand.

As he was about to go above to the altar where he was accustomed to hear private masses and (the canonical) hours, he had already mounted four steps when, behold, at the entrance of the cloister where we had come first there appeared Reginald Fitzurse clothed in mail, his sword drawn, (and) shouting: "Now here to me, you men of the king!" Shortly there were added his three comrades, their bodies and heads covered like his with mail, except for their eyes, and with drawn swords.

Seeing the armed men, the monks wished to close the door of the church; but the good man, trusting in God and not greatly fearing with sudden alarm the forces of the wicked rushing in, came down the stairs forbidding them to close the door of the church and saying, "Far

171

be it from us to make a fortress of the church of God; allow all who wish to enter God's church; let God's will be done."

Then as he came down from the stairs toward the door, that it might not be shut, John of Salisbury and all his other clerics except Robert the canon and William Fitzstephen and Edward Grim, leaving him some sought the altar and others, hiding places.

And indeed if the archbishop had wished to turn aside and free himself by the safeguard of flight, he could very well have availed himself of the opportunity of time and place not sought but right at hand. It was evening, a very long night was coming on, and there was a crypt nearby in which there were many inner recesses generally dark. Likewise there was another door nearby where, by a spiral staircase, he might ascend to the rooms and eaves of the upper part of the church; perhaps he would not have been found or something else would have happened.

But he wished none of these. He did not turn aside nor supplicate the assassins, nor did he utter a murmur or complaint in all his suffering; but awaiting patiently for the sake of Christ and the church his last hour which was at hand, he showed bravery and constancy of mind and body until the deed was wholly finished.

Behold now the murderers, borne along by their fury, contrary to their expectation seeing the door of the church open, hastily entered. And one of them said to the monks who were standing by him, "Do not move." And indeed as if bewildered and astonished by the venerability of his countenance, those bullies at first drew back when they saw the archbishop.

Afterwards someone cried out, "Where is that traitor?" The archbishop did not reply to that word.

Someone said again, "Where is the archbishop?" He said, "Here I am, no traitor but a priest of God; and I marvel that in such dress you have entered the church of God. What do you wish?"

One of the bullies replied, "That you die; you can live no longer." He replied, "I meet death in the name of God and commend my soul and the church's cause to God and the blessed Mary and the patron saints of this church. Far be it from me to flee on account of your swords; but by God's authority I forbid you to touch any one of my people."

One struck him with the flat of his sword between the shoulder blades saying, "Flee: you are dead."

He remained motionless and, offering his neck, was commending himself to the Lord. Some, saying, "You have been taken come with us," laying their hands upon him, wished to drag him from the

172

church. And so they would have done had they not feared that the people would rescue him from their hands.

He, replying, "I will go nowhere; do here what you wish and what you have been ordered," resisted as well as he could; the monks tried to restrain him; among them was master Edward Grim who first received a blow directed by William de Tracy at the archbishop's head on his outstretched arm. With the same blow both the archbishop on his bent head and he on his arm were gravely wounded.

The archbishop, wiping with his arm the blood flowing from his head, as he saw it gave thanks to God saying, "Into your hands, Lord, I commend my soul." He was struck a second blow on his head which caused him to fall forward, first on his knees, with his hands clasped and stretched forth to God, by the altar of St. Benedict which stood there. And he took care or had grace to fall honorably, covered by his cope down to his heels as if about to adore or pray. He fell over on his right hand, he who was about to go to the right hand of God.

OUTDOOR SPORTS IN TWELFTH-CENTURY LONDON

On holidays throughout the summer young men at their play exercise at archery, running, jumping, wrestling, and throwing stones. Venus leads out the chorus of maidens continuously while the moon shines overhead and they (in the dance) beat the ground with unimpeded foot. In winter on almost every holiday, before lunch either foaming boars fight for their lives, or heavy bulls or huge bears fight with dogs.

When that swamp which washes against the north wall of the city is frozen over, crowded bands of youths go forth to play on the ice. Some taking a good running start (lit., *rather quick motion taken from a running*) slide a long way; others make as it were great mill-stones from blocks of ice as seats for themselves; many running ahead and holding hands drag one sitting (on a block). Sometimes, their feet slipping, they all fall down.

There are others more skillful at playing on the ice who fit and bind to their feet, with ankle-laces, bones, in fact the shinbones of animals, and hold in their hands staves with sharp iron points. When sometimes they push these against the ice, they are carried along with as much speed as a bird in flight or a javelin thrown from a ballista.

Sometimes, moreover, two people come from opposite directions from a great distance; they crash together and raise their staves and strike one another; either one or both fall, not without bodily harm; after they fall by the force of their motion they are borne far from one

173

another, and where their heads hit the ice, they are all skinned and scraped. Often when they fall down they break a leg or arm, if they should fall upon it; but their age is one most eager for glory, and the young men desirous of victory, to be the braver in real battle, train themselves thus in mock battle.

ODO OF CERINTON

MICE IN COUNCIL

Some mice formed a plan, as to how they could protect themselves from a cat, and a certain one said wisely to the others, "Let a bell be tied to the cat's neck, and then we will be able to be on guard and hear whichever way she comes and so escape her tricks." This plan pleased all the others, and one mouse said, "Who among us is so armed with courage that she will dare to tie the bell on the neck of the cat?" One mouse replied, "Certainly not I." Another replied, "Certainly, for the whole world, I would not dare to approach that cat."

THE STUPID MEN OF WILLEBEG

Certain simple men, so it is said, were from Willebeg who had to pay taxes to their master on time, and they did not have a messenger who could carry out the business so quickly. They said in turn, "What shall we do? Because the time is now at hand." Certain ones said, "The hare is a swift animal; let us hang a purse on its neck with the taxes, and let us signify to it that it is to take it quickly to the house of our master." And they did so, and the hare with the purse and the taxes ran off to the woods as fast as it could and the men never found out where it went.

JACQUES DE VITRY

"PENNY WISE AND POUND FOOLISH"

(There was) a count named Henry, (and) after his stewards, without his knowing it, had instructed the doormen that they should allow no

174

pauper to enter, a certain boy about nine years old, about whom the doormen did not much care, came up to him and asked him, as his mother had told him, to give him something. But the count, seeing the boy without clothes, so he did not have any place to put any money, gave him one denarius, and said to him, "Go and buy a purse, and return quickly."

The boy, wishing to keep some of the money, bought a small purse with half of the money, and kept for himself the other half. When, however, he had returned to the count, the count, noticing that he had bought a small purse, asked the boy, "For how much did you buy this purse? See now that you tell me the truth."

But the terrified boy said, "Master, I bought it for one obol; take the other one if you want it." Then the count said to him, "If you had bought a bigger purse with the denarius, you would have taken it filled with denarii, and because you have wanted to keep one obolo, you will not (*only*) carry a small purse full."

A SPOILED HORSE

I have heard a certain prelate in France had a very fine horse; but his brother, a soldier, greatly desired it, to use in tournaments, and he was not able to get it in any way. Finally, with many entreaties, he obtained from his brother (the concession) that he would lend it to him for three days.

Approaching a certain secretary of the aforementioned prelate, he began to ask carefully what were the words which his brother spoke more frequently while riding. He began to think, and then replied, "My master while riding says his prayers, nor can I recall any words which he says more frequently than that which he says at the beginning, which is this: 'God, stretch out (thy hand) to help me.'"

Then the soldier began to ride the horse which had been saddled for him; and frequently repeating the above-mentioned words, as often as he spoke them, he kicked the horse sharply with his spurs, and so in three days he had so trained the horse that whenever he said, "God, stretch out (thy hand) to help me," the horse, fearing the spurs, even though he was not kicked, gave great leaps, and running wildly he could scarcely be held back.

Afterwards, when the prelate was riding the horse, his brother accompanied him to see the result. And when the prelate said, "God, stretch out (thy hand) to help me," the horse began to give great leaps and to run in such a way that he almost threw his rider. When he had done

175

this for several times, the soldier said, "Master, that horse is not suitable for you, for you are a heavy man, and if you were to fall, you would be badly injured."

Then the prelate was affected with great regret, and said, "This horse used to take me calmly with steady gait, but now — I do not know how it happened — I grieve that I have lost a good horse; but, because of what has happened, you take him; he is more suited to a soldier than a prelate." And so he obtained a very fine horse.

ROGER BACON

ROGER BACON PREDICTS SOME WONDERS OF SCIENCE

Now therefore I shall tell first of the wonderful works of science and nature, that afterwards I may designate their causes and method. In them is nothing magical, so that it may be seen that all magic power is inferior to these works and unworthy (of comparison).

And first for the shaping and planning of science alone. For devices for sailing can be made without men rowing so that the greatest ships, on both rivers and sea, may be borne along, with only one man steering, with greater speed than if they were full of men (rowing). Likewise wagons can be made (in such way) that they move without animal power and with inestimable speed, such as we think the scythe-chariots to have been, with which they fought in ancient times.

Likewise machines for flying can be made so that a man may sit in the middle of the machine, turning some clever device by which the wings cleverly constructed may strike the air in the manner of a bird flying.

Likewise an engine, small in size, for lifting and lowering almost unlimited weights, than which nothing is more useful in an emergency. For by an instrument of a height of three fingers' height and the same width and (or) of smaller size a man could free himself and his friends from all peril of prison and ascend and descend.

Also a machine could be made easily by which one man might drag to himself, by force, a thousand men, even against their will; and so for pulling other things.

Also instruments can be made for walking in the sea or rivers right to the very bottom and without bodily danger. For Alexander the Great used these to observe the secrets of the sea according to what Ethicus the astronomer tells.

Moreover these (various devices) were made in ancient times and have been made in our time, as is certain, except for the flying-machine, which I have not seen nor know any man who has seen it; but I know a wise man who has contrived how to complete this work. And almost without number can such things be made; as bridges over rivers without columns or any support, and machines and clever inventions unheard of.

GESTA ROMANORUM

THE STORY OF THE THREE CASKETS

Honorius reigned, a very rich emperor, who had one son, whom he loved very much. The fame of that ruler spread through the world, that he was upright and just in all matters.

However he kept waging war with one king and devastating his lands (lit., *him*). This king since he endured much suffering and great loss at his hands at length thought, "I have only one daughter and my adversary only one son. If somehow I could join my daughter to his son in marriage, I should achieve lasting peace."

He sent distinguished ambassadors to the emperor to ask that at least he grant him a truce for the time being, that he might be able to confer with him in person. The emperor held a council and granted a truce for one year. The king came before him in person and offered his daughter to his son. The emperor said, "I'll make the arrangement on two conditions: first, that your daughter be a virgin; second, that after your death all your kingdom go to my son." The other replied, "That pleases me well."

Straightway a document of agreement was signed. The king bade the emperor farewell. And when he had come to his kingdom, he had a ship prepared since his daughter had to cross the sea to the emperor. When the ship was ready and all things necessary prepared, the girl embarked bearing with her treasure in great supply and five soldiers with her ladies and maids.

Now when they were sailing through the sea, a great whale met them in the deep and wished to swallow the ship. The sailors, perceiving this, were much afraid and the girl particularly so. But the sailors made a great fire and kept guard day and night.

But it befell after three days that, worn out from their long watches, they slept. Suddenly the whale swallowed the ship with all its contents.

The girl when she knew that she was in the whale's belly made a great outcry. At her shouting all were aroused. And the sailors said to the girl and the soldiers, "Dear friends, be comforted; God will save us; let us take good counsel since we are in the belly of the whale."

The girl said, "Hear my advice and we shall be saved." They said, "Speak."

She said, "Let us light a great fire and some one wound the whale just as deeply as he can and through those two acts he will receive a death wound (lit., *death*) and will immediately swim to the shore and so through the grace of God we shall be able to escape." They carried out the girl's plan in every detail. When the whale felt death upon him, he made for the land.

Close to the shore a soldier was stationed, who when he had finished dinner walked toward the seashore. When therefore from where he stood he saw the whale swimming toward that place and approaching the land, he called his servants and dragged the whale to shore. They began to strike the whale with their weapons. The girl when she heard the noise spoke for all and said, "Dear friends, strike carefully and open the side of the whale; here we are in its belly, the children of good men of noble blood."

The soldier, when he heard the girl's voice, said to his servants, "Dear friends, open the side of the whale and let us see what lies within." When the opening had been made, the girl first came forth — indeed almost dead, then the soldiers and all the others. She began to tell whose daughter she was and that she was to be the wife of the emperor's son. Hearing this the soldier kept her and all her retinue with him for some days until they recovered their health.

After this he sent the girl and all her retinue with presents to the emperor. The emperor, when he saw her, said, "My dearest daughter, may it be well with you now and always. But this I say to you, my daughter, before you have my son in marriage, I shall test you by one deed." At once he had three caskets made; one was of the purest gold and most precious stones. And this was the superscription on the casket: *Who opens me will find in me what he deserves.* The casket was entirely filled with the bones of dead men.

The second was of the purest silver, covered with gems all over and had this superscription: *Who chooses me, in me will find what nature has given.* This casket was full of earth.

The third casket was of lead having this superscription: *Rather I choose to be here and be at peace than stay among the treasures of a king.* In that casket were three precious rings.

Then the emperor said to the girl, "My dearest girl, here are three

178

caskets; choose whichever you wish; and if you choose well, you shall have my son in marriage." And she looked closely at the three caskets and said in her heart, "May God, who sees all things, give me grace so to choose that I shall not fail in that for which I have worked much."

She touched the first casket and read the writing: "Who opens me, in me will find what he deserves." She thought, "The casket on the outside is precious, but what lies hidden within I do not know; therefor I shall not choose it."

Then she read the second: "Who chooses me in me will find what nature has given." She said, "Nature never granted that my father's daughter should be joined to the emperor's son. And therefore I shall not choose it."

She read the third casket saying: "It is better for me to find rest with the king's son than among my father's treasures." And in a loud voice she declared: "I choose the third casket."

When the emperor heard, he said: "O good girl, you have chosen very wisely. In that casket are three precious rings of mine: one for me, one for my son, and the third for you as a mark of your betrothal." At once he had the marriage performed and gave his son to her; and so they lived happily ever after.

Some teachers may be interested in using the "Moral" which ancient authors attached to "The Story of the Three Caskets." Teachers and schools are, of course, free to duplicate the Latin text.

MORALITAS. Carissimi, imperator est Deus, qui diu guerram cum homine habuit in tantum quod tota natura humana erat destructa per peccatum. Modo trewgae nobis datae sunt per Dominum, id est, Christum. Filia quae filio imperatoris debet desponsari est anima. Oportet ergo ut navis paretur pro ea cum nuntiis, id est, corpus in quo anima residet cum quinque sensibus et ceteris, nautae sunt ratio, voluntas, etc. Sed oportet per mare, id est, per mundum, transire. Cete grande est diabolus, contra quem debemus vigilare. Sed si nos contingit dormire in peccatis deglutiet corpus et animam. Fac ergo, sicut fecit puella; ignem devotionis accende et eum cum instrumentis, id est, bonis operibus percute, donec recedat et potestatem suam contra te amittat. Tunc servi militis, id est, praedicatores et confessores, habent eum percutere, donec puella, id est, anima, ab eorum potestate exeat et ad curiam Dei veniat. Sed est sciendum quod tres cophini ei praesentantur. Per primum cophinum potentes ac divites intelleguntur, qui habent talem superscriptionem: "Qui me," etc., id est, quando anima a corpore separetur, nihil in me Deus inveniet nisi peccata quae merui, quod est dolendum; vae qui hunc eligit. Per secundum intellegitur mundi sapientes, quorum eloquia splendunt sicut argentum et intus pleni sunt terrenis, cum tali superscriptione: "Qui me elegerit," etc. Natura semper appetit nimae contrarium et illi non maritantur Christo. Per tertium cophinum designantur boni christiani, qui sunt plumbei, id est, quod non curant de aliquo mundano; in quibus sunt tres anuli, scilicet, fides, spes et caritas; qui istos eligit, filium Dei habere potest libentius quam in thesauro mundano permanere. Studeamus.

THE EMPEROR THEODOSIUS AND HIS THREE DAUGHTERS

Theodosius ruled in the city of Rome, a very wise and powerful man, who had three beautiful daughters. He said to the eldest daughter: "How much do you love me?" And she (replied): "Indeed more than I love myself." Her father said to her: "I shall promote you to great riches." At once he gave her in marriage to a rich and powerful king.

Afterwards he came to his second daughter and said to her: "How much do you love me?" And she (replied): "As much as my own self." Indeed the emperor gave her in marriage to a certain duke.

And after this he came to his third daughter and said to her: "How much do you love me?" But she (said): "As much as you deserve, no more, no less." Her father said to her, "Since that is the case, you shall not marry so rich a lord as your sisters"; and he gave her in marriage to a certain count.

It happened soon after this that the emperor undertook a war against the king of Egypt. In fact, the king drove the emperor from his throne to a place where he could find no proper refuge. He wrote a letter signed with his seal ring to the first daughter, who said that she loved her father more than her own self, requesting that she aid him in his necessity, because he had been driven from his realm.

His daughter, when she had read this letter of his, first told of the misfortune to her husband the king. The king said: "It is good for us to assist him in this great misfortune of his. I shall collect an army and help him with all my might." She said: "You cannot do that without great expense. It is sufficient, since he is outside of his realm, to allow him five soldiers who may attend him."

And this was done. The daughter wrote back to her father that he could have no other aid from her except five soldiers in his retinue at the king's expense. The emperor when he heard this was very sad and

180

said to himself: "Alas, all my hope lay in my eldest daughter because she said that she loved me more than herself, and for this reason I placed her in a great position of honor."

At once he wrote to the second daughter, who said that she loved him as much as she loved herself (this is actually a direct quotation in the Latin), that she come to his aid in his great need. She, when she heard this, announced it to her husband and advised him to give him nothing more than food and raiment, as long as he lived befitting (such) a king; and she wrote a letter concerning this to her father.

The emperor when he heard this was very saddened, saying: "I have been deceived by both my daughters. Now I shall make trial of my third daughter, who said to me: 'I love you as much as you deserve.' " He wrote her a letter asking her assistance in his great necessity and telling how her sisters answered him.

The third daughter, when she saw her father's need, said to her husband: "My worshipful lord, aid me in this need. Now my father has been driven from his inheritance." Her husband said to her: "What do you wish me to do?"

And she (replied): "Collect an army and go forward with him to overpower his enemy." The count said: "I shall fulfill your wishes." At once he collected a great army and at his own expense went forth to war in company with the emperor. He won the victory and put the emperor back on his throne.

Then the emperor said: "Blessed the hour in which I became the father of (*begat*) my youngest daughter. I loved her less than my other daughters, and she aided me in my great distress and my other daughters failed me; for this reason I shall leave my whole realm after my death to my youngest daughter," and so he did. After the death of her father the younger daughter reigned and ended her life in peace.

This is the "Moral" attached to "The Emperor Theodosius and His Three Daughters." Teachers and schools are, of course, free to duplicate the Latin text.

MORALITAS. Carissimi, iste imperator potest dici quilibet homo mundanus qui habet tres filias. Prima filia, quae dicit: "Diligo patrem plus quam me ipsam," certe est mundus iste, quem homo tantum diligit, quod vitam suam circa mundana expendit, sed quando est in necessitate mortis tunc mundus vix cum omni dilectione quam habuit concedet ei quinque milites, id est, quinque tabulas ad modum cistae ad involvendum corpus suum. Secunda filia, quae tantum diligit patrem sicut se ipsam, est uxor tua, filii tui et parentes, qui inveniunt

181

necessaria quousque in terram positus fueris et nihil aliud. Tertia
filia quae dicebat: "Tantum te diligo quantum vales," est Deus, quem
nimis parum diligimus. Sed si ad eum venerimus in necessitate puro
corde et munda mente sine dubio eius auxilium obtinebimus contra
regem Aegypti, id est, contra diabolum, et ponet nos in nostram
hereditatem, scilicet in regnum caeleste.

AN ORIENTAL TALE

THE WITCH AND THE SPRING

King Bocre had one son and he loved him as much as his own soul,
and he did not allow him to go out of his kingdom, lest by chance some
chance for (*accident* [*or*]) trouble would overtake him. However, the
boy asked a certain wise counselor of his father to ask his father to let
him go riding so that he could go hunting. Then the counselor spoke
with the king, just as the boy wanted. The king said to the counselor:
"You go with him." The counselor said: "Gladly."

Then the king's son went out with the counselor, and seeing a stag in
a field, they ran after him. Then the counselor said: "Let the boy
alone, to follow the stag, and this for the sake of his growing wiser."
And so the king's son followed the stag, and became separated from his
friends, and he was not able to get back to his friends, since he had
wandered into a forest.

But they searched for him, and not finding him, they said to the king:
"There came a lion between us, and he devoured your son." Then the
king tore his clothing and was greatly agitated for his son.

But the boy was in the woods and saw a very beautiful girl, and he
called to her and said: "Who are you?" She in turn answered: "I am
the daughter of a king; sleep overcame me, (while) lying on an elephant,
which led me out of the way, and I fell from it and stayed here. Take me
on your horse and free me."

The boy said to her: "I also am the son of a king, and it has happened to me in the same way." The girl said: "I know the way." And
he took her on his horse behind him, and they went on and came to a
certain deserted place, and the girl said: "I will get down and wash my
feet." She dismounted, and came to a place in which she lingered.

The boy, however, wanting to see what was causing the delay, dismounted from the horse and looked through a crack in the wall. Behold, the girl was a witch, and she was standing with others and saying:
"I have brought here the son of a king."

182

Then the other witches said: "Lead the boy to this place, and we will accomplish our purpose." The youth heard this and was afraid, and returned to his horse. And the witch turned back into a girl and went out and mounted the horse. And he himself trembled from so much fear and his face was changed.

And the woman realized that he was terrified, and she said: "What do you fear?" He answered: "I have a false and evil friend and I fear him."

But she (said): "Do you not say that your father is a king?" And he said: "My father does not have power over him."

She said: "Beguile him with money and gold." The boy (said) to her: "I cannot make him friendly with money and gold."

She, however, said to him: "Cry to God about him." The boy then raised both hands to the stars and said: "O God, free me from the hands of this witch, so that I may not be under her power." When, however, she saw that she was known to the boy, she fell from the horse and broke both hips.

But he fled through the deserted territory and grew very thirsty. And he came to a certain spring, from which whoever drank, if he was a man, was changed into a woman, and if a woman, was changed into a man. And he did not know this, and he drank, and he was turned into a woman and began to weep, and was afraid to drink any more water.

And he himself remained sad that night there, and lo! a crowd of girls came there and they played and sang next to the spring. He rose up to play with them, because he thought that he had been made a witch. The girls questioned him and said: "Who are you, and where do you come from?" And he told them all that had happened to him.

One of them said to him: "Swear that you will make me your wife, and I free you and take you back to your father." And he swore to her (that he would). And she said: "Drink from the water of this spring." He drank, and was changed back into a man. She, moreover, took him and led him back to his father. He then related to his father all that he had seen. The king ordered the counselor to be condemned.

IUSTUS LIPSIUS

IN PRAISE OF A HAPPY LIFE

He is equal to the gods above and higher than mortals, who does not hope for lightly, or fear, the doubtful day of his fate.

Whom powerless ambition and hope for wealth does not stir up; whom the rash threats of kings do not make tremble with fear, nor the thunderbolt of implacable Jupiter.

But settled in one place, he laughs at the worthlessness of the common people. The day starts free from care, and the day ends free from care.

If I were allowed to shape my life according to my own plans, I would desire no emblems of power nor wealth, I would not lead the captive lines, brilliant with snow-white horses.

I would live in lonely places, I would possess gardens and fields, and by the noise of the waters I would enjoy the interests of the Muses.

And so when Lachesis shall have spun my last fates to the end, I shall die not sick, (*burdened*) or unlucky, like my friend Languis here, but in tranquility.

THOMAS WRIGHT

A FARMER GOES TO THE CITY

A certain countryman brought his lamb to the market place. Six clever hired servants met him as he was entering the town, and one of them said to the others: "We will be able to get this lamb easily from this farmer, if we wish." When the others asked him how, he said: "Let us separate from each other through the six streets, so that no one of us is with another, and each one of us will ask this farmer if he wants to sell his dog." And this was done; and they approached him in turns. And when the farmer had sworn that it was a lamb, but the others said it was a dog, finally weakened in resistance, because it had been said so many times and by so many men that it was a dog, he said to the sixth: "I do not want to sell it, but take it for nothing, and before God, do not laugh at me any more."

THE NOBLEMAN AND HIS THREE SONS

A certain nobleman in England, holding land in England and Wales, had three sons. When he saw that he was nearing death, he called the three sons to him and said to them: "If it were necessary for you to become birds, which bird would you want to be like?" The eldest replied to him: "I would be like a hawk, because it is a noble bird and lives on prey." The middle one, however, replied: "I would be like a starling, because it is companionable, and flies in flocks." Then the third and junior to the others said: "I would be like a swan, because it has a long neck, so that if anything to be said came up in my heart, I could deliberate well before it came to my mouth." The father, hearing this, said to the first: "You, son, as I perceive, desire to live by plunder; therefore I give you my lands in England, because it is a land of peace and justice, and you will not be able to ravish it without punishment. And you, son, who like society, shall have my lands in Wales, which is a land of strife and war, so you will temper the roguishness of the inhabitants by your culture. To you, the youngest, however, I assign no land, because you will be wise, and through your wisdom you will acquire enough for yourself." Therefore, when the father died, the lands were divided up as the father had ordered. Moreover, the youngest brother, relying on his wisdom, became the chief justice of England.

A WISE SLAVE

A certain master, having a slave, said to him: "Go to the market place and buy us the best meat." He, going, bought all the tongues which he found for sale from the animals in the market; when the master saw these, he was irate, believing the slave to be foolish. And wishing to test whether he had done this from folly, he said to him again after a few days: "Go and buy all the worst meat that is for sale in the market." He went again, and bought all the tongues of the animals which he found, brought them back, and cooked them, and put them before his master. The irate master asked why he had done this. He replied: "I know that no part of flesh is better than a good tongue, and no part is worse than a bad tongue." And the servant proved it wisely, as has been said.

THE TWO BLIND MEN

There were two blind men in the city of Rome. One of them cried out every day through the streets of the city, "He is well aided whom God wishes to aid"; but the other called, "He is well aided whom the Emperor wishes to aid." When they repeated this every day, and the Emperor heard it frequently, he ordered that some bread should be made, and many talents put inside; and so the bread was filled with the

185

talents, and he ordered it given to the (second) blind (man). After receiving it, and seeing the weight of the bread, meeting the other blind man, he sold it to him for the work of his boys. The blind man who had bought the bread, reaching home, when the bread was broken found it filled with talents, and gave thanks to God, and for the rest of his life he remained without begging. But the other, when he still begged bread through the city, having been summoned by the Emperor, he (the Emperor) said to him, "Where is the bread which I ordered to be given to you yesterday?" He replied, "I sold it to my friend two days ago, because it seemed to me raw." "Truly," said the Emperor, "he is well aided whom God aids," and he pushed the blind man away and threw him out.

Grammar Review for Advanced Classes

The following section is included for those teachers who would like to add periodic grammar reviews to their reading program. It utilizes the *Brief Latin Grammar* section of the text (pp. 391–438).

REVIEW OF NOUNS

Turn to the Appendix, pp. 391–394, and study the following declensions:
1) regular nouns of the five declensions (pp. 391–394)
2) the irregular nouns **deus** (p. 392) and **vīs** (p. 393)
3) the irregular forms of the nouns **fīlia** and **dea** (p. 391)
4) i-stems of the third declension (p. 393)

EXERCISES

A. Give the following forms:

1. *genitive singular:* eques, spēs, cornū, mare, vīs. 2. *dative singular:* pōns, palūs, exercitus, rēs, caput. 3. *accusative singular:* diēs, corpus, vir, pēs, fenestra. 4. *ablative singular:* pāx, mare, manus, spēs, cornū. 5. *nominative plural:* pedes, flūmen, ager, vulnus, vīs. 6. *genitive plural:* pōns, rēs, manus, cornū, fīnis. 7. *dative plural:* pēs, exitus, dea, turris, diēs. 8. *accusative plural:* cīvis, caput, cornū, rēgnum, mare. 9. *vocative singular:* dux, fīlius, servus, rēgīna, eques.

B. Translate:

1. The men were sent to Rome. 2. They lived in Italy for many years. 3. Marcus, carry the books to the ships. 4. The farmers are working in the field behind the farmhouse. 5. The horseman led the horse from the forest to the city. 6. We have come many miles to the lands of our friends. 7. Boys, look at the citizens on the bridge. 8. Many cities in Italy are built on hills.

REVIEW OF ADJECTIVES AND ADVERBS

A. Review adjectives of the first and second declensions (p. 394)

B. Review adjectives of the third declension (p. 395). They may have three endings in the nominative singular like **ācer**, or two endings like **fortis**, or one ending like **potēns**. Note that the ablative singular of all third declension adjectives ends in -ī, the nominative and accusative neuter plural in -**ia**, and the genitive plural in -**ium**.

C. Review irregular adjectives on p. 395. Note that the genitive singular of these adjectives ends in -**īus** and the dative in -**ī**.

D. Review the *Comparison of Adjectives*, regular and irregular on p. 396 and the *Declension of Comparatives* on p. 397.

E. Adverbs are formed regularly from adjectives of the first and second declension by adding -**e** to the base of the corresponding adjective. Third declension adjectives regularly add -**ter** and -**iter** to the base to form the adverb. Study the *Comparison of Adverbs* on p. 397.

EXERCISES

A. Give the Latin for the following:

1. *genitive singular:* the small body, the braver king, the heaviest shield, the only citizen.   2. *dative singular:* one horn, the largest island, a very beautiful woman, the higher tower.   3. *accusative singular:* a very wide river, a very deep swamp, a very bad son, the seventh day.   4. *ablative singular:* a very wretched girl, the brave soldier, a noble king, the strongest farmer.   5. *nominative plural:* many horses, very diligent leaders, our generals, equal strength.   6. *genitive plural:* powerful men, wild animals, higher ships, very many mountains.   7. *dative plural:* our enemies, most difficult roads, longer bridges, very good boys.   8. *accusative plural:* very fierce foot soldiers, severe wounds, happier girls, light hands.

B. Translate into Latin:

1. A very large ship was sailing very quickly to a small island.   2. The windows in our farmhouse are very small.   3. There is much water in the river at the bridge.   4. Who has seen the king's very beautiful daughters?   5. Our general is leading the very brave troops to war.   6. The farmer's only slave was working very diligently in the field behind the farmhouse.   7. The kingdom of the queen is very large and beautiful.   8. Very many large houses were seen in the city.

188

REVIEW OF PRONOUNS AND NUMERALS

PERSONAL PRONOUNS—Study the declensions of the personal pronouns of the first and second persons on p. 399. The third person pronoun *he, she,* or *it* is generally the same as the demonstrative **is, ea, id** on p. 399.

REFLEXIVE PRONOUN—The reflexive pronoun is the same in the singular and plural (p. 399).

DEMONSTRATIVE PRONOUNS AND THE INTENSIVE PRONOUN—Review **hic, haec, hoc; ille, illa, illud;** and **is, ea, id** on p. 399. Review the intensive pronoun **ipse, ipsa, ipsum** on p. 400.

RELATIVE PRONOUN—Learn the complete declension of the relative pronoun **qui, quae, quod** on p. 400.

INTERROGATIVE PRONOUN—The interrogative pronoun **quis, quid** is declined on p. 400. The plural is declined like the relative. (The interrogative adjective is declined like the relative pronoun.)

NUMERALS—Review the cardinal numbers from 1 to 20 and **centum, mīlle,** and **mīlia** on p. 398. Review the declensions of **ūnus, duo, trēs,** and **mīlia** on p. 397. The other numerals are indeclinable. Study the ordinal numbers as review vocabulary.

EXERCISES

A. Give the following forms:

1. *genitive singular:* ego, tū, is, quis, ille. 2. *dative singular:* hic, quī, is suī, ūnus. 3. *accusative singular:* hic, quī, ille, tū. 4. *ablative singular:* suī, ego, tū, quis, ūnus. 5. *nominative plural:* quī, hic, duo, trēs, mīlia. 6. *genitive plural:* duo, tū, ille, trēs, mīlia. 7. *dative plural:* hic, quis, trēs, mīlia, duo. 8. *accusative plural:* ego, quī, trēs, mīlia, ille.

B. Translate the following:

1. Quis vēnit? 2. Quōs vīdistī? 3. Peditēs quī currunt . . . 4. Nāvēs quae nāvigant . . . 5. Quōrum equī veniunt? 6. Cui librum dedit? 7. Agricolae quōs laudō . . . 8. Quod flūmen in Ītaliā est? 9. Eōrum amīcī sciunt . . . 10. Suās cōpiās dūcunt.

C. Give the Latin for the words in italics:

1. The sailors *to whom* we spoke . . . 2. The girls *with whom* I walked . . . 3. *What* did you see? 4. *Whose brother* is that? 5. The state *in which* we live . . . 6. *Whom* did you see? 7. *Which house* is yours? 8. The general's sons, *who* are

189

fighting . . . 9. An animal, *which* is running . . . 10. *What* will he say? 11. Brutus saw *his friends.* 12. I saw *his friends.* 13. We gave money *to them.* 14.*Their house* is on a hill. 15. They sent *their slaves* . . . 16. He stayed *at home.* 17. We live *in Rome.* 18. They were seen *by his son.* 19. I stood *with them.* 20. *One of the horsemen* fell. 21. He ran *for three miles.* 22. He fought *with very great courage.* 23. Come *at night.* 24. He was wounded *by a javelin.* 25. I stayed *for many years.*

REVIEW OF VERBS—INDICATIVE

A. Review the six tenses of the indicative, active and passive, for the regular conjugations (pp. 402–410).

B. Review the six tenses of the indicative of **sum** (p. 413), **possum** (p. 414), **ferō** (p. 414), **eō** (p. 415), **volō, nōlō,** and **mālō** (p. 416).

C. Deponent verbs are passive in form but active in meaning and are conjugated like the passive forms of the regular verbs (p. 410).

EXERCISES

A. Translate the following verb forms:

1. cognōscunt 2. audiēbāmus 3. māvult 4. tāctum est
5. moriēbātur 6. dedistis 7. arbitrāmur 8. ceciderat
9. cucurrimus 10. loquēbantur 11. mānserās 12. vīsus sum
13. vultis 14. posuistī 15. iussī erant 16. euntne? 17. missa est
18. cōnābimur 19. cessī 20. potuērunt

B. Translate:

1. I shall lead. 2. He has been seen. 3. We urged. 4. They will go. 5. She had touched. 6. Did he fall? 7. You (sing.) were trying. 8. He will be able. 9. They were laughing. 10. I delayed. 11. Will they come? 12. We prefer. 13. She was taught. 14. They understand. 15. I had followed. 16. They will hear. 17. Do you wish? 18. It was moved. 19. I shall have prepared. 20. You (pl.) will send.

C. Give a synopsis in the third person singular, active, with meanings of **volō.**

D. Give a synopsis in the first person plural, with meanings of **arbitror.**

190

REVIEW OF VERBS—SUBJUNCTIVE

There are four tenses of the subjunctive in Latin—the present, imperfect, perfect, and pluperfect. Review their conjugations in the verb section of the Appendix (pp. 403–412).

EXERCISES

A. Give the third person singular, present subjunctive active: **ambulō, doleō, parcō, impediō, nōlō.**

B. Give the first person plural, imperfect subjunctive active: **iuvō, noceō, frangō, impediō, possum.**

C. Give the second person plural, perfect subjunctive active: **imperō, augeō, tollō, referō, mālō.**

D. Give the third person plural, pluperfect subjunctive active: **nāvigō, respondeō, āmittō, ēripiō, sum.**

E. Give the first person singular, perfect subjunctive passive: **iūdicō, moneō, iaciō, ferō, trādūcō.**

F. Give the third person plural, pluperfect subjunctive passive: **līberō, augeō, tollō, ēripiō, veniō.**

REVIEW OF INFINITIVES AND IMPERATIVES

Infinitives—There are five infinitives that are regularly used in Latin—the present active and passive, the perfect active and passive, and the future active. The future passive is used so rarely that it is not included here.

ACTIVE	PASSIVE
PRESENT	
vocāre	vocārī
monēre	monērī
regere	regī
capere	capī
audīre	audīrī

PERFECT	
vocāvisse	vocātus esse
monuisse	monitus esse
rēxisse	rēctus esse
cēpisse	captus esse
audīvisse	audītus esse

vocātūrus esse   ——
monitūrus esse
rēctūrus esse
captūrus esse
audītūrus esse

Imperatives—Regular verbs form their present active imperatives as follows:

	SINGULAR	PLURAL
FIRST CONJ.	vocā	vocāte
SECOND CONJ.	monē	monēte
THIRD CONJ.	rege	regite
	cape	capite
FOURTH CONJ.	audī	audīte

EXERCISES

A. Give the following infinitives:
1. *present passive:* cōgō, līberō, rapiō, nūntiō.   2. *perfect active:* iungō, fugiō, transeō, aperiō.   3. *perfect passive:* vēndō, cōgō, iaciō, occupō.   4. *future active:* trādūcō, labōrō, sedeō, proficīscor.
B. Translate:
1. Nōlēbant contendere.   2. Id facere nōn poterimus.   3. Cōnsuēscit vēndere . . .   4. Putō eōs labōrāre.   5. Coāctus est fugere.   6. Nōbīs manēre nōn licuit.   7. Cōnstituimus docēre . . . **8.** Sē missūrum esse pollicitus est.   9. Oportet puerōs currere.   10. Crēdidī cīvēs monitōs esse.
C. Translate:
1. We hesitate to speak.   2. They were not able to fight.   3. He will decide to join . . .   4. They were forced to kill.   5. We are not permitted to say.   6. Do you dare to follow them?   7. She promised that she would work.   8. You ought not to cross.   9. He seems to think . . .   10. He is afraid to die.
D. Translate:
1. I think that the king dares . . .   2. We know that you are following . . .   3. He said that he would set out.   4. They hear that the citizens are brave.   5. I do not think that the army is being led.   6. Does he understand that I do not want to say?   7. He ordered the foot soldiers to cross.   8. He knew that she would go.   9. He says that he cannot remain.   10. The messenger reported that the army had been defeated.

Answer Key for Grammar Review

NOUNS

A. 1. equitis, speī, cornūs, maris, vīs. **2.** pontī, palūdī, exercituī, reī, capitī. **3.** diem, corpus, virum, pedem, fenestram. **4.** pāce, marī, manū, spē, cornū. **5.** peditēs, flūmina, agrī, vulnera, vīrēs. **6.** pontium, rērum, manuum, cornuum, finium. **7.** pedibus, exitibus, deābus, turribus, diēbus. **8.** cīvēs, capita, cornua, rēgna, maria. **9.** dux, filī, serve, rēgīna, eques. **B. 1.** Virī Rōmam missī sunt. **2.** In Ītaliā multōs annōs habitābant. **3.** Portā, Mārce, librōs ad nāvēs. **4.** Agricolae in agrō post vīllam labōrant. **5.** Eques equum ex silvā in urbem dūxit. **6.** Multa mīlia passuum ad finēs amīcōrum nostrōrum vēnimus. **7.** Spectāte, puerī cīvēs in ponte. **8.** Multae urbes in Ītaliā in collibus aedificantur.

ADJECTIVES AND ADVERBS

A. 1. parvī corporis, fortiōris rēgis, scūtī gravissimī, sōlīus cīvis. **2.** ūnī cornū, maximae īnsulae, fēminae pulcherrimae, turrī altiōrī. **3.** flūmen lātissimum, palūdem altissimam, filium pessimum, septimum diem. **4.** miserrimā puellā, fortī mīlite, nōbilī rēge, fortissimō agricolā. **5.** multī equī, ducēs dīligentissimī, nostrī imperātōrēs, parēs vīrēs. **6.** potentium virōrum, ferōrum animālium, altiōrum nāvium, plurimōrum montium. **7.** nostrīs hostibus, itineribus difficillimīs, pontibus longiōribus, optimīs puerīs. **8.** acerrimōs peditēs, gravia vulnera, fēliciōrēs puellās, levēs manūs. **B. 1.** Maxima nāvis ad īnsulam parvam celerrimē nāvigābat. **2.** Fenestrae in nostrā vīllā sunt minimae. **3.** Multa aqua est in flūmine ad pontem. **4.** Quis rēgis pulcherrimās filiās vīdit? **5.** Noster imperātor cōpiās fortissimās ad bellum dūcit. **6.** Agricolae sōlus servus in agrō post vīllam dīligentissimē labōrābat. **7.** Rēgnum rēgīnae est maximum et pulcherrimum. **8.** Plūrimae magnae domūs in urbe vīsae sunt.

PRONOUNS AND NUMERALS

A. 1. meī; tuī; eius; cuius; illīus. **2.** huic; cui; eī; sibi; ūnī. **3.** hunc, hanc, hoc; quem, quam, quod; illum, illam, illud; tē. **4.** suō, suā, suō; mē; tē; quō, quā, quō; ūnō, ūnā, ūnō. **5.** quī, quae, quae; hī, hae, haec; duo, duae, duo; trēs, trēs, tria; mīlia. **6.** duōrum, duārum, duōrum;

193

vestrum (vestrī); illōrum, illārum, illōrum; trium; mīlium. 7. hīs; quibus; tribus; mīlibus; duōbus, duābus, duōbus. 8. nōs; quōs, quās, quae; trēs, trēs, tria; mīlia; illōs, illās, illa.

B. 1. Who came? 2. Whom did you see? 3. The foot soldiers who were running . . . 4. The ships that were sailing . . . 5. Whose horses are coming? 6. To whom did he give the book? 7. The farmers whom I praise . . . 8. What river is in Italy? 9. Their friends know . . . 10. They lead their troops.

C. 1. quibus. 2. quibuscum. 3. Quid? 4. Cuius frāter? 5. in quā. 6. Quem? 7. Quae domus? 8. quī. 9. quod. 10. Quid? 11. suōs amīcōs. 12. eius amīcōs. 13. eīs. 14. Eōrum domus. 15. suōs servōs. 16. domī. 17. Rōmae. 18. ab eius fīliō. 19. cum eīs. 20. Ūnus ex equitibus. 21. tria mīlia passuum. 22. maximā cum virtūte. 23. nocte. 24. pīlō. 25. multōs annōs.

VERBS—INDICATIVE

A. 1. they learn 2. we were hearing 3. he prefers 4. it has been touched 5. he was dying 6. you gave 7. we think 8. he had fallen 9. we ran 10. they were speaking 11. you had remained 12. I was seen 13. you wish 14. you have placed 15. they had been ordered 16. are they going? 17. she was sent 18. we will try 19. I yielded 20. they were able

B. 1. dūcam 2. vīsus est 3. hortātī sumus 4. ībunt 5. tetigerat 6. Ceciditne? 7. cōnābāris 8. poterit 9. rīdēbant 10. morātus sum 11. venientne? 12. mālumus 13. docta est 14. intellegunt 15. secūtus eram 16. audient 17. vultisne? 18. mōtum est 19. parāverō 20. mittētis

C.	vult	he wishes
	volēbat	he wished (he was wishing)
	volet	he will wish
	voluit	he has wished
	voluerat	he had wished
	voluerit	he will have wished
D.	arbitrāmur	we think
	arbitrābāmur	we were thinking
	arbitrābimur	we will think
	arbitrātī sumus	we thought
	arbitrātī erāmus	we had thought
	arbitrātī erimus	we will have thought

VERBS—SUBJUNCTIVE

A. ambulet, doleat, parcat, impediat, nōlit.

B. iuvārēmus, nocērēmus, frangerēmus, impedīrēmus, possēmus.

194

C. imperāverītis, auxerītis, sustulerītis, rettulerītis, māluerītis.

D. nāvigāvissent, respondissent, āmīsissent, ēripuissent, fuissent.

E. iudicātus sim, monitus sim, iactus sim, lātus sim, trāductus sim.

F. līberātī essent, auctī essent, sublātī essent, ēreptī essent, inventī essent.

INFINITIVES AND IMPERATIVES

A. 1. cōgī, līberārī, rapī, nūntiārī. 2. iūnxisse, fūgisse, trānsisse, aperuisse. 3. venditus esse, coāctus esse, iactus esse, occupātus esse. 4. trāductūrus esse, labōrātūrus esse, sessūrus esse, profectūrus esse.

B. 1. They did not want to fight. 2. We will not be able to do that. 3. He is accustomed to sell . . . 4. I think that they are working. 5. He was forced to flee. 6. We were not allowed to remain. 7. We decided to show . . . 8. He promised that he would send . . . 9. The boys ought to run. 10. I believed that the citizens had been warned.

C. 1. Dubitāmus loquī. 2. Pugnāre nōn poterant. 3. Iungere cōnstituet . . . 4. Interficere coāctī sunt. 5. Nōbīs nōn dīcere licet. 6. Audēsne eōs sequī? 7. Pollicita est sē labōrātūram esse. 8. Vōs nōn trānsīre oportet. 9. Putāre vidētur. 10. Morī timet.

D. 1. Pītō rēgem audēre . . . 2. Scīmus tē sequī . . . 3. Dīxit sē profectūrum esse. 4. Audiunt cīvēs esse fortēs. 5. Nōn putō exercitum dūcī. 6. Intellegitne mē nōlle dīcere? 7. Iussit peditēs trānsīre. 8. Scīvit eam itūram esse. 9. Dīcit sē manēre nōn posse. 10. Nūntius nūntiāvit exercitum superātum esse.